LEND ME YOUR EARS

The Trippier family – Alexander, Edward, Ruth, George and the author.

Lend Me Your Ears

by

Sir David Trippier

The Memoir Club

First published in 1999 by
The Memoir Club
The Old School
New Road
Crook Town
Durham

British Library Cataloguing in
Publication Data.
A catalogue record for this book
is available from the
British Library.

ISBN: 1 84104 009 6

Typeset by George Wishart & Associates, Whitley Bay.
Printed by Bookcraft (Bath) Ltd.

For Ruth, Alexander, Edward and George.

Acknowledgements

I was prompted to write this book as a result of a series of coincidences.

Initially, I was approached by The Memoir Club who wished me to write an autobiography. My immediate reaction was that I would not be able to afford the time. Within the same week that I received the letter from the publishers, I was urged to write a book by an old friend, Alasdair Northrop, who is the Business Editor of the *Manchester Evening News*, and the following day another friend, David Lee, who is my barber in Manchester and whom I have known for 27 years, said, 'You should write a book.' Neither Alasdair nor David had the faintest idea that I had received a letter from a publisher earlier that week. I owe them an enormous debt of gratitude for prompting me to undertake the work.

I must also thank my wife Ruth for being such a splendid sub-editor and effective critic, Ken Clarke for writing the foreword and my P.A., Philipa Kershaw, for her endless patience in typing and retyping my illegible manuscript.

Here it is.

Contents

List of Illustrations

Foreword

by

Rt. Hon. Kenneth Clarke, QC, MP

THIS IS A VERY ENTERTAINING book by a delightful man who is one of the best friends that I have been lucky enough to acquire through my political career.

Sadly, the autobiographies of most politicians tend nowadays to be dull, self-justifying tomes. Most should have a theme as a subtitle: 'Why I was right in what I said and did throughout my career but nobody realised it at the time.' Instead David writes a cheery and self-deprecatory account of his life so far – before politics, in politics and after politics.

Sir David Trippier is one of that diminished species, a northern Tory through and through. The lad from Rochdale has become Mr. Manchester in my eyes today. He now pursues a very successful business career, proving that he can do more than make speeches about enterprise and industry – he can practise what he preaches. But his success has not changed his engaging style in any way. Few politicians or businessmen can retain the ability to write about themselves in a way which is such fun to read. He has certainly avoided the professional hazard of falling into pomposity and long-windedness, which creeps up unawares onto too many middle-aged men in public life.

He was a breath of fresh air in Parliament when he first came into the House of Commons and I began to meet him. Only his physical fitness revealed the extraordinary fact that there was a military background in his life. He nearly killed himself in an accidental fall in military training, but that did not stop him returning to hectic activity again in his beloved Royal Marines Reserve. The late nights and unhealthy lifestyle of Ministerial Office finally slowed him down a bit, but a spirit of daring do and adventure never really left him.

He first impressed me when he was lobbying me on a fairly ridiculous subject. When I was a junior Transport Minister he persuaded me, in the teeth of opposition from my dubious officials, that the name of Rawtenstall was not too long to be put on motorway route signs, even if it required signs of slightly longer size than the standard! His enthusiasms were for causes big and small. As soon as I had become senior enough to be entitled to a PPS as a parliamentary aide, I persuaded the Prime Minister and the Whips to allow me to appoint him. We began to work together as friends and we continued to do so when he inevitably began to climb the Ministerial ladder himself.

Life as a Minister can be hard and earnest for a lot of the time and not all of my colleagues would combine hard work with escapes to Ronnie Scott's Jazz Club at night as David and I sometimes did. At his desk, he had original ideas and he became Minister for Small Firms to build up the idea of Enterprise Trusts, which he had done so much to promote and develop when he was a backbencher. Urban regeneration and the environment were also his forté and he seemed destined inevitably for a high-flying career.

This book gives all the anecdotes and all the entertaining moments in what was actually a hard working career in which David made a difference. His life with Ruth and his family dominates a picture which illuminates the human side that colours the progress of a cheerful, enterprising man.

When he lost his seat, I was disappointed by my failure to persuade him to try to come back to the Commons. He was adamant that he was going back to Manchester to the next stage of his life and his career. This book is the only way in which I have known him look back with pleasure on what he has done so far.

He has obviously enjoyed it all. I trust that the chapters still to be added in a few years' time, when he has lived some more of his life, will fill out the same picture of a man who is determined to live a good life to the full.

CHAPTER I

Childhood

'Tell the truth then you can remember what you said.'

I HAVE ALWAYS BEEN SCEPTICAL of those who claim they can recall childhood incidents from an incredibly early age. My own earliest memories are relatively sparse, though I can record an overall impression that I was invariably in trouble, yet essentially happy, even while creating havoc and chaos for all those near and dear to me.

My most vivid recollection of those early days is of my career in the Wolf Cubs at Rochdale, which, though undistinguished, was certainly colourful. I believe that to this day I remain the only Wolf Cub in history to have been demoted for bad behaviour. When I was eight I was a member of the 37th Rochdale Wolf Cub Pack, which met in a converted church hall surrounded by fields. Its leading light was our highly respected Akela, Miss Kathleen Heap, the sister of the local doctor. Although relatively small, Miss Heap was buxom in build, thoroughly prim and proper, and with a back as straight as a ramrod. She had a steely glare which was all the more alarming as it was accentuated by her horn-rimmed spectacles. That famous glare was dispensed quite liberally and was guaranteed to reduce any grown man at whom it was directed within a ten-yard radius to a gibbering idiot. Truly her bark was as bad as her bite – she was a regular Cruella Deville.

In my stupidity I actually believed my career in the Cubs was blossoming. Having already gained one stripe and thereby reached the rank of 'Seconder', I was sure that I was well on my way to another, which would have promoted me to that of 'Sixer'. I was dreaming of a third stripe, which would have raised me to the dizzy heights of 'Senior Sixer' or top Cub, senior to all the rest.

Then came my downfall. It took the form of a telephone call from Miss Heap to my mother.

A keen but demoted young wolf cub.

'I've decided to strip him of his rank,' she barked. 'He's grossly ill-disciplined. When I blow the whistle for the Cubs to rally round, he invariably fails to respond because he's constantly fighting. Not that he's much good at it,' she added cuttingly. 'He's for ever picking on someone bigger and stronger than himself.'

It was true. My forays into the martial arts led regularly to my being 'slaughtered'.

My mother was devastated. She rang my father at his office and he returned home immediately. Storming into the kitchen, he knocked me down, thereby giving me the opportunity of inspecting the floor at very close quarters. No sooner had I picked myself up than he knocked me down again. 'If there is any fighting to be done,' he railed, 'it will be between you and me!'

'Yes, Dad,' I replied meekly, still lying prostrate. Slaughtered again! I was sent to bed.

As a result of the shame I had brought on the family, my mother didn't go out for two weeks. In our household this was high drama, and for me it was my Waterloo. Later I was to crawl back into Miss Heap's affections and attained the dizzy heights of Senior Sixer by winning that coveted third stripe.

The memory of that escapade was more significant than would first appear. It was a shining example of something that would dog me for the rest of my career. If there were two ways of doing something, I would always do it the hard way. Certainly I would have to learn a difficult lesson before I received any 'accolade'.

Despite these and other dramatic episodes, I was a 'happy chappy', and I owe this largely to my mother, Mary. I remember her as tall and fairly big-boned with lovely hair, the warmest of hearts shining through the kindest of eyes, a happy face and a bubbly personality. As far back as I can remember, we were unbelievably close. I have often wished that I could have been as popular as she was. One reason why she was so generally loved was that she was invariably smiling and hardly ever criticized anyone for anything. The less charitable among us found this distinctly wearing.

My mother's early life was very hard; both her parents had died before she was in her teens. She had been brought up in a butcher's family and had three brothers, Jimmy, Sam and Jack. Jimmy died of consumption at 24, having suffered ill health from birth. Her remaining elder brother Sam and younger brother Jack were the light of her life. When their parents died, they were brought up by an old family friend, a nurse known in the community as Nurse Clegg. To my mother and uncles, she was called 'Ma' Clegg and later to me and my sister Bunty she was known as Granny Clegg. She had pure white hair, a delightful soft complexion, lovely eyes, a warm heart and a great sense of fun. All in all, she was a truly wonderful person. When later in life she was bedridden, she came to live with us until the day she died.

I find it impossible to believe how the family survived after the loss of their parents at such a young age, but they did. Fortunately Sam was just old enough to work in the butcher's shop and I understand that he was helped for a time by his Uncle John, who was also a butcher. My mother left school prematurely to help in the shop and help Granny Clegg with the household chores. They had to wait a few years before their younger brother was old enough to join them and he too became a butcher. Gradually the business expanded at St Mary's Gate in Rochdale. When my mother wasn't helping in the shop, she delivered meat to customers, which in the very early years was done by pony and trap. This closely-knit family team were loving, loyal and inseparable and as a consequence the family business became a huge success. At their peak they owned no fewer than four butcher's shops and their own slaughterhouse in Rochdale.

My father, Austin Wilkinson Trippier, had, by contrast, an entirely different upbringing. For the most part he was brought up in a tiny terraced house in Arthur Street in Rochdale. His father, whom I vaguely remember, was called Herbert and worked on the shop floor as a cotton spinner. He was a small, bald-headed man, quite undistinguished but kindly. He was totally overshadowed by his wife Bertha Ellen, a cotton weaver, who was austere, incredibly serious and rather frightening. She had a severe bun at the back of her head. Apart from that, she looked like Morticia from the Addams Family. She dominated her husband and just about everything and everyone in sight. To me, as a small child, she seemed to tower over her husband. Between them they owned a few other houses in the terraced row, but she decided that they should lead a frugal life in similar conditions to their tenants.

When he was eleven, my father passed the entrance exam to Bury Grammar School and, it must be said, his life took off. He seemed to excel at most things he turned his hand to. Academically he was very competent but at sport he was an outstanding all-rounder. He became captain of both the First XI Football Team and the First XI Cricket Team. He was the Senior Cadet in the Officers Training Corps and captain of his house. When he left school and took articles with a firm of stockbrokers in Rochdale called Arthur Milne, he paid for his articles (as was then customary) with money he earned from playing football for Rochdale F.C. and later Oldham Athletic. During this same period, he also played for Rochdale's First XI cricket team.

I have always conjured up images of what he must have been like at that time. He was certainly earnest, undoubtedly ambitious and quite serious-minded, but always escaped the charge that he was too austere by being blessed with a very dry sense of humour. All his life he was exacting, critical, self-confident, sparing of praise and sadly unable to convey his deepest feelings. Although he certainly loved my sister Bunty and me, he was not overtly affectionate towards us. In many ways he was an enigma.

He was always respected, not only by me but by countless others, and was the most honest man I have ever met. His maxim was always, 'Tell the truth, then you can remember what you said.'

Of medium height, and with a perfectly shaped nose, small hands and feet, he was quite good looking. When he met my mother, he was in his early twenties. In Rochdale he was a local football hero and it isn't difficult to imagine that my mother, who was five years his junior, would have been besotted with his sporting prowess. He, for his part, would have been bowled over by my mother's vivaciousness and the fact that she introduced him into a family who were noisy, full of fun, and prepared to accept him so readily.

He must have been relieved that my mother followed him round the football circuit cheering him on. Until then his constant companion at all the games had been his own mother, who was critical to a fault. If Dad's team had lost, he hadn't played well enough. If they won, the opposition was easy. If he didn't score, she would not speak to him for several days.

When my parents were married in 1935, my father had an established practice as a stockbroker in the neighbouring town of Heywood. In those days if you left your original employer, you could only set up in competition if your office was at least three miles away. This condition remained in force for a period of no less than four years.

Their early married life seemed happy and stable, with my sister Bunty born in March, 1937. Pretty with gorgeous red hair, she was christened 'Marcia Helen' but has always hated both names. Like many girl toddlers at that time, she wore a 'Baby Bunting' outfit and became known as Bunty. The name stuck.

When the War started in 1939, my father joined the Army immediately and, due to military and other qualifications gained at Bury Grammar School, was quickly commissioned as an officer. He passed out of the Royal Military Academy at Woolwich and was immediately posted to the Northumberland Hussars, who had been converted to Gunners at the outbreak of War. The regiment was affiliated to the Royal Horse Artillery.

Initially it appeared a strange posting. A Lancastrian with a very ordinary background, he was moving into a very 'classy' and up-market Geordie regiment whose officers had been drawn from the hunting, shooting and fishing fraternity in the north-east of England. His adjutant was the Duke of Northumberland and there were at least three other titled officers to add lustre to what was a very distinguished regiment. Most of those who were not titled had serious money and, initially, my father found it hard to keep up. I have copies of letters he wrote to my mother when sailing on the troop ship to Greece, explaining that he had had to leave the card table early in the evening as he couldn't possibly afford to stay in the game. He made the point in these letters that he thought he might come into his own when the fighting started. Although that turned out to be true, he was to be greatly struck by the courage and sheer professionalism of his fellow officers, be they landed gentry or not.

He was soon pitched into the front line in Greece and Crete. In Crete he won the Military Cross for gallantry. His citation reads: 'That he and his men destroyed six enemy tanks and left several others disabled. He completely exposed himself while directing operations from an unarmoured truck.'

The *History of the Northumberland Hussars* described the events of a later battle in 1942 in North Africa which was to turn out to be a disaster:

> On May 26, 1942 Rommel, intent on reaching Alexandria, launched an attack on the line extending from Gazala to Bir Hakim with the aim of destroying the British forces with his superior tanks and artillery. Although the British and Free French troops fought with skill and courage, they lost many of their armoured vehicles to the German anti-tank guns. Rommel was eventually checked on the Alamein Line in July by Auchinleck.
>
> A survivor of the battle wrote:

> The gun position was now a dreadful place with smashed guns, dead, wounded, and burnt-out vehicles all over the place. We had inflicted much damage on the Germans but they had destroyed us. The next attack came in very quickly and soon German tanks had overrun the infantry battalion in the rear and were nosing about among the burning vehicles. Lt. Trippier and his Northumberland Hussars were quite magnificent. Under heavy fire, they man-handled their anti-tank guns across to safeguard our rear but they were all knocked out. Trippier then drove back with his truck full of badly wounded men to report that he had not a man left. As he spoke, a shell exploded beside him, wounding him severely. Trippier had a compound fracture. Taken

Major Austin Trippier M.C., the author's father, in the uniform of the Northumberland Hussars.

prisoner, he narrowly escaped having his arm removed by Italian surgeons. He was classified by the Italians as unfit to fight again and repatriated.

This account fails to mention that he had spent a year in the prisoner of war camp before being sent back to England.

For four months after my father was captured, he was reported missing. That period must have been agonising for my mother. Bunty remembers how kind and considerate everyone was and that the house was invariably full of family and friends trying to relieve the tension. As more time elapsed, it seemed likely that he was 'missing, presumed dead', and by November she had psychologically accepted the very worst. The Royal British Legion asked my mother to lay the wreath for the Legion on the memorial in Rochdale on Armistice Sunday. She bought a black hat for the ceremony.

Shortly afterwards, Charlie Cockcroft, who was the managing director of the *Rochdale Observer* newspaper, received a telegram from the War Office giving the names of servicemen from Rochdale who had been found in prisoner-of-war camps. Not certain whether my mother had left for work before her telegram had arrived, he tried to telephone her at the butcher's shop. The phone was constantly engaged so he ran down Drake Street and arrived breathless at the shop in St Mary's Gate. 'Have you heard the news, Mary?' he said.

'No I haven't. What news?' asked my mother.

'Austin has been found alive in a P.O.W. camp in Italy.'

On hearing this, my mother fainted over the lamb chops.

When my father was repatriated, although naturally delighted to be with my mother and sister again, he became increasingly restive as he continued to read the daily accounts of the War in the national newspapers. Contrary to the Geneva Convention, he signed on again after only four months. Bribing a medical officer to pass him as medically fit to fight, he rejoined his old regiment, the Northumberland Hussars, in time to join them for the 'D' Day landings in Normandy. Then a captain, he was quickly promoted to major and commanded 'D' Battery in his regiment during the north-west Europe campaign through France and Germany.

His war service, a précis of which has been given here, reads like something out of *Boys Own*. That he was lucky is not in doubt, but

Mary Trippier, the author's mother. The photograph was sent to the author's father while he was a prisoner of war in Caserta, Italy.

he returned home a very different man. Certainly he was battle-scarred, but he was also a much more rounded and sensitive individual than the man who had left Arthur Street to be married in 1935. Like some men I have met, he was reticent about discussing certain aspects of the War. When I was old enough to be conscious of these matters, I would ask him about his exploits. He would talk about his love of his regiment or the characters in it – fairly general stuff – but on the battles or his fellow officers and men who had been killed – nothing. He would be on the point of sharing his grief with me; then his eyes would glaze over and he would stand up and leave the room.

I had to wait until I was 40 before I found out why he received the M.C. I was then a Member of Parliament and a constituent had asked me to write to the Ministry of Defence Records Office to get a copy of a citation for a decoration that he had received. For the sheer hell of it, I wrote asking for a copy of my father's citation at the same time. When I received it, I was impressed.

When he was finally de-mobbed in 1945, my mother and sister were delighted and relieved to have him back home. That delight must have been short-lived as I came on the scene, being born on the 15th May 1946. This happy event was greeted by the world with an overwhelming and enthusiastic indifference. It merited two brief lines in the *Rochdale Observer* and that was all. I was born at home and delivered by Dr. Harold Knox assisted by Granny Clegg. It seems it was uneventful.

Later I was to be christened at St Aidan's Church as David Austin Trippier. Although my mother had been brought up as a Methodist and my father as a Baptist, my sister and I were to be brought up as Anglicans because during the War the elderly Vicar of St Aidan's, The Reverend B. Sockett, had regularly visited my mother and Bunty during those turbulent times, whereas the Methodist and Baptist ministers never came near. There was no malice in the decision regarding this. It was just a simple choice our parents made.

I remember being surrounded by love and by relations and friends. Our immediate next-door neighbours were the Hawkyards. Uncle Fred and Auntie Alice Hawkyard had a deep effect on my early years. Uncle Fred had a habitually cheerful expression on his decidedly round face – this despite the glass eye which he wore, replacing the one he had lost during the First World War. Auntie Alice had laughing eyes and reddish hair, turning white when I knew her. Both of them had a profound influence on me in those early days. Life to me seemed to be not only running around our family home but continually popping next door for extra pop or biscuits. They were happy days. When we moved to a larger house in Tweedale Street (which turned out to be a mistake and was of relatively short duration) I remember being worried that we would lose touch with the Hawkyards. Of course we never did, but that's what a four-year-old boy could be forgiven for thinking.

When I was six, I learned another serious lesson when I was caught acting out my secret pretend world. The lesson was that I would always get caught. My favourite pastime was to sneak away to the attic, which was an Aladdin's cave of military memorabilia, with trunks full of old army kit that belonged to my father. I would put on my father's best service dress jacket with its two rows of medals. The jacket nearly touched the floor. Then I would pull on the German officer's shiny knee boots that my father had purloined. These prevented me from bending at the knees and resembled something like waders. Then I would put on his service peaked cap. It had to be stuffed with newspaper to stop it falling round my ears. The ensemble was completed with a pair of binoculars slung round my neck and a cigar, which I had to light repeatedly because it kept going out. Off and on, I could keep one cigar going for up to three days!

One sad day my mother crept up the attic stairs and caught me standing on a soap box, smoke billowing everywhere, looking through the attic window on to the street below through my binoculars. I must have looked ridiculous – rather like a very diminutive and sad Argentinian dictator. When she enquired what on earth I thought I was doing, I replied that I was looking for Germans on Tweedale Street. Perfectly logical!

To her eternal credit, my mother never told my father. Although she turned a blind eye to the continued theatricals, she locked the cigars away in a very high cupboard. My mother told this story to Auntie Alice, who replied with the immortal words, 'As I've always said, Mary, that boy will either go far or go to prison. It could be a close-run thing.'

During this and other minor skirmishes, my sister Bunty was always supportive of me and whenever she could she protected me. Usually she just laughed. I was part of the unpaid entertainment. It was wonderful to have an older sister and we were very close. We still are, and you can't get a razor blade between us. To this day, and always in public, she still refers to me as her baby brother or little brother.

I remember that on my fourth birthday she took me to see my first film, *Annie Get Your Gun*, starring Betty Hutton. Betty must have made a profound impression on me because at every different film we went to see for the next year I kept asking when Annie was coming on.

About the same time I also remember that she rescued me from a fate worse than death. Having woken one morning and had a bath, I crept downstairs in the nude to filch some biscuits from a tin in the sideboard. The tin was in a cupboard at a high level and I had to stand on a chair to reach. Unfortunately, one of the lower drawers was partly open and I must have accidentally closed it with my knee, trapping my willy in the drawer. The drawer was stuck and I was screaming the house down. After what seemed an age, Bunty came tearing down the stairs and released me. I think I owe her my life. The doctor was sent for, magnums of cream were applied, and I was told I would live. I wasn't so sure.

However, on one occasion she turned on me. Bunty was a pupil at Bury Grammar School for Girls, which was entirely separate from the boys' school. When I went to Bury Grammar at the age of five, she would take me on the bus.

As I finished earlier than she did, I had to wait for her after school. One day I got fed up with waiting and caught the bus to go home. When she arrived much later, she was understandably livid, complaining that she had looked everywhere for me. My mother calmed everything down and said, 'Well if he's travelled by himself once, he can do it again.' Nowadays, no-one would think of letting a

With sister Bunty.

child of five wander through a neighbouring town and travel six or seven miles on a bus by himself. In those days it was fairly common and nobody thought much about it.

Bunty and I were quite enthralled by the fact that my father was an accomplished pianist. We had a baby grand piano that was a dreadful mottled colour. Sometimes Bunty and I would sit at the top of the stairs and listen to my father accompanying some of the singers who came to our house to practise. My father had the great gift of hearing a tune and being able to play it by ear on the piano.

When I was six, the whole family went to the cinema on a Saturday to see a film starring Doris Day. The principal song in the film was 'Que Sera, Sera', which at that time was topping the charts. The following morning I was up before anyone else, crept downstairs in my pyjamas and sat at the piano. I could remember the tune quite clearly and proceeded to play it. It seemed to flow quite easily. My father came rushing down the stairs, picked me up in his arms and, still carrying me, ran back up the stairs to present me to my mother, who was only half awake in bed.

'He's got it, Mary, he's got it. He can play by ear,' he said with pride. This burst of adulation made a great change from being in trouble most of the time.

From that day to this I have had hundreds of hours of pleasure and relaxation playing the piano. I recognise how lucky I am. My father was the better sight reader and was more accomplished at reading music from cold. I, on the other hand, would struggle a little more with sight reading, but had a better ear than he and a greater talent for playing without music. On rare occasions, we would play together. Often we would play for each other. I would find it an asset at parties and, perhaps most important of all, I still love playing in my drawing room with no-one to hear but me. It is pure escapism!

I suppose most young boys have been involved in gangs at some time in their younger life. Between the ages of eight and eleven I was involved in setting up three. Looking back, I think we might have been influenced by the *Just William* books written by Richmal Crompton. I think I must have been in my teens before I realised that Richmal was a woman. Incidentally, she had been a pupil at Bury Grammar School for Girls.

The first gang I organised had its headquarters in the infamous attic in our house in Tweedale Street. The three founder members of this gang were myself, Michael Howarth and Anthony Strivens. Michael was a somewhat scruffy character with a nose that never stopped running and had permanent 'candlesticks' hanging from it. Anthony was small for his age and his sharp features had earned him the nickname 'Mouse'. We were about the same age, which would have been about seven. There were four other members of the gang, but we three were the main protagonists. It was run on military lines, as you might guess. I was the Sergeant, Michael the Corporal and Anthony the Lance Corporal.

One night in the school holidays we met in the attic by candlelight. This lent a certain amount of drama to the proceedings. Unfortunately there were no cigars. We plotted that the following day we would take buckets down to the stream which ran through the nearby common and catch some frogs.

The next day we each caught about twenty magnificent frogs of all different shapes and sizes. Quite a few were of different colours and I also found some huge toads. When I returned home with my catch, I went into the downstairs bathroom. I locked the door behind me, filled the bath and basin with water, and released the frogs and toads into them. One seemed quite happy swimming in the loo. Having watched them for half an hour, I went to get some cress from the fridge in the kitchen, just in case they were hungry. Unfortunately I left the door open, thinking they would be safe. I was unaware that my mother was having a few lady friends round for coffee and I never dreamt that one of them would want to go to the downstairs loo. When the screaming started, I rushed back into the hall and saw other women joining in the chorus. They screamed and screamed – much more than even Violet Elizabeth Bott would have done in *Just William*.

By this time there were frogs jumping on the stairs, frogs in the hall, frogs in the living room. There were frogs everywhere. It was fabulous! However, my mother, not unexpectedly, was beside herself with rage. She marched me into the kitchen and for the first and only time I can remember, smacked me hard. I was made to collect all of my new-found friends, put them in the buckets, and return them to the stream on the common. With tears streaming down my face, I ambled down Tweedale Street with my buckets, swearing vengeance on my mother. I would leave home and that would teach her! She'd be sorry then. Realising that she must have learnt her lesson, I returned home after two hours. I was hungry!

CHAPTER II

Schooldays

'If you are half as good a footballer as your father, this school will do well.'

BURY GRAMMAR SCHOOL is an excellent school with a distinguished history and a fine academic record. Believed to have been originally founded in 1587, it underwent a radical transformation from 1906 onwards, when it was combined with the Girls' High School to form a single entity with new buildings. Nevertheless, the Boys' School, though adjacent to the Girls', remained separate from it and nowadays the two buildings are completely different in appearance. The old school, now wholly occupied by girls and junior boys up to the age of eight, is built of traditional old brick. The Boys' School, by contrast, is far more modern, being built in modern red brick with vast areas of glass. The playing fields cover an enormous area and add to the distinguished appearance of the schools.

The fact that I added little or no lustre to the school's wonderful reputation is entirely my fault and mine alone. I began my school career at Bury Grammar in September 1951, when I was five years old. My early years at Bury Grammar School were extremely happy and I have two schoolteachers to thank for that: Miss Renée Lemmon and Miss Joan Hamilton, who were to have a profound influence on my life. I occasionally bump into them to this day and I often feel a twinge of sympathy as I remember that they had the job of controlling such a difficult lad. In so many ways they were entirely different. Miss Lemmon had a strikingly trim figure, red hair, delicate hands and a lovely smile. She taught me to read and write and encouraged and cajoled me; and I'm sure I was not alone in having a huge crush on her. Miss Hamilton had a very high forehead, rimless glasses and a somewhat autocratic appearance. She was a disciplinarian and although she was very strict, she was much admired and respected. I have only been afraid of four women in my life: Kathleen

Heap from Cubs, Joan Hamilton, Margaret Thatcher and my mother-in-law – not a bad grouping. Although I believed I could charm Miss Lemmon with my smooth engaging chatter and sparkling repartee, it didn't seem to work on Miss Hamilton, who saw me for what I was – Trouble!

After only a couple of days at my new school, I realised that there was an established gang under the control and leadership of a boy called Gordon Swinnerton, who was a year older than me. Gordon, thin-faced and wavy haired, was the son of a local waste disposal contractor. I set up a rival gang and we thought we were the bee's knees. Girls, of course, were not admitted. There were the usual spats between the gangs, as you might expect, but there was a running feud between me and a boy called Billy Young, who was the son of a well known GP in Heywood and an active member of Swinnerton's gang. Billy and I were forever fighting and on one occasion Miss Hamilton descended upon us like the wrath of God. She severely smacked our legs and made us stand apart in the playground facing the wall for the hour-long break at lunchtime. This punishment lasted for a whole week, which was tough stuff and today, probably, in violation of the European Court of Human Rights!

In my late teens I was to rediscover Gordon Swinnerton when our lives were running on parallel lines. He was then the Chairman of the Young Conservatives in Bury and I was doing exactly the same job in Rochdale. Later on he became a very successful Councillor on Bury Council and I was a Councillor in Rochdale. This time, however, there was no rivalry. It was amazing that looking back to when we were five or six, all we wanted to do was to organise and lead. Quite sickening really.

When I was eight I moved over to the Junior Boys' School and came under the control of Tom Kershaw, who was my form master and also the Commanding Officer of the Combined Cadet Force in the school. Lieutenant-Colonel Kershaw had been a subaltern during the war, had previously been a pupil at the school with my father, and knew of my father's war record. He was very likeable but 'vertically challenged', which is why he was known as 'Tich' Kershaw. He was very strict and not beyond using the cane if the occasion warranted it. For some inexplicable reason, I avoided being on the receiving end of

Bury Grammar School. The author is in the second row from the back, third from the right. The form master is Lieutenant-Colonel Tom Kershaw. In the seated row are: Billy Young (far left), John Thorne (third from the left) and Tommy Vickerstaff (second from the right).

this but was later to suffer much worse treatment at the hands of those who had made an art form of 'thrashing'.

My next form teacher was Tom Spencer, who was affectionately known as Tom Bottle – I don't know why. Like Tich Kershaw, Tom Bottle was a born teacher, but in contrast to Tich he was very tall. Between them, it was their principle task to steer the boys in their charge through the eleven-plus, or entrance examination, to the main boys' school. The fact that they were successful with me owes much to the fact that I was anxious not to let them down. My mother once went to a parents' evening and had a meeting with Tom Spencer. Unfortunately, his nickname was a household word at our home and she called him 'Mr Bottle' all evening. He never corrected her. Her embarrassment on discovering this mistake on her return home was toe-curling but understandable.

The day before I was to take the main entrance exam, I had a serious fight with a boy called John Thorn, who was eventually to become a good friend. It must have been serious because he broke my left arm and I ended up in Bury General Hospital. Slaughtered yet again! I suppose I must have done other things than fight, but I can't remember them. If I imagined that I would escape having to take the entrance exam the following day, my father quickly banished the thought as soon as I returned home in plaster from the hospital. 'You write with your right hand, so get on with it,' he said.

It was during the year that I was to enter the Senior Boys' School that my sister married. Bunty had been going out with a man called Roddy Black, who was to become a valued member of the family. Roddy, blond and good-looking and of average height, always looked extremely fit. He was rather quiet but always charming. Although I was only nine when I first met him, I was impressed by him and a close friendship started instantly, not least because occasionally he would pay me half a crown to go and get sweets from the local shop – I'm certain, just to get rid of me from time to time. When he confided in me that he was about to ask my father's permission to marry Bunty, my heart went out to him. To confront my father was a fate I wouldn't wish on my worst enemy, never mind a close friend.

To be fair, he had four points in his favour. He too had been a pupil at Bury Grammar School, he was a first-class footballer, and had completed his Army National Service in the Royal Artillery; all experiences shared by my father. Roddy, however, had the distinct advantage over my father of having been awarded the Kay Scholarship at Bury Grammar School, which is given to the boy who comes top in the entrance examination. There the comparisons ended. My father, in giving his permission, made it clear that although Roddy's school fees may have been picked up by the school through his scholarship, he would be expected to pick up all of Bunty's fees throughout their marriage.

I remember making my first public speech at their wedding. Forced into standing up by the acting toastmaster, Vernon Shepherd, I said, amongst other things, 'Now that my sister is leaving home, can I have a dog?' My father didn't know whether to laugh or cry. The next week I got the dog.

Vernon was a very old friend of the family. Spectacled and ruddy of face, he was certainly overweight, with wonderful steel-grey hair. He was always immaculately turned out and was good fun to be with.

When I entered the Senior Boys' School the following September, I had a reception party waiting for me. Arthur Ince, who was the Deputy Headmaster and Frank Ibbotson, who was a physics master, were the only two remaining teachers at the school who had taught my father when he was a pupil there. They stood outside the main door wearing their gowns, which were flapping wildly in the wind. They looked like 'the bats from hell.' Mr Ince put his hand on my shoulder and said, 'Welcome, Trippier. If you are half as good a footballer as your father, this school will do well.'

I cringe when I remember that incident because the truth is that I was useless at football. If I ever made the second team, it was a miracle. More often than not I was dropped to the third team, which was a great embarrassment. As usual my mother was very sympathetic at my plight and would praise any success I secured in other things, however small. For my father, however, nothing else was good enough. When I made the school swimming team, he was not impressed. When I was selected for the tennis team, he though that was 'wet'. When I was chosen for the school boxing team, that was 'OK' – but it still wasn't football.

Later on, he came round a little and occasionally went to some of the boxing matches I was involved in. The fact that I never lost a fight against another school owes nothing to my skill and everything to the fact that I have very little bone in my nose. As noses go, it is just an inelegant and squashy mass of rubber. Consequently, I have never had a nose bleed in my life and it is impossible to burst my nose. In those days, any schoolmaster who was acting as a referee in the ring would stop the fight at the first sight of blood, usually from the nose. So I kept winning, sometimes by default.

On one famous occasion we were boxing against Bolton School, which is well known to be good at sport. To my horror, my opponent in the welterweight contest stepped into the ring wearing the most elaborate boxing gear I had ever seen. Whereas all we ever wore was a white vest, navy blue shorts, short socks and pumps, this chap looked as if he was a professional. He wore pucker boxing boots and matching yellow silk singlet and shorts. I was struck by sheer unadulterated terror. Apart from being a pupil at Bolton School, he was clearly a member of an Amateur Boxing Club as well.

How I got through the first round I will never know. I spent more time on the canvas than Rembrandt. His arms seemed to be twice as long as mine and I couldn't get near him, so when the bell rang to signal the end of the first round, I had taken a lot of punishment. While I sat on the stool to get the magic sponge, my second, Dr Jim Moran, my chemistry master, suggested I should throw in the towel. To be honest, I felt like it. Although he had made contact with my nose a few times, there was no blood. 'I just want one shot at his nose, and if that doesn't work I've had it,' I muttered. Early in the second round, I caught his nose on the side of my glove. Not a good blow, but fortunately good enough, and the blood seemed to be everywhere. The fight was stopped and I was declared the winner, which was ridiculous really, because on points he would have won hands down. As it was, I could barely climb out of the ring. Certainly I didn't know where I was.

In many ways, I think it is sad that boxing has been banned in schools. It was an effective way of sorting out feuding problems between lads when a master would say, 'If you want to fight – do it properly. Get the gloves on and get into the ring in the gym.'

I was to suffer punishment of a different kind when, at sixteen, I disgraced myself by running a pair of girl's knickers up the school flagpole – I refuse to say where I got them from. It was April Fool's Day and everyone could see them fluttering in the breeze. The Headmistress of the Girls' School seemed amazingly distressed and telephoned my headmaster, John Hansford, expressing her anger in a decidedly one-sided conversation. The whole school was held back in the morning assembly until the culprit owned up. After what seemed like an age, I stuck my hand up and, to thunderous applause, which I liked, I was marched to the Headmaster's study for the usual punishment, which I did not. The Headmaster threw open the two doors of his cupboard and revealed a row of canes of different thicknesses. There must have been at least a dozen. 'Which one would you like, Trippier?' asked the Head.

I pointed to the thickest one. 'That one, please Sir.'

'I thought you would choose that one,' he said, 'I'm going to give you this one.' He then took down the thinnest and most painful. I vividly remember that when I bent down and he administered six of the best, I could see him by looking between my legs. Before each stroke he would take a little run at me, rather like a bowler taking a short run up to the crease. This was six of the very best ever!

Returning to my classroom immediately afterwards, I remember steeling myself not to shed a tear. That would have been a colossal loss of face. As it was, my face was simply drained and I could hardly sit down. I was in agony! Needless to say, my father never knew or I would have been punished again.

Although there was no direct connection between the Boys' and Girls' Schools of Bury Grammar, sitting virtually side by side to each other as they were, it would have taken more than the Berlin Wall to stop the pupils on either side of the barbed wire from socialising together. My first girlfriend at the Grammar School was Sylvia Ellis. Small of stature, with an elfin face and remarkably good legs, she was endowed with an underlying toughness that belied her somewhat delicate appearance. Clever and especially witty, she still plays a very special role in my life. Sylvia's father, Bernard, was a great character who was in textiles and in his spare time bred Arab horses. At a school Christmas Fair, supported by both schools, I introduced Sylvia to David Kay, who was not only a good friend but also my form prefect.

Not much taller than Sylvia, he had a cheeky face and markedly dry sense of humour. I never dreamt that they would eventually marry. I still see Sylvia and David today and their son Toby is my godson. Sylvia would always run a gimlet eye over any girlfriend I passed in front of her, and she must be a good friend, because if she didn't think the girl right for me, she would never hesitate to tell me.

When much later I was to introduce Ruth to her before we became engaged, I think it was the only time in her life that Ruth was really nervous. Fortunately they got on like a house on fire. Sylvia was already practising as a barrister and realising that Ruth wanted to qualify in the same profession, persuaded her to join Gray's Inn, which she subsequently did.

My social life during my schooldays was either in Tottington or Greenmount in Bury. It was a little difficult when I lived so far away in Rochdale, but the parties were too good to miss. Most Friday evenings there would be a party at Tommy Vickerstaff's house in Tottington in a converted attic meant to resemble a night club. Alternatively, the party would be at Sylvia's house in Greenmount. All of this was a relief from the academic side of the school, at which I did not excel. I remember the hateful school reports which my father waved in my face. Bunty had gone through the same pain during her school years. He always seemed to be standing in front of the fireplace thundering away, growing larger by the minute and terrifying me out of my wits. I suppose his anger couldn't have been as effective as it should have been, because I just wouldn't work hard enough.

In later years I was to experience a reversal of roles when, as an angry father, I faced my youngest son George, who also goes to Bury Grammar School. We sat at either end of the dining table and I was armed with his school report and the bill for his school fees. Straining for the necessarily high decibel level which would put the fear of God into any eight-year-old, I said, 'George, in this hand I have your school report, which is dreadful. In this other hand I have the bill for your school fees. Your mother and I have to work extremely hard to pay these fees and we don't think we are getting good value for money.'

George blinked back at me: 'Dad – I'm trying to eat as much as I can.'

On the point of cracking up with laughter, I swept out of the room to recover my composure in the loo. I think I needed a little more practise at playing the domineering father.

Looking back on my school years, I realise what a fool I was. To this day I have no qualifications except 7 GCE 'O' levels. Some would say, 'But what else would you have done with your life, David, if you had taken 'A' levels or perhaps gone on to university?' – a question I don't know the answer to. But I do know that life would have been more rewarding if I had achieved some tangible academic success. Fortunately I have always thought well of those who did achieve that success, so I have never been bedevilled by a chip on my shoulder. All this does help to explain why I admired Ruth for sticking at it and why I so enjoyed seeing her go through university and qualify at the Bar. It also explains why I can never be blasé about our children and their education. I suppose when one has been daft enough to leave school at sixteen, one is rather keen that one's children shouldn't make the same mistakes.

For me, the most rewarding part of being at Bury Grammar School was the Cadet Force. The C.C.F. was affiliated to the Lancashire Fusiliers and I enjoyed every minute of it. In this respect at least, my father and I were as one – we both loved anything military. In this force I could have my own uniform for once and I was determined to shine. Several of the masters were officers in the C.C.F. and Lieutenant-Colonel 'Tich' Kershaw was a huge success as the C.O.

Having just joined the C.C.F., which was not obligatory, the school welcomed a new Classics Master called Geoff Bennett. He was later to become the Commanding Officer, but at that time had recently left National Service, where he had been commissioned in the Lancashire Fusiliers. He was also an officer in the Territorial Army. Smart as paint, with a ready wit, Geoff Bennett had been a former pupil at the school, made Head Boy and played for the First XI football and cricket teams. To many of us he was a hero. To this day I recognise that he was, for me, a role model.

For a time, I seriously considered applying for a commission in the Regular Armed Forces but decided to pursue a career in politics. I would, however, later be commissioned in the Territorial Army and then the Royal Marines Reserve. In that way, I was to enjoy the best

Geoff Bennett in the uniform of the Lancashire Fusiliers. Later he became Lieutenant-Colonel Bennett T.D., C.O. of Bury Grammar School C.C.F.

of both worlds. It has to be said that Geoff Bennett, although he never knew it, was the inspiration for this. In the same immortal words I often use when talking about my bank manager, 'The debt I owe him can never be repaid.'

When my three sons were to go to Bury Grammar School, they had exactly the same experience that I had had aged eleven. There were still two masters that were teaching there who had taught me – Geoff Bennett and John Bisson – both popular, both respected.

Almost thirty years after leaving Bury Grammar, when I was the Minister for the Environment, the school invited me officially to open the extension to their new science block, which was a great honour. I couldn't help feeling the irony of the situation, as I was notably weak at science subjects when I was a pupil.

Two years later, and shortly after I was knighted, the Headmaster, Mr Keith Richards, who is a great success at the school, invited me to speak and present the prizes at the Annual Prize Giving Ceremony in the school hall. In my speech to the school and the parents, I explained that life had been difficult for me when I initially went to Bury Grammar School, having to follow a father who had achieved so much there. Then, in dramatic tones, I said very slowly, 'But there is one thing my father has never done at this school. He has never been invited to present the certificates and awards at Prize Giving. So this is a momentous night for me.' I then went on to reveal what had transpired when I went to see my father, who was then 83, to tell him that I had been asked to perform this great honour and that at last I was about to do something he hadn't done. Surely he would be impressed. His eyes reflected his genuine pleasure at the news, but once again he disguised his true feelings with his customary sharp wit. He smiled and said, 'David, most normal people achieve something significant at that school whilst they are still attending it. You have had to wait until you are 46 years of age before they have recognised you.' I couldn't stop laughing – it was true!

CHAPTER III

Stockbroking

'Buy me 100,000 ICI shares and 200,000 Shell.'

FROM ABOUT THE AGE OF 14, I had wanted to become a stockbroker and join my father's firm. My mother, however, was not so keen on the idea. She thought that the heavy responsibility of investing other people's money and worrying as to whether you had given the right advice had had an adverse effect on my father's health. Quite often he brought his problems home with him as he could never leave his responsibilities back at the office. Fortunately I could, and was temperamentally more suited to the profession than my father ever was. In truth, I have always enjoyed stockbroking. The Stock Exchange excited me and even now – having returned to broking – it holds a fascination for me which few professions could equal.

When I started working for my father in Rochdale, I was paid £15 a week, and that figure didn't rise much over the next few years either. My father seemed oblivious to inflation to the day he died and was constantly amazed at the price of things. It wasn't that he was mean with money, he was just careful – extremely careful. For as long as I can remember, he would dispense his largess to his children and grandchildren at birthdays and Christmas by stuffing a £5 note in an envelope. These were highly prized, while £10 notes were as rare as rocking-horse droppings. My mother was exactly the opposite – generous to a fault, she would give you her last farthing if it gave pleasure. It is nothing short of a blessing that she had her own income from the butcher's shops. It amused her, as well as Bunty and me, that she would go to extraordinary lengths to persuade my father that she was more frugal than he was. I don't know why she bothered, for he never believed it.

Her elaborate ploys would mean that we often plotted together, which was good fun. My mother would take me on one side and say:

'I have bought a new dress, David. I've hidden it under the bed. When you see me wear it, back me up by saying something like 'That always looks nice, Mum, but why don't you get something new?' Often there were so many carrier bags pushed under the bed that they would be coming out of the other side – still my father feigned ignorance. This was harmless stuff and anyway, I would always support her. She deserved to spend her money in the way she wanted and it gave her such pleasure.

My mother always looked immaculate and my father, for his own part, perpetuated the myth of her frugality and frequently exclaimed how amazing it was that she was so well dressed and spent so little money. My mother and I were always close, but as I grew older, and particularly in my late teens, we were great friends. We would talk endlessly about anything and everything, usually in the evening when she was ironing or washing up. Over a gin and tonic and one of my cigarettes – she never smoked on her own – she would advise, sympathise and make me laugh. However close I might have been to my father, he knew, but never resented the fact, that we were as thick as thieves. You don't have to be a rocket scientist to realise that in temperament and outlook I was much more like my mother. I even looked like her. At the same time, I obviously inherited my ambition from my father, and a healthy dose of cynicism, in contrast to her unswerving belief that everybody was kind and if you couldn't say something nice about them, you shouldn't say anything at all. My profligacy I obviously inherited from my mother, and I'm glad about that. At the same time, I can't help feeling that it would be better if I had achieved a little more balance between the two extremes. My sister is also more like my mother than my father, so it appears that the strict régime which Grandmother Trippier sought to impose on the family has run its course. Thank God!

Shortly after starting work, I met Adrian Bennett, who was to become my closest friend and eventually to be my best man at my wedding. I met Adrian at a dance hall in Rochdale called the Carlton, which was holding a dance for a foreign exchange visit with the French town Angoulême. That night Adrian had an immense advantage over me. He spoke excellent French and was making a good impression with the girls. My chat-up lines were incomprehensible, so when I overheard Adrian, I decided to get in on his act.

Adrian wore horn-rimmed spectacles and had light brown wavy hair, which even then had tinges of grey in it. Though he looked like an academic, he was in fact an electrical engineer at Whipp and Bourne in Rochdale. In so many ways we were opposites, which is probably why we got on so well. We certainly shared the same 'wacky' sense of humour, although his wit was sharper than mine. We became a double act and enjoyed the social high life, going around the Manchester night club scene and going out with girls. In contrast to me, Adrian was an accomplished sportsman and a particularly good footballer. Later, when we took up golf, he was superior to me in that too. Although he wanted to do well in his career, he was not remotely ambitious. My parents, as well as the wider family and other friends, adored Adrian. He must have spent almost as much time in our house as he did in his own.

On one occasion we had agreed to play a round of golf at Rochdale Golf Club and were to meet on a Sunday morning on the first tee at 8.00 am. I waited for about an hour and he still hadn't turned up. As Adrian's house was very near to the golf course, I walked over to find out what had happened.

I was treated to a very frosty reception by Mrs Bennett, who informed me that Adrian was very ill in bed. I was allowed to go upstairs to see him and was shocked to see that his face was badly bruised and he had a number of cuts on his nose. Apparently the previous evening he had attended a special reception at the Rochdale Town Hall for the football league of which his firm was a member. As Whipp and Bourne had won the silver cup for the championship, and as he was the team captain, he was expected to drink the contents of the cup 'down in one'. It was handed to him at the top of the stone steps. However, what he thought was beer turned out to be whisky. Having completed the appointed task, he beamed at the cheering crowd like an imbecile and instead of collapsing in a heap on the spot as a normal decent chap would have done, fell down the stairs, rolled past the Mayor and the various dignitaries, and continued at an increasing speed down 48 steps to the reception area below. Fortunately someone caught the cup. Having discovered that he was alive and almost well, the party carried on dancing round him. His football friends had deposited him on his doorstep at about 3.00 am, and not being able to find his key, he had remained there until his mother collected the milk at about 8.00 am, by which time he should have been on the first tee.

When I was certain he would eventually recover, I reminded him that he could never drink spirits – a comment which I now realise was not very helpful. I told him that had he been out with me, none of this would have happened. 'Now that's a problem,' he said, 'I've told my parents that I *was* out with you.'

I was incredulous. 'Why?' I asked.

'I don't know. It sounded better to say that you were there and could vouch for the fact I didn't disgrace myself.'

'Terrific', I said. 'OK, leave it to me.'

I went down the stairs and Mrs Bennett was standing in the hall – arms folded across her bust, a sure sign of anger and righteous indignation. 'A word with you, David,' she said through gritted teeth.

'Yes, Mrs Bennett' – 'Here we go,' I thought.

'Sit down', she said. I sat on the settee. Mr Bennett, who was a great chum, was sending me heart-rending signals of sympathy behind his wife's back. He was plainly embarrassed for me. 'It is clear to me that you are having an adverse effect on Adrian,' she told me.

'Yes, Mrs Bennett.'

'You know he can't drink spirits, but you persist in allowing him to drink them and make a complete fool of himself.'

'Yes, Mrs Bennett.' Then, as an afterthought, I went on, 'I don't think he made a fool of himself.'

'Rubbish', she said. 'Do you know his great-grandfather was an alcoholic?'

'No, Mrs Bennett.'

'Well he was, and laughing boy upstairs is going the same way. It will stop, David, and you will stop it. He is a disgrace and after last night, I now realise that the bad influence on him is you.'

'Yes, Mrs Bennett.' I then slunk out of the house looking suitably chastened. Whilst walking home, I was spitting rivets. How could he do this to me? By the time I reached home, I consoled myself with the thought that this is what friends were for. I had to stick by him, but I decided to give the Bennett household a wide berth for a few weeks. Months later, when his mother was in one of her better moods, Adrian confessed to her that I hadn't been with him when he met his Waterloo. Every time I saw Mrs Bennett after that I was treated like a king. No apology was forthcoming, instead she killed me with kindness.

When I was twenty-one, I acquired my first vehicle, a second-hand Mini van which appeared to be rather boring at first sight. It was medium grey in colour and needed some bells and whistles to pep it up. Adrian and I converted the dashboard in a rather dramatic way. We designed a walnut dashboard and fitted it, added a clock, a temperature gauge, other sophisticated measuring devices and a music tape deck. Adrian was the electrical genius behind all of this and I was just his assistant. When it was finished, it looked like the cockpit of a VC10. However, despite all this, it still lacked 'pulling-power', so we converted the rear of the van by fitting a thick rug, easy cushions and psychedelic lighting. It was called 'the passion wagon' and became quite famous for reasons I won't go into. Suffice to say, the van was not so much mine as ours, and Adrian had ready access to it when he wanted it.

In those days, most provincial firms of stockbrokers had a close liaison with a London firm in order that we could deal on the London Stock Exchange. The firm we used was called Grieveson Grant, which was a huge firm with a first-class reputation. I was informed that two of their senior partners were visiting their country-mice colleagues up and down the country and they were to visit our firm in two days' time. I was very worried about this meeting for two reasons. First of all, business was very quiet at the time and comparatively few orders were being put through Grieveson Grant. As we were such a small firm, it wouldn't have surprised me if they had wanted to sever the connection, which would have been disastrous for Austin Trippier and Company. Secondly my father was away on holiday and I would have to handle the meeting alone, and would undoubtedly be blamed for any adverse consequences.

I prepared for this meeting in two ways. First I arranged for Adrian to telephone me with a bogus order to buy shares during the interview with Grievesons. At least that would give them the clear impression that we were fairly busy. Secondly I was keen to let these distinguished gentlemen know that we were a 'high tech.' office by showing off the brand new dictaphone I had purchased. These machines had just come on the market and I knew that it would impress them if they saw ours in action and witnessed at first hand my masterly handling of the equipment.

On the day of the race, the meeting went horribly wrong. One of the two gentlemen was Sir Alexander Spearman, who must have been at least six foot two inches tall with distinguished iron-grey hair and a suit which represented twelve months' salary to me. He was a former M.P and was very charming. During the discussion Adrian telephoned at the pre-arranged time and I pressed the button to put him on the loud speaker so that his important order could be heard by the assembled throng. Doing his best for me, Adrian decided to exaggerate the value of the orders he gave me. It was ridiculous, and would have terrified Wall Street, never mind Rochdale. He said, 'Buy me 100,000 ICI shares and 200,000 Shell.' Sir Alexander's eyes were popping out of his head. He was obviously wondering whether we were dealing with another London firm and he was missing the cream.

When later they were to ask me to demonstrate the brand new dictaphone, I was delighted. With alacrity I pressed the button to play back a tape of a letter I had dictated the day before. This turned out to be a disaster as the lyrics of 'There's A Coach Coming In' from the recent musical *Paint Your Wagon* burst forth into my small office and I sank deeper into my chair. Sir Alexander shot back in his and after what seemed like a long silence, my treasured guests took their leave. They walked out of the office looking strained and bewildered and it was nothing short of a miracle that we kept the account with Grieveson Grant for many years afterwards. They obviously had no intention of severing the connection, so in retrospect my ham-fisted efforts to impress were unnecessary.

In 1972 I persuaded my father that we should merge with a Manchester firm of stockbrokers called Pilling and Co. It was clear that the profession was changing dramatically and the future would lie in more firms expanding in the large cities up and down the country. Things had moved on from the time immediately after the Second

Author sitting behind his stockbroker's desk. The infamous dictaphone is on the left.

World War, when Rochdale had no fewer than eight firms of stockbrokers. Those firms had grown with the high turnover of textile shares in the area, and at one time we even had a Stock Exchange of our own in Oldham. Sadly, with the demise of cotton, the number of firms in Rochdale went down to three. After the merger, my father remained in Rochdale while I moved to St Ann's Square in Manchester. The friends and business contacts I made in that wonderful city were to have a profound and lasting effect on my life. For me, the newly merged firm of Pilling, Trippier and Co. was a great success and I remained a partner until I became a Minister in 1983.

One other major event in my early stockbroking career was noteworthy. When all the Stock Exchanges were merged into the United Stock Exchange, we were canvassed as to whether we would be prepared to admit women as members. The Stock Exchange was the last bastion of male chauvinism and its doors were closed to women. There were no women stockbrokers, which was ridiculous in an emancipated age in which women had proved their success in so many professions. Every one of the 4,500 members had a vote in the Stock Exchange ballot and every time there was a ballot, I would vote for women to be admitted and every time my father would vote against. When I challenged him on his stance, he would argue that women would not be a success in the Stock Exchange and that the language would have to be cleaned up on the Stock Exchange floor. Eventually, when the vote was won by those of us in favour, my father never dreamt that later his own daughter would be admitted as a member and become a stockbroker. That was a happy day for me and I was very proud of Bunty.

My father was ecstatic and he threw a small party for her in our offices. When, tongue in cheek, I asked him why he had not thrown a party for me when I was admitted to the Stock Exchange, he said, 'David, this is different. This is a great day.'

Nearly choking, I said, 'But you kept voting to stop women becoming stockbrokers.' 'Did I?' he said in a bemused way, staring into the middle distance. 'Anyway, never mind that now. Don't forget, blood's thicker than water. Open another bottle of champagne.'

CHAPTER IV

Introduction to Politics

'Presentation Is Everything.'

IT WOULD BE WONDERFUL if I were able to say that I joined the Young Conservatives because of my passionate political commitment to their cause. The truth is that I didn't. At the age of nineteen, I don't think I had any clear political views at all. The nearest I ever got to political commitment was when I was a candidate in a mock election at school organised by a history master called Mr Hodgkiss. It was probably one of the first mock elections held in any school in the U.K. Certainly they only became fashionable many years later. Michael Booth in my form was to stand as the Conservative and Jimmy Holden was to stand as the Socialist. They couldn't find anyone to stand as the Liberal, so I volunteered; a decision which turned out to be a huge mistake.

A few days before the big debate in school, Jimmy and I went to the reference library in Bury to work on our speeches. We hadn't a clue what to say and while Jimmy was delving into works by Aneurin Bevan, Hugh Gaitskell et al., I was combing through Jo Grimond's biography and selected speeches of Lloyd George. On polling day, passionate speeches were made by all three candidates. It was clear that my speech didn't hit the spot and instead of the thunderous applause I had confidently expected, there was a deadly silence and I came bottom of the poll. I think I made the dreadful mistake of 'banging on' about the case for proportional representation and I lost the attention of the audience. I'm not even sure that at that time I myself understood proportional representation any more than they did. No serious politician could have had such an unpromising start to his career. It would be many years before my election results improved and the improvement was painfully slow.

Notwithstanding my shameful defeat, my mother was pleased I

stood for the Liberal Party as she was a member of the Rochdale Reform Club. Like many people in the town whose families had attended Baillie Street Methodist Church, they gravitated to the Liberals. My father was a staunch Conservative but not an active member. He was choked when my mother helped Ludovic Kennedy in a famous Rochdale by-election. Although he didn't win, he did well. Strong rumour had it that when Kennedy spoke at a public meeting in the Town Hall, his beautiful wife Moira Shearer, who was a ballerina and star of the film *Red Shoes*, crossed her legs on the platform and five hundred men swung their votes in favour of Ludovic. Heady stuff!

My mother could not drive and consequently my father always drove her everywhere. However, he drew the line at giving her a lift to the polling booth on an election day because he knew she would vote Liberal. She would stand patiently waiting for a bus whatever the weather, and he would smile and give her a wave as he drove past.

My first introduction to the Young Conservatives came as a result of gate-crashing a party in Rochdale. Adrian Bennett and I had been at a night club called the Cellar Club in the basement of the Town Hall. We decided that we needed more action and I remembered that there was a party at Elizabeth Wild's house in Cutgate – her parents were very friendly with my father and mother. The problem was we weren't invited, although I knew her slightly. On knocking on her door, Elizabeth opened it and seemed genuinely pleased that we had come.

The party consisted of a heaving mass of Rochdale Young Conservatives. Some I knew, many I didn't, but they were a lively and attractive bunch and we had an excellent evening. There were several people at that party who became, and remain, extremely close friends. Kaye Lindley was lovely and lively then as now. She had already met her future husband, Dennis Everett, a trainee solicitor. Keith Walker, another trainee solicitor, had not yet met his future wife and had to search as far afield as the Heywood Young Conservatives to find Susan. With such matchmaking, it was not surprising that the Young Conservatives Association was locally nicknamed the 'marriage bureau'. At that party I was introduced to a charming girl called Susan Nelson. Like Elizabeth Wild, she went to Rochdale Convent

Grammar School. She was very bonny, with a good figure and dark hair in a bouffant style. We hit it off immediately and she invited me to a Y.C. meeting the next Friday. I wasn't exactly keen to go to the meeting, but I was very keen to see Susan again.

The Conservative Party Headquarters in Rochdale consisted of a large meeting room, a reading library, an office for the agent, and on the top floor, a Conservative Club with bar, billiard tables and a lounge. The Y.C.s had invited a speaker called Bob Connell, who was the Chairman of the Manchester City Young Conservatives. He was good and I found myself agreeing with most of what he had to say. When he sat down, I asked a question which I hoped was sensible. The following week I was put on the Branch Committee, which would teach me not to open my mouth.

Looking back at the house party and my first Y.C. meeting, I realise how much I owe to Susan Nelson and Kaye Lindley for introducing me to another world. I never dreamt that it would eventually lead me into such a rewarding and exciting career in politics. I was soon swallowed up by the success of the Young Conservatives in those days. I enjoyed the politics as much as I enjoyed the social life, and both were equally demanding but great fun. We organised money-raising events, went away for hiking holidays to the Lake District or North Wales, and there was always a party going on somewhere.

On the political front, we canvassed at local and general elections. The opportunity often arose to meet some Conservative Members of Parliament and occasionally a Minister, but the thought that later I might become one myself never dawned on me. I did believe that I might possibly go on the local Council and that was as far as my horizon stretched.

I gradually climbed up the political ladder in the Y.C.s and eventually became the Chairman. During the whole of this time, our Friday night meetings were very well supported, with at least fifty people attending, and I found that my confidence in public speaking was growing all the time. I enjoyed the cut and thrust of debate and found that there was nothing so satisfying as to make a speech which was well prepared and held the attention of the audience, whilst at the same time convincing them of your argument and hopefully entertaining them. I also discovered that I was able to speak with very few notes – sometimes with none. By happy coincidence for me, there was a correlation between making speeches and piano playing. The trick with playing the piano by ear is subconsciously to commit to memory the tune you are trying to play. The trick with speeches was to commit to memory the most significant points you wished to make and without the prop of notes, deliver the speech in a fluent and articulate way. Presentation is everything.

During the time I was in the Young Conservatives, I was lucky enough to win the North-West of England Courier Cup for Public Speaking, which was a competition organised for all branches of the Y.C.s in the north-west. John Kay, who is a great friend, was my chairman for the competition. Tall and be-spectacled, and somewhat Victorian in appearance, he was no mean speaker himself. After delivering my prepared speech, I had to answer questions on the topic from the judges for twenty minutes.

Flushed with this success, we entered the public speaking competition of the Rochdale Youth Music Festival, open to anyone under twenty-one years of age. For this we had to have a third member of the team, who would give the vote of thanks. Joanne Tomkinson, who was a Y.C. and former pupil at Bury Grammar School, performed this role beautifully and again we won the cup. Later, when age determined that I should leave the Y.C.s and become a card-carrying member of the senior Association, John and I entered the big league and won the Conservative Party's cup for public speaking in the north-west.

As some of this success attracted local and regional publicity, I decided to have a heart-to-heart conversation with my mother concerning her membership of the Liberal Party. I dared to suggest that some people were having a lot of fun at our expense because we seemed to be a politically split family, and to my astonishment she agreed to leave the Liberals and join the Conservatives. I would love to think that this was all due to my success in persuading her of the merits of Conservative philosophy, but I think I was assisted by the fact that Jo Grimond had retired as Liberal Leader and she wasn't anywhere near so obsessed by his successor, Jeremy Thorpe. At any rate, my father was delighted to be running her to the polls in his car.

Whilst in the Y.C.s, I learnt some valuable lessons which were to stand me in good stead in my later political life. In all organisations there is a great deal of plotting and conniving going on behind the scenes and the Y.C.s were no exception. Such activity was, and remains to this day, the least attractive and most pernicious side of politics in all parties. Although no party has a monopoly of expertise in this field, the Y.C.s in Rochdale were high in the league of gerrymandering and intrigue. Although it was all fairly harmless stuff at that level, I suppose it is a condition of politics that there are those who love to be 'fixers' behind the scenes rather than leaders with the much greater responsibility of setting an example and building up team spirit.

I owe a great deal to John Sandiford, who was the Machiavelli of the Rochdale Y.C.s. True to his character, he was somewhat sinister in appearance despite being tall and well built. He wore his hair short and invariably smoked a pipe. A man of great ability, he loved the intrigue and fixing and was Warwick the Kingmaker, never the king. Fortunately, he was usually on my side. The reason I will always be grateful to John is that he was the first person to teach me that political naivety was the downfall of the unwary and that quite often there were forces at work which one needed to be aware of. If you didn't square up to them, they could topple you. From time to time in my career I would encounter a relatively small number of people who would pat me on the back and at the same time shove a knife in it. I'm glad I learnt this lesson when I was so young, because I now think I can spot them a mile off. They are difficult to describe, but so is an elephant, and I've never failed to recognise one on sight.

One of the other members of the Y.C.s who was to become a long-standing friend was Stuart Clough. He was going out with a girl called Susan Topper, who, I thought, was the most attractive girl in the Y.C.s – at this time I was still seeing Susan Nelson. Stuart and I ended up swapping our girl friends and, however unlikely it sounds, the new arrangement was to the complete satisfaction of all concerned and there was no acrimony whatsoever. In fact Susan Nelson remains a friend to this day. Later on she married another friend from the Y.C.s, John Howard, who was a Chartered Account.

I was besotted by Susan Topper with her classical features, fine bone structure and aristocratic nose. She was small with stocky legs and an

A group of Rochdale Y.C.s. From left to right: John Howard, Susan Nelson, Stuart Clough, Christine Matterson, Jacqueline Grice, the author, Dennis Everett, Kaye Lindley.

attractively trim waist. She was a staff nurse at the Rochdale Infirmary and won several awards in various disciplines in nursing, which she was very modest about. I was unaware of this success in her chosen vocation until my mother happened to go to a nurses' prize-giving ceremony at the Town Hall when Susan swept the board, winning most of the prizes, and was the star of the show. She soon became a Nursing Sister and was probably the youngest Sister to be appointed in Rochdale.

Susan was very vivacious and with her good looks she would never fail to turn heads at any gathering. I was as pleased as punch to be going out with her but there was one problem which was to be my undoing in the relationship – she was three years older than I and was undoubtedly well established in her chosen career. When we started our relationship, I was only nineteen, still a trainee stockbroker, and, in short, really only a clerk. As this was a period long before I was to acquire my own vehicle – the infamous grey mini-van – I was dependent on my father lending me his car when we went out. At the time it didn't seem to matter to either of us because we had wonderful times together.

The rot set in when Susan joined the Army and became a lieutenant in the Queen Alexandra's Royal Army Nursing Corps. To be brutally frank, I was largely responsible for her joining, for my grand plan was that she would complete her two years' short-service commission and then we could be married. By the time Susan went to Catterick for her initial military training, I was twenty and thought I would have to wait at least two years before having the slightest chance of becoming a stockbroker. I know that my motivation for persuading Susan to join the Army was wrapped up with my obsession with matters military. In truth, Susan was reluctant to go but believed that it would work out in the end. After all, scores had gone away when National Service was compulsory and had returned to marry their sweethearts. The difference here was it wasn't the man who was going away, and I soon learnt that the phrase 'absence makes the heart grow fonder' is tommyrot.

Not surprisingly, the male officers were attracted to Susan like moths to a flame. At that time there must have been twenty times as many male officers as there were women and these men were mostly fresh out of Sandhurst, with smart uniforms, sports cars of their own and probably more than £15 per week in their pockets. How could I have been so stupid as to push her into the arms of so many rivals? They couldn't fail to fall in love with such a lovely girl, who looked so elegant in her grey uniform with the bright red cape adding just that extra hint of magic.

The regular telephone calls and letters to each other become more infrequent and my visits to her garrison postings and her return visits to Rochdale grew fewer and fewer. Eventually she met an officer in the Royal Signals who was of her own age and much more mature than I was then. She came home to Rochdale to tell me that she was to become engaged and she handled the meeting with great skill and her customary charm.

I had known for a long time that the relationship was coming to an end, but I was still devastated. I tried to put a brave face on it, but for months after our last meeting I was thoroughly miserable. I lost my sense of humour, I was depressed and I couldn't pull myself out of it. I disguised my true feelings from everyone, except of course my mother, for there was no point in trying to hide them from her – she knew me too well. My mother gave all the right advice – I would get over it – there are hundreds of other girls out there – she was never right for you anyway. Of course, at twenty, I didn't believe a word of it. She was right, of course, and I did fall in love again, but not for another seven years.

Many months later, just when I thought I was getting over the affair, I saw the photograph of Susan's wedding in the local paper. She and her husband looked blissfully happy, she was as lovely as ever and he was handsome – damn him. I rushed from the kitchen to the bathroom and was physically sick.

In the death-throws of any relationship people can be forgiven for saying hurtful things. I cringe when I think of some of my cut-off lines, but although I've not seen Susan for thirty-three years, I would wager she will smile, as I do, when she recalls her final 'coup de grace': 'David,' she said, 'you are a clerk now and you will be a clerk for the rest of your life.'

CHAPTER V

Local Councillor

'Oh my God – get me our election manifesto.'

WHEN I WAS TWENTY-ONE, I stood as a candidate in the Rochdale local elections for Falinge Ward. The Conservative Ward Committee in Falinge was very strong and its Chairman was Mrs Florrie Widdup. She was a sizeable lady with spectacles and tight bun at the back of her head. She was widely considered formidable. Her daughter Barbara was stocky and wore rimless glasses and heavy brogues. Together they were the backbone of the party in Falinge. They lived and breathed Conservatism and were very knowledgeable politically. Both were also very witty and good fun to be with.

Falinge was the Ward which Cyril Smith represented as a Councillor. By this time he had been elevated to be an Alderman and therefore did not have to seek re-election. The Conservatives held two of the three seats in the ward: their members were Councillor Edward Collins, a local solicitor and Councillor Ronnie Bridden who worked at Whipp and Bourne with Adrian Bennett. Edward was later to stand as the parliamentary candidate in the General Election of 1970 and although he was unsuccessful, he had a higher percentage of the votes than any Tory candidate before or since. Cyril was to stand in the same general election and although unsuccessful on that occasion, he was soon to become the Member of Parliament in the by-election in 1972 caused by the demise of the Labour MP, Jack McCann, who had been a very popular Member.

I didn't win the seat in Falinge and I was unsuccessful largely due to the fact that Frank Abbott, who was the Liberal Councillor defending his seat, had a very strong local following and was popular as well as hard-working. He was a butcher on Spotland Road and knew my mother very well.

Having failed in Falinge in 1967, I was then selected to stand in the following year as the candidate for Brimrod Ward for the local elections and this time was successful. The backbone of that Ward was Ida Woolfenden who was the Secretary. Tall and very smart, she enjoyed periods of self-flagellation, to the great amusement of those in her company. But to me she became a close and valued friend. Everyone worked their socks off to ensure I was elected and I had a first-class working relationship with the other two Councillors for the Ward, Councillor Alan Thompson and Councillor John Fletcher.

The Labour candidate whom I defeated was Derrick Walker. In the past he had been the Leader of the Labour Group and was the principle exponent of a harebrained scheme to build an Arts Centre over the beautiful Memorial Gardens in the town. As I had promised the electorate that I would do everything to stop this happening, I had to start the campaign shortly after taking my seat in the Town Hall.

Rochdale Town Hall is one of the finest in the country. Although it is a Gothic reproduction, it is a masterpiece and a credit to those who had the foresight to build it 180 years ago, and I was very proud to be a member of this Council. I quickly found that the quality of debate was very high and although this high standard was set and maintained by relatively few of the members, I realised that all members, whatever their Party allegiance, had a part to play and were motivated to do all they could for the benefit of the County Borough.

It should be recorded that no town council had sent as many Members of Parliament to Westminster: Sir Tom Normanton, Michael English, Sir Cyril Smith, Roger Stott and Ernest Thornton. Later, when local government reorganisation had taken place in 1973, the boundaries of the new Metropolitan Council embraced Middleton and Heywood as well as many of the outlying villages surrounding the area. This enabled the wider Rochdale area to claim that other former Councillors had become M.P.s: Jim Callaghan (not the former P.M.) from Middleton and Jim Dobbie from the same town. At the time I joined the Council, it had not occurred to me that eventually I would be joining this list.

The principle player in the Rochdale Council when I was a new member was undoubtedly Cyril Smith. Larger than life at 29 stones in weight, and a gifted orator with a sharp mind, he and I were to become firm friends despite our political differences. Our friendship stemmed initially from the fact that during the War my mother had always made sure that Cyril's mother had sufficient meat for the family, including Cyril and his brother and sister. They were a very poor family without a father to support them. Cyril never forgot my mother's kindness and he was kind to me because I was Mary Trippier's son. It also allowed me to escape his pulverising onslaughts when he was minded to stick the knife into the Conservatives.

The Conservative Leader on the Council at that time was Alderman Tommy Rose. Tommy, with his short stature, white hair, red face and eyes forever twinkling at you through his spectacles, was like one of the more delightful characters in a Charles Dickens novel, and always ready with a new joke to share with you. He lost no time in taking me under his wing and becoming my political godfather, doing all in his power to further my cause. I was flattered to be his friend.

It was clear from the early days on the Council that relatively few were party-politically minded. However, I certainly was and found that the debates were more highly charged when the subject matter overflowed into national politics. This was inevitable and mainly good fun. Fortunately personalities were usually kept out of the debates and frequently after the dust had settled, a cross section of Councillors and Aldermen from the three parties would adjourn to the Flying Horse pub to sink a few well earned pints.

I found the work that I had to do for individual constituents in my ward to be demanding but enjoyable and in most cases I found I was able to sort out a number of problems. It certainly meant that the telephone rang a lot and with committee meetings of the Council, I was out most evenings.

I recall a very unsavoury incident when I was sent a dead rat in a jiffy bag through the post with a note attached which read, 'How would you like this running round your house?' I was on the case immediately, half of me dreading what would be coming through the post next.

The campaign to save the Memorial Gardens in Rochdale was to become the single most important campaign I was ever to run at a local level. It took an inordinate amount of time and the organisation of the campaign was designed to attract support from individuals and voluntary bodies who had never dreamt that they would feel so vehemently about anything. There were three distinguished luminaries who were to join me in defeating the plan to dig up the Gardens and build an Arts Centre: Berkeley Moir, who was the senior partner in Moir and Bateman, Architects, John Taylor, a solicitor with Standring Taylor, and Lady Morrison, who lived near the centre of the town and was the widow of Herbert Morrison, the former Labour Cabinet Minister.

A former Lieutenant-Commander in the Royal Navy, Berkeley was an absolute gentleman to his fingertips, distinguished in appearance, with his balding head, though what hair he had was a little too long at the back. To look at him, you would have taken him at first glance for an architect. John too had been a Naval officer, and had won the Distinguished Service Cross for his bravery during the War. He was unusually tall and stooping, and sometimes slightly clumsy. Lady Morrison was a stocky and somewhat formidable lady, and a no-nonsense kind of person. Together we initiated a petition which attracted over a hundred thousand signatures and there was no shortage of people to collect these signatures. We were fortunate in enlisting the support of the *Rochdale Observer*, BBC Television in the north-west and Granada TV, and together with help from local radio stations and other local newspapers, the campaign gathered momentum and became the principal talking point in the town.

It was significant that the Gardens were not only very attractive but also surrounded the memorial built to honour those who had given their lives in the two World Wars. Naturally, this sparked a reaction amongst the Royal British Legion and many other ex-service organisations in the town. The memorial itself was a replica of the cenotaph in Whitehall. Behind this was a garden for the blind which was very popular with the local Blind Society, as their members could enjoy a wide variety of sweet smelling flowers. It was sad that they couldn't see them as well for they were beautiful.

The issue of the Memorial Gardens was hotly debated in the Council Chamber and it took all the skill of the then Mayor, Alderman John Fox, to maintain order. I was a great fan of John Fox. He was a Liberal, a former headmaster, and had an outstanding service career which spanned the two Wars. He was decorated with the Military Cross – not just once but twice, and had concluded his Army service as a Major. He was always immaculate and as straight as a ramrod.

I think he was a little unnerved by the fact that I seemed to be taking on the majority of the Council on this issue, although he was sympathetic to the crusade. Another Liberal colleague of his, Councillor Tom Chadwick, was not only sympathetic to our cause but, along with Berkeley Moir, was instrumental in galvanising the Rochdale Civic Society to oppose the Arts Centre. The vast majority of the Conservative Group on the Council were gathering behind me in increasing numbers, with the Labour Councillors embarrassed into silence when they saw how the whole town seemed to be outraged by the proposal.

Lady Morrison and I travelled by train to London to present the petition to a Minister in the Department of the Environment. Although the Minister was only the first rung of the Government ladder, I was impressed by his grasp of the issues. It was Michael Heseltine, who was young, dynamic and clearly going places. I never dreamt that his office in the DOE where we had the meeting would much later be occupied by me. It was clear that Michael thought that the Arts Centre proposal was quite daft and made clear that the Government would oppose it if it ever saw the light of day.

The final death knell which resulted in the scheme becoming buried for ever was a presentation I gave to the planning committee, showing plans drawn up by Berkeley Moir revealing how an Arts Centre could still be built in the Town Centre while retaining the Memorial Gardens in their entirety. In the event, the Committee, and later the full Council, shelved the Arts Centre plans and subsequently they were dropped. We had won. It was a truly wonderful victory, the outcome of a fight that had been hard fought. Even though all of us who had campaigned for so long were tired out, it was thoroughly worth our efforts.

There was no doubt that the campaign had given me a higher profile than I would have thought possible after such a short time on the Council. Only then did I think of becoming a Member of Parliament. I had discovered that if one wanted to be a responsible member of society, then one had to be active in trying to shape it.

After Local Government reorganisation, the outlying districts and rural areas that surrounded Rochdale, which had became part of the new Metropolitan Borough, invariably returned Conservative Councillors. Although we didn't have control of the Council – that was still in the hands of the Socialists – our numbers had swollen and it was perfectly possible for us to take control in the next few years. There were to be other benefits as more Conservatives came into the Council. New members included Keith Walker, my old friend from the Y.C.s, who represented a Heywood seat, and his wife Susan, who represented the same Ward.

One of the most significant events which was to happen as far as I was concerned was the election of Mary Tomlinson as a Conservative Councillor for my own Ward. This had increased in size and was now known as Brimrod and Deeplish. Mary was a most attractive woman, small and deceptively delicate in appearance, yet a 'workaholic', full of energy and forever dashing here and there. She was a great asset and brought considerable political clout to the Council as she had been the Chairman of the Women Conservatives in the town. She would later rise to become the Chairman of the North-West of England Area Conservatives and was awarded the CBE in 1991. She is godmother to our second son Edward and she and her husband Bill are very close friends. Mary took to Council work like a duck to water and in no time she was making her mark. Always conscientious, she would take up every single complaint or problem brought by the electorate in the ward. Nothing was too much trouble.

It was clear at this time that we had a persistent and habitual complainer on our hands. The gentleman in question would telephone Mary or myself from his flat in Ashfield Valley. This was a difficult area for us to look after, with highly concentrated tower blocks, masses of vandalism and graffiti, and a fair amount of criminal activity to boot. Our constituent was constantly complaining that he was being victimised by several neighbours and would telephone at all hours of the day or night wanting one of us to visit him to calm him down. If it was dark, I would never let Mary go by herself for fear of her safety. Although he would always receive a visit, he would practise his own brand of blackmail by threatening that if one of us didn't go round immediately, he would commit suicide by jumping off the twelfth floor. This went on for months.

The Leader of Rochdale Council outside the Town Hall.

After a protracted burst of these phone calls – quite often at two o'clock in the morning – my charm was wearing thin and I was fast coming to the end of my tether. Finally I snapped. When he rang at half past two, yet again with the same story and threat of suicide, I said, 'I will come in the morning.' When he told me he was going to jump, I retorted, 'O.K., jump', and then hung up. However hard I tried to get to sleep, I found I couldn't. Pacing around the bedroom, I was beside myself with worry that I could be wholly responsible for his death if he carried out the threat. Much to my relief, when I called on him the next day, he was fine and after that incident we were only bothered in more civilised hours.

In 1974, I became the Leader of the Conservative Group on the Council. Although I thought we would do quite well in the subsequent May elections the following year, I never thought we would take control of the Council, but I was to be proved wrong. As the results came through to the Party H.Q., they were being chalked up on the blackboard – clearly not the stuff of high technology – and result after result showed a Conservative gain. The sudden thought dawned on my dull brain that we were in danger of winning this election. We would then control the Council and I would become the Leader of it.

'Oh my God,' I said to John Fletcher, 'Get me our election manifesto to remind me what promises we gave the people. We are going to have to deliver them.'

CHAPTER VI

The Cavalry

'What does your worst enemy think of you?'

THOSE WHO KNOW ME WELL would assume that I have spent the whole of my twenty-two years' service in the Reserve Forces in the Royal Marines. However, prior to that I was an officer in the Territorial Army. In 1967 I joined as an Officer Cadet in the 40/41st Royal Tank Regiment in Oldham. It was a first-class regiment and was equipped with Centurion Tanks. Shortly after I signed up, Harold Wilson dramatically reorganised the TA and much of its new role was in Home Defence. We were informed that we were to be merged with the Duke of Lancaster's Own Yeomanary, whose previous role had been reconnaissance – very similar to the role of my father's regiment, the Northumberland Hussars. After the War, his regiment was re-rolled from Artillery to Armoured Cars.

My Squadron Commander was Major Robin Greaves and the squadron officers' mess in Oldham was most impressive. Robin was a friend to me and did a great deal to ensure that I would take a commission after basic training. As a result of a serious accident in his mid-twenties, he had lost an eye and his party trick on Mess nights was to remove his glass eye and wash it in a pint of bitter! In another amusing incident at that time, Robin had his sports car completely squashed when a Centurion Tank unexpectedly rolled off the back of a tank-trailer on Salisbury Plain. Happy days!

The Commanding Officer of the 40/41st was a regular soldier named Lieutenant-Colonel Alan Parks, who was the epitome of what every CO should look like: steel-grey hair, tall and elegant. The Second-in-Command was a Territorial named Major Brian Mallalieu, who had a senior position in the Oldham Metropolitan Borough Council. Both officers had seen war service. Another senior officer, who was also a stockbroker in Manchester, was Major Michael Seal, who was an excellent officer and, sadly for me, was about to retire, having decided not to be part of the merger with the Cavalry. The other subalterns were determined to continue and all of them remain friends of mine to this day: David Ingram had been a regular officer and was in Insurance. Ted Clucas eventually left to become a pilot in the RAF and later became a very successful businessman in Jersey. David Rodger was the Mess Secretary and for a time I was his assistant. During David's service in the TA he wore more cap badges than anyone I have ever known, and he ended up as a Major in the Royal Engineers with an MBE to his credit.

The merger with the Duke of Lancaster's Own Yeomanry was to go much more smoothly than anyone had thought. It was something of an experience for the Royal Tank Regiment Officers, who were a lively lot but a far more eclectic mix than the officers of the cavalry regiment with whom they merged, whose officers were drawn from the hunting, shooting and fishing fraternity. The DLOY wore uniforms that were more flamboyant and one of their aims in life was to ensure that no two officers would appear in the field or on the parade ground wearing the same kit. In many ways my experience was similar to my father's when he joined the Northumberland Hussars. I found that I liked and respected them and although their Mess functions were really wild – wilder than anything I had experienced in the Royal Tank Regiment – many of them were extremely able, intelligent, capable and successful businessmen.

When the merger took place, the new Commanding Officer was Lieutenant-Colonel Norman Phillips, who at the time was a director of Wilson's Brewery. Colonel Norman was very much the country gentleman, with dark hair brushed down severely on either side of his parting. He was very professional and it is largely due to him that the two regiments with rather different traditions should have come together so successfully. He had been a regular soldier and for a time had served in the Royal Horse Artillery.

After I was passed by the regimental board of the new Regiment for a commission, the recommendation was endorsed by the Commanding Officer and I had to present myself before the Army Commissioning Board, which was to hold interviews for a host of candidates from the north-west of England. The chosen venue for this interview was at the Royal Artillery Headquarters in Manchester. The experience was very nerve-wracking; the President of the Board was a full colonel and he was flanked by four other senior officers who were determined to weed out those who did not hit the mark.

One member of this Board interested me a great deal. He was a lieutenant-colonel and his questions were more aggressive than anyone else's. In the middle of his cross examination of me he fired off his favourite question, which he had obviously rehearsed with all the other candidates.

'What does your worst enemy think of you?' he said.

There was a dreadful pause as my brain went into overdrive. What on earth could I say? This was a catch question. Obviously everyone had enemies. I decided to make a joke out of it.

'I think he thinks I'm an absolute bastard, Sir.'

'Why is that?' he barked back at me.

'He believes his wife is in love with me.'

There was a silence. Then the President of the Board burst out laughing and said, 'We had better move on to the next question.'

As everyone on the board with the exception of the lieutenant-colonel who had asked the question was either smiling or laughing, I thought I might just have got away with it. I returned to the waiting room, where there were at least half a dozen candidates left who were waiting for the result of their interviews. I only knew one of them slightly.. He said to me, 'Did they ask you what does your worst enemy think of you? I told them I had no enemies.'

'I suspect that there's only one wrong answer and that's it!' I told him. The most important man who ever lived was nailed to a cross. Even he had enemies.'

'Oh yes', he said, 'I've failed.' And sadly he had.

I received the news that I had passed the Board, and was commissioned in the Duke of Lancaster's Own Yeomanry (Royal Tank Regiment), which must be the longest title of any regiment in the British Army (but probably someone will prove me wrong). I was delighted with the news and my father smiled and nodded approval, which was his equivalent of doing cartwheels. However, the cartwheels did not last.

Not long afterwards a time came when we were completely at loggerheads. The final battle-lines were drawn, there was to be no give and take and no quarter given. All this fuss concerned a horse called Chieftain.

On a regular basis several officers and Senior NCOs from the Regiment undertook serious instruction at a riding school at Buckley Hill owned by an autocrat named Captain Milton. This was entirely voluntary and we would turn up on Saturday mornings when we didn't have a military training weekend in the field. It was a perfectly natural thing for those of us in the cavalry to do. I became an enthusiast and developed a love of horses which has never left me. It was great fun to gallop through Tatton Park from time to time, but I particularly enjoyed the jumps over the fences in the riding school, and despite repeated falls, some more painful than others, I gradually became proficient and decided to buy my own horse.

Not being expert enough to select a horse which would be suitable, and particularly one that would make a good show jumper, I relied heavily on the expertise of Bernard Ellis, the father of my former girlfriend, Sylvia, whom I had met at Bury Grammar School. He had been an amateur jockey and because of his successful textiles business, he was able to concentrate on his real passion of breeding Arabs. He was small, good looking, witty and his knowledge of horses and their ability was excellent. We had a lot of fun combing the countryside together, visiting stables which had horses to sell. Eventually he found me a fine hunter which had just arrived from Ireland. Just short of 16 hands, he was beautiful and I was thrilled. Bernard quickly saw his enormous potential.

Having purchased the horse, I therefore arranged stabling at Bamford. I let my mother into the secret but instinctively knew my father would not approve. My mother and I discussed methods of concealment – the time-honoured remedy of hiding purchases under the bed was hardly appropriate in this case. When my father found out, he was furious. He never liked horses or wanted to be near them, and his only experience of riding them had ended in a disastrous fall. He didn't speak to me for weeks and on this occasion did not come round easily. The only saving grace was that my enthusiasm was being stimulated by my friends in the Yeomanry. This he couldn't deny and

Ruth with Chieftain.

although he may have been the toast of another Cavalry regiment, his success owed nothing to horses whatsoever.

I spent countless hours training Chieftain to jump fences and often my mother would come and watch. Sometimes she would be picking up the fences we had knocked down; at other times she would pick me up.

One day I had been out riding with a girlfriend called Joanna Gartside who had her own horse, Minstrel. She was a wonderful rider and far better than I. The rain was teeming down and Joanna beat a hasty retreat to her own home. I called in at my home and parked the horse in the garage for some respite from the harsh weather.

When my father came into the garage to see what was going on, he was amazed at the enormous size of Chieftain, who must have looked fearsome as he was steaming and hungry. My father backed away and fell over a wheelbarrow. Then the inevitable happened. Chieftain decided to unload the contents of his stomach all over the garage floor. 'Get him out,' my father shouted. As I turned the horse round, he stood on my father's foot and he screamed with pain. Fortunately his outburst did not cause Chieftain to lash out and kick him. He had a marvellous disposition – alas my father did not. Reluctantly we rode back into the storm and the two of them were never reconciled.

When eventually I had to sell Chieftain (because of pressure of business and politics) he was bought by a gentleman called Mr Appleyard, who lived at a farm near Harvey Smith, the Olympic show jumper, in Yorkshire. Mr Appleyard had a string of show jumpers as well as a whole host of riders who could concentrate many more hours on developing Chieftain's potential, which Bernard Ellis had spotted a few years before.

Mr Appleyard changed Chieftain's name to North Star because he had a white blaze on his nose. This upset me a little as I thought Chieftain was a fine name. He soon became a Category 'A' show jumper and in his heyday won at the Great Yorkshire Show. He was then valued at many thousands of pounds. I had bought him for £400 in 1969 and sold him for £600 in 1972. Not exactly my best investment, but the hours of pleasure I had with that horse were beyond price.

Years later Ruth and I visited a horse show in Yorkshire and Chieftain was there. I blew up his nose and he recognised me. I said to Mr Appleyard, 'This is my horse.'

'No', he said with typical Yorkshire charm, 'He's mine, lad!'

My commissioned service in the Cavalry was to be of short duration. Once again there were going to be defence cuts and the DLOY were sadly to be reduced to a relatively small cadre. This, loosely interpreted, meant that it would be a permanent unit forming the nucleus for expansion at need. All of us who were in the Regiment were saddened by this bitter blow. Although a number of years later the DLOY were to be revived as a full regiment, I thought that I had to move on as I certainly wished to make a significant contribution somewhere.

A number of officers, senior NCOs and men were transferred to the Royal Engineers, who were to take over our Drill Hall. Although the Sappers are a Corps for which I have the highest regard, I would have been totally out of my depth as I was not an engineer and, worse still, I was technically dim.

Although there might have been other Regiments in the TA that I might have applied for, I had recently met up with some Royal Marines on a weekend's training at a Military Camp at Leek in Staffordshire. I wrongly assumed that they were regulars, as I never knew that there was a Royal Marines Reserve. They stood out in a crowd because they wore the green beret which is the hallmark of the Commando. They were extremely smart, very fit and switched on. I spoke to one of their officers, Major David Ellis, who kindly invited me to their Drill Night in Birkenhead to meet their Commanding Officer, Lieutenant-Colonel Tom Sherman.

My meeting with Colonel Sherman was to be of great significance. That was the first meeting of many which have taken place over the last thirty-one years, and many can vouch for the fact that despite the difference in our ages, Tom Sherman has always remained one of my closest friends.

Tom certainly looked the part with his greying hair, bristling moustache and steely blue eyes, which for some of the time could look kindly when he was genuinely pleased. On other occasions, when he was genuinely fierce, his gaze could rip the top off a pressure cooker. He had seen considerable action in the War, not least of all in the Commando raid on St Nazaire. After a lengthy interview, he made it clear that he could accept my transfer to the Marines Reserve, but it would be wholly conditional on me qualifying for the green beret on the Commando course. If I failed this, then I would have to leave.

I asked him what the Marines might feel about someone joining them from the Army and his reply was clear and to the point: 'They won't mind at all as long as you get the green beret. After all, I was originally in the Army, in the King's Regiment, before I volunteered for the Army Commandos. I only transferred to the Royal Marines Reserve after the War, when the responsibility for providing Commando forces moved entirely across to the Royal Marines.'

When I discussed the offer I had received with my father, he was very concerned about the risk I was taking. 'The challenge of the Commando Course is daunting,' he told me. 'If you fail, the Army could be forgiven for not having you back.'

I suppose life is full of risks and I had to accept the challenge. I never dreamt that what was to follow would stretch me to the very limit.

CHAPTER VII

The Green Beret

'Abandon hope all ye who enter here.'

MOST PEOPLE WOULD BE surprised to hear that apart from my family, I treasure my association with the Royal Marines more than anything else in my life. Whatever success I may have achieved in politics or business remains very important to me, but it pales by comparison with my love and admiration for the Corps and its Reserve Forces. I have never been so proud of being in any other organisation as I am of being a member of the Royal Marines family.

For over three hundred years the Royal Marines have fought with heroism and distinction in all corners of the world. Undeniably they are amongst the finest fighting troops in the world today and conventional tactics have never been their hallmark. Dedication, cunning, guile and unwearying determination are their stock in trade. They are simply different. The principle reason why they are different is that in a modern consumer-orientated society, where discipline is scorned and the scramble for wealth is foremost in the minds of our youth, the green beret of the Royal Marine Commandos remains a symbol of excellence, dedication and professionalism; an accolade for those who push themselves beyond the limits of normal human endurance. The green beret is not for sale. Thousands have sought to attain it but along the way many have wilted and failed. It is a classless symbol of fortitude and achievement.

Perhaps above all else the Royal Marines are a family and they never forget it. The Royal Marines Reserve are part of that family and there is a mutual respect between those in the regular corps, whose full-time career is totally committed to the service, and those of us who have to hold down a demanding civilian job whilst still maintaining the high standards demanded by the parent Corps. Either way, both the Regulars and the Reserve have to attain the green beret. There is no escape.

My initial reaction to my transfer to the Royal Marines Reserve was one of shock and I found the physical and the military training to be very demanding from the start. Nothing in my life has stretched me physically or psychologically as much as the Commando course. The weapons and equipment were bang up to date and the same as those used by the Regular Corps.

Not everyone realises that the Royal Marines are part of the Royal Navy and that fact was made crystal clear to me when my commission had to be re-issued by the Admiralty. I also found the rank structure confusing at first. Officer ranks in the Marines equate to their counterparts in the Navy, although we use Army titles. A captain in the Royal Marines would be the equivalent rank to a naval lieutenant-commander and a major in the Army. Even though I was only a second-lieutenant, I was the equivalent of a full lieutenant in the Army and paid at the same rate. The pay was good and we received exactly the same rate of pay as regular Royal Marines for every hour we served. In addition there was a handsome tax-free bounty paid annually if you had met all the statutory training commitments. In those days this would entail at least 30 drill nights, 12 weekends and, once a year, 14 days' continuous training, usually with a regular Commando Unit. Despite the obvious attractions of the money, I have never met anyone who joined for the cash.

The terminology was very nautical. I had been used to the Army cookhouse whereas in the Marines, that was called 'the Galley'. Marines referred to bedrooms as cabins and floors as decks and a night out as a 'run ashore'. Our attached ranks, such as doctors and chaplains, were Naval officers. They too had to be Commando-trained and wore green berets.

I soon realised that promotion was going to be very difficult. Royal Marines Reserve, Merseyside had one lieutenant-colonel, one major, three captains – one of whom was the Officer Commanding the Detachment in Manchester – and a glut of lieutenants and even more second-lieutenants. I can't say I wasn't warned, for my father had told me that promotion in the Marines was renowned for being slow.

The intensive training for the Commando course was under the direct supervision of Sergeant Major Jerry Lynn, who was a tough but kind-hearted Senior NCO. Like Colonel Sherman, he had been in the Army Commandos during the War. To my amazement, despite Mr Lynn's seniority and age, he did not expect us to do anything he could not do. The speed march, with full kit and rifle, covered six miles and had to be completed in an hour. The twenty-mile yomp over difficult terrain had to be completed in seven hours. The Tarzan course consisted of climbing several ropes, abseiling and completing regains to get back on the rope from a position where you were simply hanging from the rope by your hands. In addition, there was an endurance course which was to become my pet hate.

The Second-in-Command of the Unit was Major David Ellis, who was very popular with everyone. He was the youngest officer to be commissioned in the Royal Marines during the War and served in 48 Commando. Immediately after the War, David Ellis went to Cambridge University and after that, set up his own insurance broking firm. He had film-star looks and was very fit. Later on he became the Commanding Officer. Like Colonel Tom Sherman, he would never compromise on standards but was always approachable and friendly. Their attitude was reflected by the spirit of the officers' mess and everyone was very kind and supportive. Despite all this, I was secretly conscious of the fact that although I was an officer, I still had not passed their test. I was not yet a Commando.

David Ellis suggested to me that, if I wished, they could 'fast track' my training and I would go on an earlier Commando Course at Lympstone in Devon in four months' time. The reason behind the suggestion was that they badly needed another officer who was Commando-qualified in Manchester. If I passed, I would be the Second-in-Command to Captain Paul Banks. As the normal time to prepare for Lympstone was a year, I had to think about this idea very seriously. I was just about fitting everything in as it was, with the business the most important thing. I decided to accept the challenge, primarily because I needed to get the course behind me. This now meant that every available minute of my spare-time I had to spend training, and much of this was done running over the moors known as Owd Betts in Rochdale. Most of the time I had to carry the kit, with additional weights to compensate for not carrying the rifle. If I was doing road training, cars would sometimes stop and their drivers, obviously feeling sorry for me, would offer me a lift which I reluctantly refused. I went to a local gym for weight training and regularly swam in the Rochdale baths. I also gave up smoking.

One of the other junior subalterns who was training for the green beret was Charles Hillock. With wavy hair, slightly thinning on top, he had an open, pleasant face, revealing a slightly crooked set of teeth when he smiled. He had been commissioned only a few months after me but was two years younger. We became firm friends and it made life more bearable that we were sharing the pain together. Charlie was to go on the next Commando course after mine, but he was a home-grown Marine from the very beginning and had undertaken the Phase 1 Basic Officer's Training at Deal in Kent, which I had escaped, having done my basic training in the Territorial Army. Charlie would constantly refer to me as the 'donkey walloper', which is a term – I hope of endearment – used to describe someone who is, or has been, in the cavalry. When I went near him he would sniff the air and say, 'Does anybody else smell horses?' He became one of the finest Commanding Officers that RMR, Merseyside has ever seen.

When the four months of intensive training was over in June 1969, I had to present myself at the Commando Training Centre in Devon for the two-week-long pass out. By this time I had a more salubrious car to travel in, having acquired a second-hand MG Midget, racing green in colour.

When I checked in at the guard house and drove into the base, I was impressed by the appearance of the Training Centre. Most of the buildings were new and everything was spick and span. The accommodation for officers under training, however, was far from new. When I walked into the old wooden hut, there was a sign above the door on which was written, 'Abandon hope all ye who enter here.' I thought that was a good start to what turned out to be a living hell.

Having unpacked my kit in a cabin in which you couldn't swing a cat around, I met the four other officers who were to share fourteen days of agony with me. All the other officers were from RMR, City of London. Two of them were medical students about to qualify soon as doctors in the Royal Naval Reserve and then become attached to the Marines. Graham Hill, who worked for an Insurance Company, was the one who stands out in my memory. He certainly looked the part and was extremely fit. He was undoubtedly the most popular officer on the course, and he had a natural charm which never deserted him throughout the fortnight.

First thing on the Monday morning, we paraded with approximately thirty other ranks from the five RMR Centres. By this time everyone of us was 100% fit after so much training. We were also apprehensive and particularly so when the regular training team appeared on the parade. These men, one captain and three senior NCOs, were hand-picked to pass or fail those of us who had aspirations to be like them.

In the brief presentation, which was given by the Captain, there were two shocks to the system. First of all, as trainees we would be expected to run everywhere in the camp. Even if we were only going a short distance from one building to the next, we would never walk but run. If we were ever seen walking anywhere except inside a building, we would be on a charge and made to run further and faster than we had ever thought was possible. The second shock was that the five officers on the course would be expected to complete the four parts of the Commando course in record times. Everything we did would be timed to the second. Although those who were not officers might pass the individual tests within the time limit laid down by the Royal Marines, that was not going to be good enough for the officers, who should set an example and must beat the time limits by a substantial margin in order to pass. The last point made by the Captain was not lost on the Marines, who either grinned or laughed. The officers did not. We simply studied invisible marks on the ground.

After the briefing, we collected our rifles, from which we were rarely detached for the rest of the course, and the work began in earnest. By the end of the first day, I was already in trouble. Running through the base to change my kit quickly, I saw the fearsome sight of the Regimental Sergeant Major walking towards me on the same road. He was as big as a public convenience and smart as paint, with a silver-tipped cane under his left arm. This man might not be an officer but he was the most senior NCO and sat on the right hand of God. He saluted me and said, 'Good evening, Sir.'

I returned the salute whilst still running and replied, 'Good evening, Regimental Sergeant Major.'

He called me back and, still smiling, said, 'As I'm sure you know, Sir, it is not done for you to return my salute whilst you are still running.'

'My apologies, but if I stopped running, you would put me on a charge.'

'Correct,' said the RSM. 'Just goes to show you can't win in this life. Now if you would be so kind, I would be grateful if you would run round the parade ground. Incidentally, your accent is familiar to me. Do you come from Lancashire, Sir?'

I beamed at him, certain in the knowledge that here was a kindred spirit from my own county and that he might let me off the punishment.

'Indeed I do.'

'That's a great pity. I'm from Yorkshire myself. I think that means you run twice round the parade ground. Good evening, Sir.'

The next few days were taken up with weapon training with rifles, sub-machine gun and the general purpose machine gun. There were exercises, trials on the Tarzan Course, Assault Course and Speed Marches. All of this to improve performance and timing. The part I enjoyed and was good at was the Tarzan Course, which entailed a lot of swinging through the trees like apes. Obviously there is something in my ancestry. Unfortunately on the third day I came a cropper on the cat crawl, which entailed lying flat on top of a very tight rope with one foot hooked over the rope behind your backside and the other leg trailing down at right angles. I was pulling myself along in fine style until the chap in front of me reached the end and stood on the rope to help him get on to the platform; when he lifted his weight off the rope, it twanged and jumped and I went spinning into the air and landed in a heap at the feet of the Sergeant Instructor. He was standing in front of about twenty men who had just completed the Tarzan course. Everyone winced and I was badly winded.

'Very entertaining, Sir,' said the sergeant. 'Not so much Tarzan – more like Jane. Go back to the beginning and do it all again.' The lads were shouting encouragement and cheering me on as alone I had to complete the aerial gymnastics in record time.

On the fourth day I was to encounter the Parade Adjutant. Like the Regimental Sergeant Major, Adjutants are delivered at birth in pristine condition and both are to be avoided at all costs. Immaculate at all times and destined for high office, the Adjutant was a Captain and at Lympstone at that time – would you believe – rode round the Commando Training Centre on a horse. He wore a spotless lovat jacket, a green beret, pressed breeches, leather gloves and black shiny knee boots. Nobody dared call him a 'donkey walloper'.

For a Royal Marine to ride a horse is quite a shock to most people. It preserved the tradition of the old days, when officers in the Royal Marines Artillery would ride on horses. This adjutant spotted me – worse luck – and pointed his riding crop at me. 'What was the year the Royal Marines were first formed?' he asked.

'1664, Sir.' He seemed disappointed with the right answer and rode off into the sunset.

'Thank God for that,' I murmured to Graham Hill. 'With my record of getting into trouble in the last few days, I thought he was going to ask me how many joined in 1664 and what their names and addresses were.'

Later on in life, Major General John Mottram – who was to become a good friend – told me that when he was the Parade Adjutant at Lympstone in 1959, he was riding immediately in front of the Royal Marine Band at a pass-out parade when he lost control of the horse, which was disturbed by the music. He backed into the band, the horse kicked the double base and Marine bandsmen, instruments and pith helmets were flying in all directions. Good stuff – probably no-one could photograph it for laughing. Often described as a 'man mountain', General Mottram was very tall and built like a weight-lifter. In 1980 he became the General Officer responsible for Training and the Reserve Forces in the Royal Marines.

As the course ran on up to the middle weekend, the strenuous demands on all of us were taking their toll. Some people were dropping out on a daily basis and being RTU'd (Returned to Unit). To make matters worse, I was finding it difficult to sleep at nights. Before Lympstone I had been cynical when told that people could be so fit they couldn't sleep. Now I was experiencing it. Part of it must have been the psychological pressure not to fail. The lack

The Tarzan Assault Course at the Commando Training Centre in Devon.

of sleep was debilitating and often nerves were taut. This was all part of the process and we were being judged on how we would handle it.

On the Saturday we were put through the Endurance Course. For most Marines it is very firmly wedged in their memories for all time and I was no different. I hated every minute of it and as I had to do it three times, it became a recurring nightmare.

The Endurance Course is situated on Woodbury Common, about four miles from the Training Centre. The course candidates were split into groups of four, which is a normal Commando grouping, and we were expected to help each other get through. In fact the instructors were watching carefully to ensure that no individual was simply looking after himself.

The groups set off at different times and we launched ourselves into the infamous Peter's Pool. This was not so much a pool as a swamp with deep mud, guaranteed to sap the strength in your legs as you tried to run through it. It was impossible to keep running, but you had to keep your legs moving or you would be up to your waist in no time. In winter the instructors have to crack the ice to make it harder for everyone – no skating allowed!

After this came the water tunnel, which has claimed the lives of a number of people over the years, and there was a Naval Doctor stationed at this obstacle in the event of a crisis. This evil under-water invention was a huge waste pipe approximately twelve feet in length and just wide enough to allow a man with his equipment to swim through. If your equipment got stuck on the rim of the pipe or wedged in the tunnel, you were in serious difficulty. This was obviously the reason for the deaths by drowning.

However, the worst was yet to come. We then had to crawl into underground tunnels of varying lengths and very narrow widths. Some were very long and, to make this more realistic than a walk in the park, the instructors had thrown small pebbles on to the floor of the tunnels which played havoc with knees and elbows.

At all times you would be expected to keep your rifle barrel clean, because when you had spent what seemed like hours in these tunnels, you had to run the four miles back to the Centre and fire live ammunition on the range. You also had to keep hitting the bull or near to the bull to pass the Endurance Course. By that time you were lucky if you could see – never mind see straight.

Having completed the course, I was filled with a deep and solemn loathing for the whole performance. I could hardly walk and nor could Graham Hill. Under the watchful eyes of the instructors, we doubled away to the officers' cabins for a shower. When we were out of their sight, we hid behind a hut, unable to move, and I rested my back against the wall and slid to the floor. I was finished and I believed at that moment that I couldn't go on. The course was killing me; it was non-stop. One gruelling test of stamina after another without a break. I didn't need this. I was a stockbroker. That was my career. Hang the Marines! I never said anything to Graham as we helped each other to trot back to our bunks. Four more were RTU'd that afternoon.

The following Sunday morning we were given some time off, which was a blessed release. There was a huge parade to celebrate the Royal Marines' success in the battle at Zeebrugge. The parade took place on the square with everyone in blues uniform; the band, the Commandant, the Adjutant plus horse – the full works. I was enthralled by the event and had never witnessed such a fine display of drill in my life. Wives and children were sitting in the stands and Graham and I, with the other officers, were doing the same. We were told to keep in the background and wear civilian clothes.

To my astonishment, Graham whispered to me, 'I'm having great difficulty with this course. I'm not sure I'm going to be able to crack it.'

'I feel the same way,' I told him, 'but I thought you were doing quite well.'

'What do you think we should do?' he said.

Looking at the men on the parade ground, whom I envied, I said, 'I can't let this get to me, Graham. I can't afford to fail. I was thinking last night that I probably should throw the towel in, but I couldn't face my father. Worse still, I couldn't face myself in the mirror. Every time I saw a Royal Marine uniform, I would feel sick because I had not been up to it. All these men have done it and I admire them, but I never really realised how tough it was going to be and we're only halfway through.'

'I suppose it's mind over matter. They don't mind and we don't matter.'

I laughed and said through clenched teeth, 'Perhaps we will matter if we get through. Let's finish the bastard.'

That was the turning point for both of us. Although Graham was sympathetic, he was supremely fit and I knew he wasn't experiencing the difficulties that I was. Until then I had been wrestling with my own private hell, never dreaming that he was feeling the strain to the same extent. The fact that he was feeling the same pressure helped me to realise that I certainly wasn't alone in the effort required to meet this challenge.

'Know thyself' is not a bad maxim. I was beginning to learn things about myself and if I was to like what I learnt, I had to square up to this immediate problem. If I failed, there might be other things in my life which would defeat me because I would have taken the easy way out. It might have been the simplest thing to drive out of the camp gates on that Sunday afternoon without a backward glance. The problem was that I would have left my pride and self-esteem behind and that couldn't be done!

The events of the second week, including the final tests, were less memorable for me as I doggedly drove myself on and on. Having come to terms with myself, it was easier to sleep and the brain was more engaged with the body.

Approximately two-thirds of the original course had qualified. No officer had fallen by the wayside and most of the other ranks from RMR Merseyside had got through. Before the final pass-out parade on the Friday morning, the whole course, including the instructors, went for a wild run ashore in Exmouth. I cannot remember much about that.

However, I do remember that the Royal Marine Military Police were called out to the Chinese restaurant we ended up in. Sergeant Jock Ross, who was the principal instructor, had enjoyed a few scoops of ale during the evening and washed it down with a few whisky chasers as befits a true Scotsman. The Military Police had been summoned by the irate Chinese restaurant owner, who took exception to Sergeant Ross doing the highland fling on top of one of his tables. When the Royal Marines MPs burst in through the door,

Commissioned in the Marines, 1969.

the Military Police Sergeant recognised Sergeant Ross straight away. 'Hello, Jim,' said Sergeant Ross as the dancing stopped immediately.

'Hello Jock,' said Sergeant Jim with a smile. 'Perhaps you had better come down.' At this point Jock fell off the table. Sergeant Ross was a small stocky man, good-looking and cast in a 'Rambo' mould. He had a granite chin.

The Chinaman wanted Sergeant Ross arrested. 'Can't do it,' said Jim, 'One of the finest Marines I've ever met.' As the MPs started to leave, Jim said, 'Well done lads. The green beret is something to celebrate but try and keep it down a little.'

The following morning we were lined up on the parade ground and the Commandant of the Commando Training Centre, Colonel John Parsons OBE, MC, came to present each one of us with the green beret. There was a dustbin strategically placed near the Colonel. As each one of us was called out, we marched out and stood to attention in front of him, giving the usual salute. Sergeant Ross, who had staged a remarkable recovery, read out the individual reports, the green beret was handed over, and the recipient then threw his blue beret in the dustbin. When I went up, my report was fair and reasonable. It did make the point, however, that I had found the course difficult to begin with. The Commandant leant forward and said, 'What do you do in civilian life?'

'I'm a stockbroker, Sir.'

'Oh a pen pusher, eh? Well, very well done.' He handed me the beret and vigorously shook my hand. I felt ten feet tall.

When I drove back home to Rochdale, I don't think I'd been so pleased to see my parents for many years. I had lost one and a half stones in two weeks. As I showed them the green beret, my father filled up and was unable to speak. He kept grinning at me like a Cheshire Cat. He knew what it all meant.

My mother's remark took the biscuit. 'That's wonderful, dear,' she said, 'Can't you get one of those green berets in the Boy Scouts?'

I was speechless.

CHAPTER VIII

The Hazards of Marine Life

'Tell it to the Marines.'

HAVING SUCCESSFULLY COMPLETED the course at Lympstone, I took up my new post as the Second-in-Command of the Royal Marines Reserve Detachment in Manchester. The Detachment shared a huge Drill Hall with the Royal Corps of Transport, who were amazingly tolerant of their naval cousins, and although the area of the Drill Hall which we occupied was relatively small compared to the RCT, there was no friction and we rubbed along together very nicely.

The Officer Commanding Manchester was Captain Paul Banks, whom I would eventually succeed. In appearance he was good-looking with somewhat sloping shoulders. He was a good rugby player with a loud voice and a hysterical laugh, whose mirth frequently continued after everyone else's had ceased. Paul was a passionate fan of the Royal Marines. He had served in the Corps during National Service and been at Suez. He was remarkably fit and was a Heavy Weapons Officer. Whatever spare time he had was devoted to building and tuning sports cars.

The Manchester Detachment's speciality was, and still remains, Heavy Weapons, and along with the City of London RMR, we had 81mm Mortars. This made us quite unique in the RMR and brought a new dimension to Commando training, as the speciality, and indeed the technical language used, were not widely understood by the rest of the RMR. When later I was to qualify as a Heavy Weapons Officer myself, it felt as if I had been admitted to a rather exclusive club, whose members had developed a passion for heavy fire power delivered by a close-knit team of professionals who were determined to excel in accuracy and speed in getting mortar bombs down on the ground. The Manchester Detachment, commonly called MANDET for short, was to distinguish itself in Cyprus by winning a live firing

The Officers' Mess, Royal Marine Reserve Merseyside, 1969. Back row: the author (third from the right), Charles Hillock (second from the right). Front row: Lieutenant-Colonel Tom Sherman (centre), Major David Ellis (third from the left).

competition against all the mortar troops in the regular Corps. That resulted in MANDET receiving a congratulatory letter from the Commandant-General of the Royal Marines, General Sir Ian Gourley.

Until I qualified in Heavy Weapons, my principal task was to train candidates for the Commando Course, and it was a very pleasant change to become an instructor and do everything I could to ensure that those whom I thought were ready for Lympstone were not RTU'd during their course.

MANDET had more than its fair share of characters, the most outstanding of whom was Sergeant Tex Tobin, whose principal responsibility was the Mortar Troop. He had hooded eyes which concealed the cynicism with which he viewed anything and everything he encountered (including all other Marines and particularly young officers). However, he had the pleasantest of smiles and a great sense of humour. He eventually became a Sergeant-Major and received the BEM. Tex Tobin was the cleverest senior NCO I have ever met in either the Royal Marines or the RMR. He has a very agile mind and a sharp wit. Working with him was a treat and I can't remember anyone making me laugh as much as he did. In his civilian job he was the Regional Organiser of the Union of Communication Workers, having started his career as a postman. He was quite a powerful man in the Trade Union movement and he would love to wind me up because I was a Conservative Councillor. For my part I wound him up by insisting he was a Conservative masquerading as a Socialist. He has always been a good friend to me and our close relationship is as solid today as it ever was. Undoubtedly he was the backbone of the Detachment until the very day he retired in 1984.

Twelve months after completing the Commando Course, I volunteered for the Parachute Course, which was then available to all Marines. This was an intensive course run by the Royal Air Force at Abingdon near Oxford. Whereas the Parachute Regiment had their own system of selecting those who were fit enough to undertake the course, Royal Marines were exempt from this because they had completed the Commando Course.

I enjoyed every minute at Abingdon. The physical side of the work was relatively easy compared to Lympstone, but the drama was as high. There were four officers and thirty men on the course. Three of us were RMR Officers and the fourth was a Lieutenant-Colonel in the United States Army who was on attachment to the American Embassy. I never really knew how he managed to wheedle his way on to the para course, but he was fairly fit and very good company. The vast bulk of the men were in the Parachute Regiment, TA. There were only six other ranks who were Marines and two TA soldiers in the SAS.

We all got on remarkably well together for most of the time. As I was the most junior officer on the course, I was the Orderly Officer. On one occasion I received a call in the middle of the night telling me to go down to the All Ranks' Mess because fighting had broken out between the Paras and the Marines – which was senseless as the Paras outnumbered the Marines five to one.

I stormed into the Mess to break up the fighting. Marine Gallagher, who was one of my own men from Manchester, was to be found, with difficulty, under three Paras who were knocking nine bells out of him. Raymond Gallagher was a relatively small, engaging chappy who fancied himself as John Wayne – in civy street he was a joiner. He was never so happy as he was in a fight, and could start a row in an empty house. Surveying the scene in the All Ranks Mess – which resembled 'Custer's last stand' – one didn't have to be a rocket scientist to work out that someone from the Parachute Regiment would have said something derogatory about the Royal Marines and Gallagher would have responded with some cutting remark. Although I liked him a great deal, he was 'a mouth on a stick'.

The whole event had its amusing side. The fighting stopped when I walked in and the perpetrators – be they Paras or Marines – stood there brushing themselves down and grinning stupidly at me. No-one was prepared to name anyone else; no-one was prepared to say who started it and no-one was badly hurt. I wouldn't put any of them on a charge because it would have meant that they were kicked off the course, but I told the obviously guilty parties that they would pay the RAF for any damage and pulled Gallagher on one side to talk to him outside.

'What the hell are you playing at Gallagher? You are outnumbered five to one. You could be seriously injured.'

But Sir, you once said to me that Royal Marines would choose to die on their feet rather than live on their knees.'

'Yes, you idiot, but I was talking about Marines who were fighting an enemy. These Paras are on our side.'

'I'm glad about that, Sir. They are great lads and good fighters too.'

'If you don't put a zip on your mouth, I will get the Royal Air Force to RTU you.' Then as an afterthought I said, 'If you think they are great lads, I'd hate to see what would happen if you didn't like them.' I then marched off.

There were no more incidents and Gallagher was tamed. He invariably led the singing in the four-ton truck which came to collect us after our parachute jumps on to the Dropping Zone, and undeniably he was the most popular man on the course. I remember thinking that I would always be happy to go to war with Gallagher, especially because he was on my side.

There were only four on the course who were RTU'd, simply because they refused to jump from the plane. Anyone who tells you that they are not nervous when they are about to jump out of a plane is telling porkies, but the exultation of gliding through the air still makes up for that.

The landing can be dangerous, as I was to discover during a parachute drop on the Isle of Anglesey in the dead of night a few years after I'd earned my parachute wings at RAF Abingdon. Having taken off in a Hercules from RAF Valley, we were to parachute into a large field near Beaumaris. There was hardly any moon and vision was fairly limited. When I jumped out, the 'chute' opened rapidly and I glided down quite gracefully until a gust of wind carried me away from the objective. However much I tried to correct the fact that I was trailing away, it was obvious that I could not avoid landing on a spot which was shimmering through the gloom. It looked like a lake and I was glad, as anyone who knows anything about parachuting knows that water is the easiest landing you can have. The trouble was that it turned out to be not a lake, but the black shiny corrugated iron roof of a barn. I smashed into the roof at a fast rate of knots. I then juddered down the corrugated iron, the silk parachute catching on the roof, leaving me dangling over the side in my harness. There was blood everywhere.

The military ambulance, affectionately known as 'the blood wagon', came tearing across the field. I was lifted down and rushed to the hospital in Bangor. Nothing was broken but I had a nasty gash, which would have to be stitched, above my right eye. Needless to say, the ambulance was superbly equipped, as the medical orderly cheerfully informed me, before detaching a paper clip from a sheaf of papers and deftly placing it on my wound to stem the blood.

The hospital staff telephoned an Indian doctor who was on night duty. They had clearly woken him up, as he was pretty bleary-eyed.

'What have you been doing?' he asked.

'I've just jumped out of this plane.'

Interrupting me, he said, 'What – why didn't you wait until the plane landed? Was it on fire?'

I gave him one of my glittering smiles. 'Don't worry about it, I do this for fun. Just stitch me up please.'

One of the great benefits of being in the RMR was that each year my 14-day continuous training could be spent as an individual officer attached to the Regular Corps. For instance I would replace a regular officer in a Commando Unit who would be due for a spot of leave. This could apply equally to the senior NCOs, NCOs and Marines in the RMR as much as it applied to the officers.

In those early days of my military experience, the Territorial Army would train differently. Usually they would go on what they called 'a camp' and train as a complete regiment or battalion. Both systems had much to commend them but I would argue that an individual posting to a regular unit was more demanding. Quite frequently the unit concerned would be going on a major exercise, sometimes a brigade exercise. Certainly for someone like me to slot into a post such as Mortar Troop Officer in 42 Commando, where the NCOs and men had been used to their own regular officer and I was going to be with them for only two weeks, would put me on my mettle. They would expect me to be up to the mark and very professional. Some of the men would have had no experience of serving alongside someone from the RMR and would be fascinated by the fact that I had a separate job, and indeed a separate existence, in civilian life.

One of the most enjoyable attachments I had with the Regular Corps was in Singapore in 1971. I joined 42 Commando, which was

The author receiving the Zeebrugge Plate for Commando skills from Colonel Tom Sherman.

– and still is – part of the 3rd Commando Brigade. I was the Mortar Troop Officer and, having only relatively recently qualified in Heavy Weapons – at yet another fortnight's course at the Commando Training Centre at Lympstone – I was bang up-to-date and hopefully useful. Like many of the men in the mortar troop, I had been taught by Lieutenant Jerry Wells-Cole. He was one of the tallest officers I had ever met in the Corps and incredibly kind to me. He would later become a full Colonel and the Commandant of the Commando Training Centre.

I was also more confident of doing my job in Singapore because of the teaching I had received in Lympstone at the hands of Colour-Sergeant Eric Blythe, who was a great character of Cockney origin and had forgotten more about heavy weapons than most people would ever learn in a lifetime.

Shortly after arriving in Singapore, I was to go on exercise in Malaysia, where we completed two amphibious landings from Naval ships on separate islands in the Malay Peninsula. I was stationed on the Royal Fleet Auxiliary Ship *Sir Galahad*, which later, in the Falklands War, was badly hit and sunk.

For the first time in my life I met the Gurkhas, who were attached to the Brigade. They were first-class troops with an enviable tradition of distinguished service with the British Army. I learnt a great deal during that exercise which was to stand me in good stead later on, when I attended a course on amphibious warfare. The opportunity to serve abroad came fairly frequently. I have served in Norway on a number of occasions, in Malta, and also in South East Asia.

Some years my two weeks' training was spent in England, on compulsory training courses in which it would be necessary for me to pass the course in order to climb the ladder of promotion. These included the Company Commanders' Course at the School of Infantry in Warminster, and eventually the Staff College Course at the Royal Naval College, Greenwich.

I realise that I have had some wonderful experiences in the RMR. Some were serious – some hilarious – so I know that for most of the time, I have been lucky. I have not been so lucky with the accidents that I have had with the Marines, but it is hardly a 'risk-free environment'.

Apart from my parachute accident in Anglesey, I have had several accidents on exercise not important enough to mention here. My 'pièce de resistance' was falling off a 'death slide' in Ashworth Valley in Heywood. I fell 30 feet on to some rocks and was in hospital for three weeks.

A death slide is something that most people have seen at Army exhibitions. The participant hangs on to a pulley sliding down a very tight rope, which will normally be at 45 degrees to the horizontal. Our death slide was a much longer rope stretched across a small valley which had a narrow river running through it. At one end the rope was tied to a tree on top of a cliff and at the other it was secured to another tree across the river but on lower ground. On this fateful Sunday morning, we were training our Phase 2 Marines for the Commando Course. Worse still, we had a visit of approximately 20

Fusiliers from the TA in Bury, who had been brought along by their Company Commander, Major Brandon Fowden, who was a friend of mine. They were to participate in adventure training, which we had organised for them.

I grabbed the short rope hanging from the pulley and pushed myself off the cliff edge. Someone had to test that the main rope was tight enough and as the officer, I was expected to set the example. I gathered momentum as I came nearer and nearer to the ground. I flew over the river and then tragedy struck – I started to slow down. The rope certainly wasn't tight enough and I gradually came to a halt at a point where I remained hanging with my hands clutching hold of the pulley. The rocks were immediately below and I was left swinging in mid-air.

This wasn't funny and thirty feet is a long distance to drop on to rocks. Colour Sergeant Tobin, as he was then, went white and ordered the men to untie the rope from the tree below me. There simply wasn't the time to do this and my strength was deserting me by the second. Tobin shouted, 'Jump on my back and I will break your fall, Sir'. There was no doubt, I could have broken his back and I said, 'No'. I told everyone to keep clear and I dropped on to the rocks. I broke my ankles, all of my toes and my left arm in three places, including the scafoid bone, a nasty break which occasionally in cold or wet weather reminds me sharply of the escapade.

When Colour Sergeant Tobin ascertained I was alive, I was carried off to the hospital by other Marines whilst he turned round to the assembled throng, who were still getting over the shock with eyes popping out of their head.

'Right', he shouted. 'You have just seen my officer's deliberate mistake. Now who's next?' Nobody moved.

Later that afternoon ten Marines came to visit me in hospital after my limbs had been readjusted and put back in some semblance of order. The nursing sister looked on this onslaught with a jaundiced eye. She had great authority and could have completed the Commando course quite easily. For certain she was not going to be intimidated by ten Royal Marines.

'Only two visitors to each bed – unless you are family,' she said.

'We are his family,' replied Colour Sergeant Tobin and they all

Sgt Major Tobin (left) and Corporal Gordon Corfield.

marched down the ward. The other patients thought there was an invasion.

In all times of stress and strain, the Marines always have to come out with some witty crack to ease the tension. The prize went to Lance-Corporal Corfield, who was an excellent man, an accomplished boxer and had a charming way with words. Looking at me in traction with two legs and an arm held up in the air, he bent down and picked up my boots, which had been placed neatly under the locker by my bed.

'Now these are good boots, Sir. You won't be needing these for a few months but they would look good on me.'

No sympathy. No recriminations. No offer of help. Just – we'll make him laugh – which I did. Bloody Marines!

The very next day I was visited by my Commanding Officer, Lieutenant-Colonel David Stanley, who had been a close friend for many years. In fact I had joined the Marines several years before he came to the unit, as he had spent much of his T.A. service in the Parachute Regiment, where he became a Major. I had met him through politics when he had stood as Parliamentary Candidate, and I effectively recruited him into the RMR. He was immediately dropped in rank to Captain, which is the Marines' equivalent to an Army Major, and to his eternal credit, he passed the Green Beret course at a somewhat mature age. His wavy hair had gone prematurely grey, which added to the distinction of his aristocratic good looks. Endowed with immense charm, he had the knack of remaining highly popular even while addressing his fellow officers as though he was the country squire and they were all behind with their rent. He quickly rose to become the Commanding Officer of the Unit and I secretly looked on him as my prodigy.

On visiting me in the hospital, and seeing all the traction wires and my body encased in plaster, he was more sympathetic to my plight than had been my own men – but not much.

'My God, David, I see you've been showing off again. You will have to put in an insurance claim for all this lot.' God save me from my friends!

When later I was to become Member of Parliament, I kept up my training in the RMR for the first five years in the House of Commons. I was an active member of the Royal Marines Parliamentary Group, which drew its members from those who had served in the Royal Marines and were M.P.s or members of the House of Lords. It was a club within a club. The chairman when I joined was Major Sir Patrick Wall M.C., the M.P. for Haltemprice. Later it was Major Sir John Biggs Davidson, who was the M.P. for Epping Forest, and later still I became the chairman. We were the most active of all the ex-service clubs in Parliament. We had to defend and preserve what is still a small Corps which regularly came under scrutiny when the axe of defence cuts was being wielded.

Every year, the Royal Marines Group would be invited to dinner at Stationers' Hall by the Commandant-General of the Royal Marines and his senior officers. We would then organise a return match in one of the dining rooms in the Palace of Westminster. We all wore ties which were distinctive. Later I would redesign these and they were popular not only with the Parliamentarians, but with all the doorkeepers who were former Royal Marine senior NCOs. The official dinners helped both the Corps and the Parliamentarians to keep up-to-date with what was going on.

I met some very impressive people in the Corps during this time. I first met Michael Wilkins when he was on a massive exercise with the United States Marines Corps in Norway, where I was the Liaison Officer for him and he was the Brigade Commander. He would eventually become the Commandant-General. He was an enormously tall man – possibly six foot three – but was unusually spare of frame with immensely broad shoulders, which made him look as if he had retained the coat hanger in his jacket. His teeth were slightly protruding and had been somewhat damaged by a lifetime of pipe-smoking. He was utterly charming and great fun as a friend and companion.

When we first met, on H.M.S. *Fearless*, the Commando Carrier, I said, 'I have never been a Brigade Liaison Officer before, Sir, but I will try to make the best fist of it I can.'

'Well, David, I've never had a Liaison Officer before who has been a Member of Parliament, so it should be interesting for both of us.'

It was and I learnt a great deal. It was nothing short of a tragedy that after Mike's retirement, and having secured the job of becoming Lieutenant-Governor of Guernsey, he was to contract cancer and died before his term of office expired.

Whilst on exercise in Norway, I also met Robin Ross, who was the Commanding Officer of 40 Commando, and David Pennefather, who was the Brigade Operations Officer. Both of these were to become Commandant-Generals in their time. In so many ways they were entirely different in both appearance and approach, but both had immense ability and it was easy to see that they would go far. Both became good friends. Robin Ross was quite outstandingly bright and a 'workaholic'. Naturally smooth in manner, he had a tendency to erupt when things needed to be kicked down the road. David Pennefather too had a razor-sharp mind. He was small and somewhat serious in outlook, but exuded confidence in his ability to cope with anything and everything.

One of the pleasant tasks I enjoyed in Parliament was to show the

Royal Marines who were on the Young Officers' Course around the Palace of Westminster when they took a break from Lympstone to come up to London. They thought it was a highlight for them. I thought it was the other way round.

For a return match, one of the course batches invited Ruth and me to their Passing-Out Parade at Lympstone. It was a great thrill and we were treated to the very best of Royal Marines hospitality by the Commandant, Colonel Henry Beverley OBE, and his lovely wife Sally. Later Henry would also become the Commandant-General and they remain good friends today.

For the first time in my life, I met General Sir Peter Whitely and his wife. Sir Peter was a legend in the Corps as he had been one of the few Commandant-Generals who went on from being the C.G. to be given a four-star appointment in N.A.T.O. When I met him at Lympstone, he was the Lieutenant-Governor of Jersey and was invited to take the salute at the officers' 'pass-out' because his son Christopher was passing out in the batch. Chris was to become a Major and was awarded the MBE during his attachment to RMR Merseyside.

One month before I was made a Minister by Margaret Thatcher in 1983, I received a letter informing me that I was to be awarded the Royal Marines Reserve Decoration. This was awarded for long service as an officer in the RMR and my life of undetected crime and cowardice was to be recognised by a medal presentation ceremony organised to coincide with the official opening of our new headquarters at the South Atlantic Building in Birkenhead. There would be a Royal Marine Band and a huge crowd of supporters.

The V.I.P. who was to perform both ceremonies was the then Commandant-General, Lieutenant General Sir Steuart Pringle, Bart, K.C.B. The medals presentation was a double celebration for me, as Sergeant-Major Tobin was to receive the BEM, which he richly deserved. We were very lucky that General Pringle was in office at the time. He was a household name as he had suffered terrible injuries and lost a leg when his private car had been blown up in London by the IRA. I knew him well and had visited him in Hospital in London, where I had left him with a bottle of House of Commons whisky. He was a very brave man and naturally modest. Our Commanding Officer at the time was Lieutenant-Colonel Tim Courtney, who was a regular and a larger-than-life character. His enthusiasm for everything was infectious. He had wanted to name our new headquarters after Sir Steuart Pringle but the General had turned down the request. He thought it better to honour those who had served in the Falklands War. I greatly admired him for this.

On the appointed day, I had been a Minister in the Department of Trade and Industry for only one week. The General pinned the medal on my tunic and said he couldn't remember a time when a Marine had been made a Minister. He then went on to ask me a number of questions, one of which was, 'Is your father here, David?' I said that he was and the Commandant-General said that he would like to meet him at the buffet reception later. Then General Pringle walked up the steps to the saluting dais to address the assembled throng and officially open the South Atlantic Building. He started his speech by saying, 'You have just witnessed a rare sight. I have just enjoyed asking a Minister a number of difficult questions. My experience is that it is usually the other way round.' Good stuff!

Later on in life, I was to become General Pringle's boss when I was the Minister for Heritage and he was doing a superb job as the Director of the Royal Naval Historic Dockyard at Chatham.

The ceremony at Birkenhead marked the end of my active service in the Royal Marines Reserve, because when I became a Minister I was required by the Government to resign my commission. Quite apart from the fact that no Minister could possibly devote the time required to comply with the statutory training in the RMR, I could not receive two incomes from the Crown. The principal regret that I have is that later, when in terms of age, service and promotion I would have been in the zone to become the Commanding Officer of Royal Marines Reserve Merseyside, I was still a Minister and therefore effectively de-barred from holding that position.

The Royal Marines more than made up for that when, after losing my seat, I was appointed the Honorary Colonel of the Unit in 1996. In the past, the position had only been offered to ex-Commanding Officers or those of similar standing in the Navy. Some have served in that capacity for many years and it is a sobering thought that I am only the fifth Honorary Colonel since the War. This meant that I followed a line of distinguished predecessors which included the following: Colonel Harold Barnes OBE, VRD, Colonel Tom Sherman OBE, VRD, DL, Colonel Bill Slater CBE, VRD, and Commodore Rodney Walker RD, DL. It is a great honour and I am particularly grateful to Lieutenant-General Sir Robin Ross KCB, OBE, the Commandant-General at the time, for inviting me to take on the role.

I have been privileged to be Honorary Colonel whilst two great friends have been Commanding Officers – Lieutenant-Colonel Mark Rundle and Lieutenant-Colonel Brian Hough.

Lieutenant-Colonel Mark Rundle is a Regular, and later became the Director of the Royal Marines Reserve. To my certain knowledge he is the only former C.O. of an RMR Unit whose enthusiasm for the Reserve ensured that he would be appointed Director of the whole of the RMR in the country.

Lieutenant-Colonel Brian Hough is an RMR Officer whom I have known for longer than Mark Rundle. He has been an enormous success as the Commanding Officer and is shortly to retire, when I understand I will be working with another regular C.O.

There were two regrets that I had at my 'dining in' night in the officers' mess. The first was that my father was not there to see it as he had died three years before. The second was that I couldn't shoehorn myself into my old uniforms, so extensive alterations were undertaken. A source of shame to me and even more so to my wife!

All of this means that I am back on the inside track, enjoying every minute of my association with the Marines once again. It also gives me the opportunity to repay the great debt of gratitude I owe them by being useful from time to time.

When I was awarded the Royal Marines Reserve Decoration in 1983, I had to ask the Prime Minister for permission to attend in uniform. Technically I should have resigned my commission on the day I became a Minister, which was a week before the event.

As this was a matter of protocol, I had to write to Sir Robert Armstrong, who was then the Secretary to the Cabinet, head of the Home Civil Service and Margaret Thatcher's right-hand man.

In my letter I asked for confirmation that I should resign my commission. Then I asked permission to wear my uniform on one last occasion, explaining the ceremony that was to take place. Finally I

Honorary Colonel: Colonel Sir David Trippier, R.D., J.P., D.L.

stated that in the unlikely event of hostilities breaking out, I would wish to resign as a Minister in the Government and be called up by the Royal Marines.

The reply from Sir Robert was swift and to the point.

'Dear Minister,

I have received your letter and have discussed it with the Prime Minister.

The Prime Minister regrets that you will have to resign your commission in the Royal Marines Reserve but confirms that this will be necessary.

The Prime Minister has agreed to you attending the ceremony to receive your decoration in uniform.

In the unlikely event of hostilities breaking out – the Prime Minister will tell you what to do.'

CHAPTER IX

The Rochdale By-Election

'A prophet is not accepted in his own land.'

When I was a Member of Parliament, it was always a good story in an after-dinner speech to say that it was a miracle I was ever elected. I had distinguished myself by being the only Conservative candidate in the history of the nation who had stood in three elections and substantially increased the Labour majority on each occasion. When I stood in my home town of Rochdale in the 1972 by-election, I also substantially increased the Liberal majority. Not a bad record!

It is true to say that Rochdale is hardly a Tory seat, but the fact that the Conservative Association selected me as their candidate meant a great deal to me. It was of special significance because the age-old saying, 'a prophet is not accepted in his own land', is invariably true.

When the sitting Labour MP, Jack McCann, died, the vast majority of the electorate – including me – were very sad. Although Jack never reached the higher echelons in politics, he was a good constituency member and, having a very sunny disposition, he was always approachable.

From the moment that campaigning started for the by-election, Cyril Smith was the red-hot favourite. He had a head start because he had fought the last General Election in the seat and although he didn't win, he polled well and was re-adopted by the Liberals. The Conservatives and Socialists had still to select and adopt their candidates.

I was encouraged to put my name forward by Alderman Rose, the Conservative Group Leader on the Council. When the Conservative Association invited applications for the candidature, approximately 300 people applied. Although it was clear it was going to be a tough battle for the Conservatives, a by-election gives the candidate a very high profile nationally because the eyes of the country are on that result, in this case especially as there were no other elections taking place to distract attention.

When I went for my first interview at the Conservative Headquarters, there was a panel of twenty of the great and good who were senior members of the local party. Anthony Garner, who was the North-West Area's agent, was there to ensure that everything was conducted along the strict lines of the Conservative Party procedure. It appeared that I was the only local person to apply. I was also conscious of the fact that for some of the panel, I would be too young. I was only twenty-six at the time. On the positive side, at least I knew everyone on the interviewing panel well. On the negative side, they knew me very well.

By their process of elimination, I found that I was short-listed with two others, Peter Morrison, who was later to become the MP for Chester, and John Cockroft, who was to become the MP for Nantwich. The final selection meeting was attended by every paid-up member of the Association. It seemed like a cast of thousands and everyone had a vote. In the time-honoured tradition, each of the prospective candidates gave a speech for twenty minutes and answered questions for the same length of time.

When I was told that I had won the selection, I was ecstatic and so were my parents. The second reaction I felt was one of fear. The following day the national press, radio and television would come to an early morning press conference and I had to shine. The press conference went well and the national, regional and local newspapers were fair to me with the exception of the *Guardian*, which was not impressed by my hair style at the time. They described it as making me look like a fallen pop star. My hairstyle was to prove a disadvantage at a later date, not just in politics but in my personal life. I eventually changed it on the advice of a future agent and never looked back, personally or politically.

Ted Thurgood, who was a Deputy Central Office Agent from Manchester, was attached to the Rochdale Conservative HQ and became my agent. He was first-class, very likeable and witty. As the campaign progressed, it was clear that the media were particularly interested in Cyril Smith, not only because he was the favourite, but because he was 29 stones in weight. Were he to be successful, he would be the largest MP ever to get elected.

With a glint in his eye, Ted Thurgood came out with the most stunning and terrifying suggestion I have heard from an agent. He said, 'If we are to recapture some of this lost publicity and put you in the limelight, David, you will have to get engaged to a Rochdale lass who is bigger than Cyril Smith.' Now I'd made a lot of sacrifices for the Party in my time, but I drew the line at that.

Shortly after being selected, I had to be officially confirmed as the candidate by Conservative Central Office in Smith Square, London and to travel down to be interviewed by Bill Elliott MP, who was a Vice-Chairman of the Party responsible for candidates. The reason for this was I had never applied to go on the Official List of Candidates, where the selection process was somewhat lengthy and demanding. In short, I had bypassed the system.

Bill Elliott was a gentleman and could not have been kinder. He was the MP for Newcastle-upon-Tyne North and had been in the Whips' Office. It wasn't so much an interview – more of a fireside chat. He shook me warmly by the hand and said, 'Congratulations, David. Although it will be a difficult fight, it's a wonderful thing to be selected in your own town. I was lucky because it happened to me. I didn't get in and it will be a miracle if you do, but we are here at Central Office to help you in whatever way we can.

I returned to Rochdale to hear that the Labour Party had just selected their candidate. He was called Lawrence Cunliffe and came from Farnworth, near Bolton. His nerves must have been fraught because he had the job of keeping the seat for his Party. Although he failed to do this, he later became the Member of Parliament for Leigh.

Ostensibly, the Labour Party should have won easily. In 1972 there was a Conservative Government in power and Ted Heath was the Prime Minister. It was hardly a popular administration and the principal Opposition party should have done well in a by-election, but all the opinion polls showed that Labour was not doing well.

A further complication was that the National Front, under the banner of the British Campaign to Stop Immigration, had nominated a candidate, Jim Merrick. Nobody knew where he came from or what he stood for, but we soon found out. His policies were outrageous and offensive. He not only believed in a complete halt to immigration, but in compulsory repatriation.

Although the three main Party candidates were to conduct a clean campaign throughout, Jim Merrick had no such intention. He also attracted the worst kind of supporters and many of his lieutenants were violent from time to time. The media also focused on this because it was the first time in any general or by-election that the English National Party – or National Front as it was to be called later – had fielded a candidate.

The only break I had in the Election was on the first Sunday of the campaign, when the Royal Marines Association in Rochdale was to have its new standard dedicated at the Parish Church. This event had been organised for three months and had to go ahead. I was the Branch President and it was a very memorable day. The Manchester Detachment provided the Guard of Honour, we had a band and a

Sharing some views with Chancellor of the Exchequer, Tony Barber, at the 1972 Conservative Party Conference.

large contingent of ex-Royal Marines who were on parade. It must have been one of the finest parades that Rochdale has ever witnessed and I was glad to have a respite from politics for a change.

One of the benefits of being a candidate in a by-election is that you have no difficulty in getting senior figures in the Party to come and speak for you. As the Tories were in power, this often meant Ministers, and there was quite a galaxy of talent: Jim Prior, who was Chairman of the Party; Mark Carlisle, who was a Home Office Minister; Chris Chataway, who was a Minister in the Department of Trade and Tony Barber, who was the Chancellor of the Exchequer. All the public meetings were packed and I was questioned on every subject known to man and a few that man had not thought of.

The highlight of the campaign for me was a major speech I had to deliver in the middle of the by-election at the Annual Conservative Party Conference being held in Blackpool. I was anxious to make a speech in the Social Services debate. Sir Keith Joseph was the Secretary of State for Social Services and would reply. I had never made a speech at the Conference before so it was a very dramatic experience for me. In fact it turned out to be wonderful. When the Chairman called me to the rostrum, he introduced me as the candidate who was fighting the Rochdale by-election. I suppose this was pretty obvious to most people as I was the only one in the Conference Hall who was wearing a huge blue rosette, so I was either a candidate or a prize bull. Some would say the latter. The reception, even before I spoke, was tumultuous, which was a good start. I then made an impassioned speech calling on Sir Keith to give a Christmas Bonus to all the pensioners in the land. Although I had thought about it for some time, nobody seemed to have suggested it. In his reply to the debate, Sir Keith thanked me for my suggestion and said he would think about it seriously. In fairness, that's all he could have said.

In the following Budget delivered by the Chancellor, Tony Barber, all pensioners were promised a £10 Christmas Bonus. You could have knocked me down with a feather! Sadly this was many months after the by-election was over but that didn't matter. Anyone who tells me that Ministers don't listen to the rank and file on some occasions are wrong.

On polling day all the candidates were tearing around with frenetic energy. In the late evening the votes were counted in the Town Hall. Cyril Smith won handsomely and richly deserved to. Lawrence Cunliffe was second and behaved in a very dignified way. I was third while Jim Merrick polled an astonishing seven thousand votes, which had clearly been gleaned from the votes which would normally be cast for the three major parties. Had the voters who supported Jim Merrick seen his henchmen at that count, I think they would have had second thoughts about voting for him. My sister Bunty was pushed down the Town Hall steps by the Merrick tribe but I think that was the only incident. The police were quick to move in and sort it out.

In the speeches which followed the count, I congratulated Cyril on winning and predicted that he would be an able MP and a worthy representative for Rochdale. To this day he has never forgotten that speech and refers to it from time to time. It is only right that I should praise the local newspaper, the *Rochdale Observer*, for its scrupulously fair reporting throughout the by-election. None of the three principal candidates had cause to complain about the coverage. Norman Thornton was the editor at the time and, to his credit, he attended most of the public meetings in the town.

With Cyril Smith on This Is Your Life *in 1988.*

In the editorial written by Norman Thornton immediately after the by-election, he castigated Jim Merrick and his party; he praised Cyril and said that although I had not been successful in Rochdale, he was convinced I would be elected to Parliament for another seat.

When eventually that prophecy was to come true and I travelled to the House of Commons to take my seat, the first MP to congratulate me and show me round the Palace of Westminster was not a member of my own party, but none other than Cyril Smith.

When Sir Cyril was the star of the BBC's *This Is Your Life* and bounced by Michael Aspel with the famous Red Book in the Rochdale Town Hall, I had a walk-on part. When I strode across the stage to greet him, he got a little carried away and despite his enormous bulk, picked me up as if I was a rag doll and gave me a big bear hug. Amazing behaviour for two protagonists who had fought each other in 1972, when he not only defeated me but metaphorically sat on me. A very painful experience.

CHAPTER X

Ruth

'She will sort you out.'

IT IS THE TRUTH THAT my life only really took off when I married Ruth. Our first meeting was to become legendary amongst our close friends because it was fairly unconventional. In fact it was a blind date.

I was prompted to telephone Ruth out of the blue as a result of a conversation I overheard between my parents. I had just returned from a lively weekend with the Marines and was reading a newspaper in the sitting room. They had just returned from a Sunday lunchtime drinks party which was organised to raise money for charity by Keystone Lodge in Rochdale. Both my father and I were members of the Lodge, as was Ruth's father. In the de-briefing that follows every party, my mother was positively raving about a girl called Ruth Worthington whom they had seen at the party. My parents were friendly with Ruth's parents, Alec and Joan Worthington, and I knew and liked them both. I did not know Ruth or anything about her.

My mother said what a lovely girl Ruth was, how clever she was supposed to be, and that she had not seen her for many years. She also reminded my father that when Ruth was a baby, she had wheeled her round in a pram. When she was about five years old, and my mother and Joan Worthington were having their regular coffee meetings in the Bon Bon Café, my mother would always slip the best cream cakes to Ruth under the table. Although I pretended to be absorbed in my newspaper, I was riveted by my mother's description of her. I was also impressed by the fact that my father – who was never the most effusive man on earth – agreed with everything she said. I never said anything. My evil mind stored away all these facts and I made a mental note to ring up this amazing girl and ask her for a date.

The following Saturday morning I was recovering from a row that

I'd had the night before with a girl I had been going out with called Joanna Gartside. Joanna was a lovely girl and very dramatic – hardly surprising as she was then studying drama in London. One of her more outrageous creations was a green wig, which she wore with aplomb.

On the Saturday night there was to be a fancy dress dinner party at the Officers' Mess in Birkenhead. Under normal circumstances Joanna's green wig might be appropriate but for once the row had been fairly dramatic and I decided that the relationship was at an end. However, I could not go to the dinner party alone. I had a reputation to consider and I needed another partner to take out that evening. I thought of Ruth. Although it was short notice, I telephoned the Worthingtons and her mother answered. She told me that Ruth was helping at a centre for disadvantaged children in Royton, but when she returned she would ring me. I was fascinated. This amazing girl that my mother had described was also engaged in voluntary work with the disadvantaged at the weekends. What next?

When Ruth returned my telephone call, I came out with all my best chat-up lines, which had never failed in the past, but then I'd never tried them with Ruth. In other words, they'd never been seriously scrutinised or marked for sincerity, honesty and originality.

Although she was very polite, she repeated my request back to me very slowly. 'As I understand it, you are asking me to go out with you to a military function in fancy dress. Not next week, or next month, but tonight.'

This girl was quick on the uptake.

'I'm terribly sorry, but I have a prior engagement.'

I gulped. I wasn't used to this – she was turning me down. 'I understand perfectly. Perhaps I could telephone you again and take you out for a meal, giving a lot more notice.'

'That would be nice.'

I put the phone down and walked into the hall, bumping into my mother, who said, 'You look white. Are you alright?'

Shaking, I said, 'It's just stupid arrogance on my part because 27-year-old men are not used to being turned down by girls, but that is what has just happened.'

'It's good for the soul,' said my mother. 'Who were you asking out?'

When I told her it was Ruth Worthington, my mother was livid. Not since the frog incident had she raised her voice to me in anger. 'You are joking. Ruth Worthington is not the kind of girl you go out with. She is nice and good and clean. What are you thinking about? Even if you had been successful, it would have been like all your relationships – on one minute and off the next. It would ruin the close friendship your father and I have with Joan and Alec Worthington. Good God, she is only seventeen, man! Are you completely mad?'

I stood open-mouthed – too shocked to say anything sensible. My mother exhaled and then, like every mother the world has known, swung into protective mode. In a hushed whisper she asked, 'Why did she turn you down?'

'I think it was because I asked her to go to the Mess function, which is tonight. Perhaps I didn't give her enough notice.'

My mother broke into hysterical laughter. 'Not enough notice because it's tonight – not next week, but tonight! God give me strength! I admire that girl. I always said that there was something special about her. So is that it? Knowing you, I can't believe you left it like that.'

'Well I've tried to leave the door open by saying I would ring and give her more notice when she wasn't washing her hair or going out with some other chap.'

'Mmm,' she murmured. 'Well I give you fair warning. Ruth Worthington will not be messed about. She may be only seventeen, but she could easily sort you out.' She then stalked off into the kitchen, mumbling something about 'Men!'

When I telephoned Ruth the following week, I gave her two weeks' notice to go out for dinner and she agreed. On the appointed day I turned up at her house not knowing what to expect or what she would look like. Needless to say, it was exactly the same for her, as she had never consciously seen me.

Although I do believe there is such a thing as love at first sight – this was not it. Although, she was undoubtedly beautiful, with a superb figure, she was wearing a very dark – almost black – lipstick, which was very fashionable at that time, but I didn't know it.

We went to a restaurant called 'The Old Mill' at Ramsbottom near Bury. There was never a break in the conversation all evening. She was a wonderful conversationalist, very witty and great fun. Halfway through the evening I remember thinking I had never enjoyed talking with anyone so much. I found it difficult to keep remembering that she was only seventeen. I felt embarrassed because I had telephoned on the first occasion in desperation, and on the second occasion in fascination, because like all men I simply could not believe I'd been refused.

Although I had enjoyed a wonderful evening, I was still very conscious of her age. When I looked at her, I felt I was the sugar daddy without the sugar. I was so concerned that she was seventeen, I wasn't certain that it was legal for me to be going out with her. By then I had been adopted as the Parliamentary candidate for Oldham West. In my mind's eye I couldn't really see how her age, the lipstick or the fact she was still at school could make her an ideal partner at Conservative functions. On the other hand, neither would Joanna in her green wig. I faced a huge dilemma: how to end the evening on a friendly note and let her down easily? After a chaste kiss on the cheek, I came out with a phrase which, when I think of it now, makes my toes curl. 'Ruth I've enjoyed such a wonderful evening, I'm sure we could be just good friends.' In response she shot me a sideways glance that would have felled a weaker man.

'Really,' she said, 'How very nice.' Crunch!

The following week Ruth went on holiday with her parents to Sicily for three weeks. The day after she left to go abroad, I had the accident on the death slide which left me incapacitated for a few weeks.

She only heard that I had been injured when she returned to England and then she telephoned my mother to ask how I was and offer to drive me around from time to time. I was delighted she had telephoned and thought that at least she must be interested in me. On the other hand, I didn't want to get carried away with the offer she had made because I knew that Ruth adored my mother and would go to enormous lengths to be nice to her.

Either way, when I was home and mobile, I telephoned Ruth, thanked her for the offer and arranged a date at a dinner dance to take place in a few weeks' time at the South Meols Tennis Club in Southport. The event was a great success. Ruth looked lovely; there was no black lipstick but she did have a crepe bandage on her ankle. She told me that she had been injured playing squash. This was a white lie. The truth was that she couldn't dance, and although she had arranged some secret dancing lessons, she didn't think she would be sufficiently proficient in time for the Tennis Club dance. It was many months later that I learned the truth about the fabricated injury and only after she had learnt to dance very well.

One incident at South Meols stands out in my memory. Two of my closest friends, Jimmy and Jane Gartside, were in our party and knew Ruth, but only slightly. Both Jane and Jimmy were to become Conservative Councillors on Rochdale Council, with Jimmy eventually becoming Chairman of the Conservative Association and Jane a very successful Mayor in the town. While Jane and I were queuing at the buffet, she turned to me and said, 'You know, David, I think Ruth is terrific. It's the best relationship you've ever had and she will sort you out.' This was the second time I had heard this prophecy. First from my mother – now Jane.

The following week Ruth and I were to go to Keystone Lodge Ladies' Evening in Rochdale. This was an excellent evening and both Ruth's parents and mine were there. Ruth had obviously completed her crash course in dancing, as this time there was no crepe bandage. Dennis and Kaye Everett – two good friends I had first met in the Y.C.s – were in our party and Dennis pulled me on one side. 'You know, David, Ruth is too good for you, chum – she is super. I'll tell you what, buggerlugs, Kaye and I think . . .'

'I know, I know – she will sort me out.'

'How did you know what I was going to say?'

'Everyone is saying it. I obviously need a lot of sorting out.'

'You are not kidding.'

The truth of all of this was that until Ruth came along, I had never settled down with one girl for very long. I just went from one girl to the next and secretly I was basically unhappy, although no-one would have guessed it. Everyone thought I was just playing at being a playboy. Even Dennis and Kaye were getting exasperated, never knowing which girl would turn up on my arm next for a dinner

'The Gang of Ten' – good friends for many years. Back row, left to right: Dennis Everett, Keith Walker, Stuart Clough, Jimmy Gartside, the author. Front row: Ruth, Jane Gartside, Christine Clough, Susan Walker, Kaye Everett. Edward is in the middle.

party. My mother was also seriously fed up with me gallivanting around the town with so many different girls.

Only a few weeks before I had met Ruth for the first time, my mother had a bad experience while travelling on a bus into Rochdale town centre. Two ladies were sitting together a few seats in front of her. My mother overhead one lady ask the other whom her daughter Anne was going out with at the moment. 'David Trippier,' replied Anne's mother.

'That's funny,' said the first lady. 'I thought my daughter Julie was going out with him.'

My mother was so embarrassed by this that she got off the bus a stop before the terminus for fear that the two ladies might recognise her. When I arrived home from the office that evening, my mother related the story to me and said, 'It's getting beyond a joke. It's certainly no longer funny. You are going to ruin your reputation.'

All of this had now changed because of Ruth. Whenever we were going out together, I would look forward to it for days. I had never been so happy to see someone in my life.

Every year the Royal Marines had a Ball which was held in the Drill Hall in Manchester. This was very well attended, with all the men in mess kit or blues uniform; and there was a steel band and a pipe band. It took a lot of organising and I was always slightly apprehensive and very anxious lest everything should fail to go like clockwork. A marquee was put up on the huge parade deck and the whole show was quickly off the ground.

This was the first time I had taken Ruth to any Royal Marines function. Although she seemed to get on well with all my friends, it was quickly apparent that she was going to become a particular fan of the Marines. She liked the military way of getting things done and the Marines' sense of humour, which was invariably outrageous. I was very impressed that instead of clinging to me because she didn't know anybody else there, she quickly got stuck in by helping me organise all the last-minute details, and then helped to serve the food and assisted with the change-over of bands. By the end of the evening she had danced with Colour Sergeant Tobin and several of the Marines. I could tell she had genuinely enjoyed herself. I had one anxious moment when she returned from dancing with Corporal Donnolly, a pugnacious and witty little Scott with an accent so thick I could hardly understand him. 'What did he say?' I asked.

'Oh I don't know, I couldn't understand a word, but I just smiled and agreed with everything. He was very nice.' I had no doubt that he'd been very nice, but I trembled to think what she had agreed to!

Ruth was a great hit with Colour Sergeant Tobin. Tobin had always been the self-appointed protector of my back and my front, but he saw no reason to intervene and protect me from Ruth

At the end of 1973 I was selected to be the prospective parliamentary candidate in Oldham West, which was a more winnable seat than Rochdale had been. At that time I met Eric Taylor, the Chairman of the Conservative Association in Oldham. He was an enormous man, often known as the 'gentle giant'. His wife Jenny was tall, graceful and highly attractive with a beautiful face. Both of them were invariably impeccably turned out. Eric was to become my closest friend and ally – later he would become the North-West Area Chairman. He asked a gentleman called Alderman Frank Bolsom, who had been the Conservative Party Agent in Oldham for many years, to come out of retirement and act as my agent for the General Election, which we predicted would take place in only a matter of weeks. Frank Bolsom was a wonderful agent, very distinguished looking with a rich sense of humour. He pulled me to one side and suggested that I should change my Billy Fury hair style, which had been the subject of the critical article in the *Guardian* during the Rochdale by-election. I decided to comply and when the job had been completed, I found that Ruth saw me in an entirely new light.

The General Election was going to be held in February 1974. Ted Heath had been battling with the miners, who were on strike; we had a three-day week and the Prime Minister decided to go to the country on the election platform of 'Who governs the country?'

Immediately prior to the first week of the campaign, Dennis and Kaye Everett had invited Ruth and me to a Round Table dinner dance at the Midway Hotel in Castleton, Rochdale. I knew by then that I was falling head over heels for Ruth and it was a wonderful evening for us both. We went back to a friend's house for coffee after the dance. When I was driving Ruth home afterwards, she said that she would come and help me canvas during the campaign, which was not going to be that easy for her as she was in her final year at school with 'A' Levels looming in the summer. I knew how conscientious she was about her studies, so I realised that she could only come out and work in the campaign at weekends. Nonetheless I was delighted that she was going to help me.

Throughout the election, the opinion polls were against us and although the team of workers in Oldham were second to none, polling day was going to be bad news for the Party. In the event, the results were poor for Conservatives up and down the land. Michael Meacher, the sitting Labour MP in Oldham West, was returned with an increased majority. However, I had mixed feelings that night. Although the result was very disappointing, my personal life was happier now than any time in my life. If I could hold on to Ruth, my life would become complete. After the count, we went back to our Campaign Headquarters at the Conservative Club in Stanley Road,

Oldham to thank all my supporters and workers. Later still, Ruth and I went to my house for coffee. I then told Ruth that I loved her and she confirmed that she felt exactly the same.

A few weeks later, Ruth came to stay overnight at our house. This was of more significance than one might imagine, as no girlfriend had ever stayed overnight before. On the Sunday morning Ruth came down for breakfast and my mother was cooking the bacon and fussing round her. My father was buried in the *Sunday Times* and had completely forgotten that Ruth had stayed overnight. He was shocked and lowering his newspaper, he peered at her over his reading glasses. As he continued to stare at her with his mouth open, my mother said, 'Now you know Ruth very well, Austin, don't you?'

My father seemed mesmerised by the fact that Ruth was at his breakfast table. Like most fathers from that era, he had always remained aloof from girls that I might have gone out with. In any event, he couldn't remember their names. He closed his mouth and in a shocked whisper he said, 'Did you stay here last night?'

'Yes, Mr Trippier.'

'You mean you stayed upstairs in this house?' he repeated.

'Yes I did.' My mother loved it and winked at Ruth.

'Incredible,' said my father and returned to his reading. He occasionally peeped over his newspaper at her just to make sure she hadn't disappeared in a puff of smoke. I could almost see his brain turning over and he would be thinking, 'This is getting serious. She's stayed overnight – Wow!'

By this time Ruth's 'A' level examinations were creeping ever nearer. She had always wanted to study law at Manchester University, but initially had not been accepted. She did have an offer from Hull University and I was very worried about the fact that she might be so far away for three years. Although it seemed a long time ago, I still remembered how I had suffered in my relationship with Susan Topper when we were geographically so far apart. I didn't want it to happen again.

I discussed it privately with my mother, as usual over the ironing board in the kitchen and she was very sympathetic to my dilemma. She said, 'I know that Ruth doesn't want to go to Hull either.'

'How do you know?' I asked.

'Because her mother and I have had a long chat about it on the telephone. Joan acknowledges that you and Ruth are besotted with each other and she told me that if Ruth can't get into Manchester University, she might go to Manchester Polytechnic instead. I only want to say to you, David, that she must make that decision. You should not try and force her. That girl has set her heart on studying law and becoming a barrister and you should not interfere, but rather be supportive.'

'Is Joan annoyed that Ruth might turn down Hull just to stay in Manchester?'

'No. She accepts that Ruth would be very unhappy if she had to go away. The very best thing that could happen is for Ruth to do better in her 'A' levels than is predicted, and then she might get into Manchester University.'

That is precisely what happened. Ruth did well in her 'A' Levels and, having badgered the admissions tutor for a day and a half, she was admitted and never looked back. I now realised how tenacious Ruth was. Whilst she was waiting to find out whether Manchester would admit her, she waited at the Law Faculty all day long. When there was no decision, she returned early the following morning. By lunchtime Ruth popped her head into the Admissions Tutor's office to ask for the umpteenth time whether there was any news. The Tutor was out, but a secretary smiled at her and said, 'You will be pleased to know that I have just telephoned your mother to say you can come. Now – will you *please* go home.'

For months now I had been planning to ask Ruth if she would marry me and I decided that the question should be popped at Manchester Airport, where Ruth had a holiday job interviewing passengers arriving at the airport. Before I drove to the airport to pick her up, I confided in my mother that I was going to ask Ruth the crucial question. 'Oh – wonderful,' she said. 'Do you think she will say yes?'

'I think so, but you never know. It means more to me than anything in the world.'

When I arrived at the airport, Ruth was standing at the top of a long escalator waiting for me. What was to follow should have been filmed. It was a farce.

I shouted to Ruth to wait for me where she was and I stepped on the escalator going up. She hadn't heard me and stepped on the escalator going down. We passed in the middle and I couldn't say anything for laughing. I signalled for her to wait at the bottom and I got on the other escalator going down. She got it wrong again and was on the escalator coming up. This was becoming ridiculous. When we were about to pass each other for the second time, I called out to her, 'Will you marry me?'

Laughing, she said, 'Yes.'

Two elderly ladies were travelling on my escalator and one said to the other, 'I think we have just heard a proposal. That chap has just asked that girl to marry him and she said yes.' They looked back at me and I was beaming and nodding at them. They started clapping and others within earshot were laughing. When Ruth and I look back at this daft incident, it's always important that we remind our friends that although the exchanges were not dissimilar to the final stages of the film, *Crocodile Dundee*, my question was popped in 1974, long before that film was made.

Having been out with Ruth to celebrate that evening, I returned home late to find that although my father had retired to bed, my mother was anxiously waiting up for me to hear the news. When I told her that Ruth and I were to be married, she was ecstatic. She could not have been more thrilled and kept hugging me. The following day my mother died. She simply fell asleep on the settee watching the television and never woke up. It was as if she could rest now she knew I was 'sorted out'.

CHAPTER XI

A Wedding and a Funeral

'Are you going out with a schoolgirl?'

THE EFFECT OF MY MOTHER'S death was devastating for all of us. My father simply could not take it in. Bunty and I were very much the same. Bunty's husband Roddy and their two children, Heather and Iain, were beside themselves with grief. How we ever survived those first few weeks after my mother's death I will never know. For my own part I felt that I had been robbed by her premature death. Worse still, I can't help feeling bitter about the fact that my children were robbed because they never knew her. I can't feel thankful enough that Ruth knew her so well.

The tragedy was she was only 59 years of age. She had a history of minor heart problems but they had never surfaced to such an extent that any of us would have taken the warnings seriously, and that applied particularly to my mother herself, who was always so full of life. Bunty and I did our best to comfort my father, Roddy comforted Bunty and Ruth comforted me.

Although Ruth and I had agreed to become engaged, it was totally inappropriate for us to announce the fact officially for a few weeks. In any event, there was so much work to do for the whole family: clearing my mother's affairs up, arranging the funeral and generally preparing to face the future without her being at the centre of our very existence. Right across the whole family, we all busied ourselves with work, and it helped.

As my mother had been so well liked, it was no surprise to see so many at her funeral. However, my father only invited family members to our house afterwards. It was significant that he invited Ruth – my father now saw her as one of the family.

It was clear at that time that there would be another General Election soon. Harold Wilson had won the February election, but with only a tiny majority. He would want, and expect, to get a ringing endorsement from the electorate for the policies he had introduced and it was clear to everyone that with his slender majority he would not survive.

I had been officially approached to stand again for the Conservatives in Oldham West. The offer had to be made by the Chairman, Eric Taylor, and he was kind enough to visit me in my stockbroking office in St Ann's Square only two weeks after the February election. This was several months before my mother died.

This meeting was to become famous in the Trippier annals, and on many occasions in the future Eric and I would refer to it and have a good laugh. If anyone referred to it more than we did, it would be Jenny, Eric's wife. Jenny Taylor became such a close friend that she would later become a godmother to our youngest son. She has dined out on the story more than anyone.

It transpired thus: Eric started the discussion by saying that the Executive Committee of the Association had agreed that I should fight the seat once again. Although he realised that the contest would be a difficult one and I was unlikely to win, he did not want me to desert them. I replied that I would not dream of deserting them and I valued their confidence, support and particularly their friendship. I also made the point that I should hate it if anyone thought that I was a carpetbagger. Eric said he was delighted with my decision and stood up to leave. He then sat down again and came out with some fairly inane comments about the general political situation. Later he stood up to leave for the second time and moved to the door. He promptly turned round and came and sat down again, looking very troubled.

'Eric, there is something worrying you, why don't you tell me about it?'

After a pause, he said, 'David – I know this can't be true, but rumour has it that you are going out with a schoolgirl.'

'It's true,' I told him.

'What! I don't believe it. Who is it?'

'I think you might know her. It's Ruth Worthington. She is in the Upper Sixth Form at Oldham Hulme Grammar School.' Eric was a Governor at the school.

He thought for a second. 'I do know her. Very bonny girl – is it serious?'

'Yes. It's very serious.'

'Mmm,' he murmured. 'Is she hoping to go to University?'

'In a few months' time.'

Eric's face brightened. 'Well,' he said, 'If you can keep it under close wraps for a few months until she leaves school, everything will be all right. It's not done for a Conservative Parliamentary Candidate to go out with a schoolgirl, but it's perfectly acceptable for him to go out with a University Student.'

'I'm sorry about this. I think I must have a hang-up about gym slips!'

Having completed his mission and secured my assurance that I would keep matters under close wraps, Eric stood up and moved to the door for the third time. 'I hope it works out between you two. That girl is something else and you would be a lucky man to marry her. I will tell you this, if Jenny and I are not invited to the wedding, there will be a bloody row.'

I laughed. 'You will be.'

Shortly after my mother died, Ruth went on holiday to Iran to stay with an old friend of her mother's who was living there with her husband and family near the city centre in Tehran. I joined her for the last two weeks of the holiday and we had a wonderful time. This was before the Revolution in Iran, but you could detect that there was trouble bubbling beneath the surface.

Joan Worthington's friend Enid was English and had married an Iranian called Farouk Mahboubian. Farouk was concerned that because Ruth and I were not married, certain proprieties had to be observed. I was not allowed to sleep in the main house but had a bed in a small summer house at the other end of the garden. Every night when I left everyone to return to my solitary confinement, I would lock the summer house door behind me and Farouk would let out the guard dogs to roam the garden all night. These dogs were sufficiently fierce to quell anyone's ardour.

When Ruth and I returned to England, we agreed that I would ask Ruth's father's permission to marry her. This was never going to be a fraught meeting as I knew Alec very well and we were good friends.

Alec was extremely slim and fit, full of zest for life and generally looking as though he was enjoying himself. He was always optimistic, no matter what crises might arise. Joan, my prospective mother-in-law, was a highly intelligent woman. Quite small and with delicate hands, she had a distinguished look about her. She was particularly keen on family values and the importance of the family.

It was fairly clear to me that Joan had been let into the secret by Ruth and there were a few knowing glances before I was ushered into the sitting room. Alec was watching the television and I didn't know whether he had been tipped off before the meeting or not. Apparently not, as he talked about football for half an hour and I couldn't get him to focus on the business in hand. I never interrupted him for fear of being thought rude, and it was clear that he hadn't a clue as to the purpose of my visit.

Ruth appeared on the path outside the house and stared at me through the window. I could clearly see her, while her father could not. She pointed to her watch and then started tapping it. I got the message but for the life of me I couldn't get round to broaching the subject with Alec. Worse still, I was in danger of laughing hysterically as Ruth appeared for the second time at the window and in sign language was telling me to get on with it. She smiled and put both her thumbs up. Then she pretended to look severe and turned her thumbs down. Still Alec rabbited on. Ruth returned to the window with a bottle of champagne and two glasses. The next minute she put her hand round her throat as if she were throttling herself. 'Yes or no?' she mouthed through the window. When Alec wasn't looking, I waved her away.

Eventually there was a pause in Alec's flow. 'Alec', I said. 'Ruth and I would like to get married. I would be most grateful if you would give your permission.'

Without a moment's hesitation he said, 'Of course, David. It was always a foregone conclusion.'

I dashed to the door, where by then Ruth and her mother were eavesdropping. The champagne was then served and everyone was hugging each other.

During the evening's celebrations Joan extracted two promises from me. The first was that whilst the wedding would take place in August

Ruth's parents, Alec and Joan Worthington.

the following year, it should be after Ruth was twenty on the 9th of that month. It seemed more respectable that she should be twenty and it was still only a twelve-month engagement. I readily agreed. I'd hate to think what would have happened if I hadn't. The second request was even easier. Both Joan and Alec wanted me to support and encourage Ruth to complete her law degree and go to the Bar. The thought that I might not support her in what was her long-standing ambition had never crossed my mind. Again, I readily agreed. With the engagement ring purchased the following Saturday, the announcement was made and our wider families and friends descended on us to offer their congratulations.

The General Election was held in the October and Harold Wilson secured the endorsement he was seeking. The result was worse for me than in the February, and that was reflected throughout the country. For both Ruth and I it was sad for us to leave Oldham West. I may not have been successful in either of the elections, but we had made many new friends and had had so many happy times with them. On the night of the count, when it was clear that once again I was going to be defeated by Michael Meacher, he was kind enough to say to me privately that if I was determined to become an MP, then he was sure it would happen.

One of the many happy memories of our engagement was house-hunting. Ruth and I eventually agreed to buy an old farm called Bethany Farm, Newhey in Rochdale. I bought it for £16,000 and it had 16 acres of land. A great deal of work had to be done on the property to renovate it and whenever we could find the time, we were working our backs off to develop our dream home. My father, who was not only supportive of Ruth but protective of her too, thought that buying such a run-down property was a mistake. 'Why couldn't you have bought a flat in the town centre where Ruth wouldn't have had to work so hard in doing it up? A run-down farm is no place for such a young wife to look after.'

Months after we had bought the farm and it was beginning to look as if it had enormous potential, my father drove round to pay us a State Visit. Ruth's father, Alec, who loved working on the farm with us, thought it convenient to disappear up a chimney rather than hear what my father had to say. Eric Taylor was visiting at the same time and did a marvellous job in explaining how it would all come right in the end. The Taylors' farmhouse was a showcase and he was trying to convince my father that when he and Jenny had bought Friarmere House, it had been in an even worse condition than Bethany Farm. My father looked at Ruth and me, both covered in muck and dust from head to foot. He grinned, pointed at a rope which was hanging down from a beam in the barn and said, 'I suppose if you get fed up with it, you could always hang yourself.'

Later when the work was completed and we were so proud of what we had accomplished, my father asked Ruth to invite his friends round to Bethany for a party. He simply wanted to thank them for being kind enough to entertain him on so many occasions since my mother had died. When they arrived at the party Ruth had organised, my father had the brass neck to conduct tours round the farm, claiming all the credit for thinking of the conversion in the first place. We were just pleased that he seemed so proud of it.

The wedding took place on the 23rd August 1975 at St Thomas' Church in Thornham. Ruth looked radiant and her mother looked very elegant. Alec was as proud as punch. My father and Bunty were quite emotional and very kind to Ruth. The bridesmaids were Katherine Grady, a close school friend of Ruth's who later became a G.P., her cousin Anne and Bunty's daughter Heather.

Adrian Bennett was the best man and the ushers were Philip Hacking, another of Ruth's cousins, Charlie Hillock from the Marines, Dennis Everett, Keith Walker and John Kay from the Y.C.s. The reception was held in Rochdale Town Hall and Ruth's uncle, Alan Lynskey, who was Joan's brother, proposed the toast to the bride and groom.

Uncle Alan was a headmaster and a confirmed Socialist. In his witty speech he explained his bewilderment that his favourite niece was marrying a Conservative. He said that he was afraid he had wasted his time when she was a baby and he used to wheel her round in a pram reciting the famous sayings of Clement Attlee, Aneurin Bevin and Hugh Gaitskell. He also referred to the time when I had fallen asleep in his house while he was talking to me. His speech went down a treat. In my reply I apologised for the fact that I had fallen asleep but I recalled that at the time he was reciting the sayings of Clement Attlee, Aneurin Bevin and Hugh Gaitskell – all good knock-about stuff. It was a lovely day for everyone. It was just so sad that my mother wasn't there. For all of us, including Ruth, her presence would have made it a perfect day.

We shot off for a honeymoon at the Lygon Arms in Broadway and having spent a few days there, we travelled to London and stayed at the Army and Navy Club. We only had a week's honeymoon as we were both anxious to get back to Bethany Farm to see the new carpets which had been laid.

Wedding Day. Left to right: Keith Walker, Heather Black, John Kay, Anne Lynskey, the author, Ruth, Adrian Bennett, Philip Hacking, Kath Grady, Dennis Everett, Charles Hillock.

Our wedding had been the cause of some amusement in the Manchester area because of a newspaper article that was written on us both a few days before the wedding day. It arose from my stag night, which had been held in a Manchester Night Club and organised by John Kay. Most of us travelled to the Club in coaches and there must have been about fifty of us. Like most stag nights, it got a little out of hand and one of my friends, who was a zany character called Julian Blincoe, set off a fire extinguisher. It then deteriorated.

Unknown to me, my Marine friends had brought a ball and chain to the party. The ball was incredibly heavy and made of solid steel. The chain and the manacle were of the same material, with a padlock which was one of Chubb's finest inventions. At about midnight I was wrestled to the ground with six Marines holding me down. Charlie Hillock and Tex Tobin fastened the manacle round my ankle and locked the padlock with the key. I then had to carry the ball around with me for the rest of the night.

When we were travelling back to Rochdale on the coach, Charlie threw the key out of the window on to a building site. The boys made the coach driver stop outside Ruth's house and the Marines threw pebbles at her bedroom window to get her to witness their fine handiwork. She couldn't stop laughing. When I arrived home and tried to go to bed, I couldn't get my trousers off as they weren't wide enough to go over the ball. Charlie was staying the night at our house and made plaintive efforts to pick the lock with a blade of grass. Charlie was in a very happy state. I slept with my trousers on and thought I was going to have to carry the damn thing round with me all week and probably down the aisle at the wedding. My father was undoubtedly impressed by events, but for me the joke was wearing a little thin, as the manacle was starting to rub against my skin. Charlie drove me down to the nearby Woodyard Garage so that we could ask one of the mechanics to use his big cutters to cut through the padlock. All the mechanics at the garage fell about laughing, but eventually they cut me loose.

The greatest embarrassment was that an old friend of mine called Alan Tweedale was filling up his car with petrol when I arrived, still attached to the ball and chain. Alan was a senior reporter with the *Manchester Evening News* and was weeping with laughter. Despite my entreaties, he wrote the story, which appeared on the front page of the *Evening News* that night. The headline ran, 'Council Leader Manacled to Ball and Chain.' So now everyone knew about it.

On the Wedding Day, immediately after the buffet, Adrian, as best man, read out the telegrams. The one that stole the show was from the Marines. It simply read, 'Please can we have our ball back?'

CHAPTER XII

Member of Parliament

'How we avoided being burnt out before the Election was a miracle.'

I HAD APPLIED TO BE THE Conservative Candidate for Rossendale in 1975, two months before Ruth and I were married. This was advertised by Conservative Party Central Office and sent to those who were on the 'Approved List'.

I was very anxious to be selected as the candidate for the seat for two reasons. The first was that everyone knew the seat was winnable. They had only recently had a Conservative Member of Parliament, Ronald Bray, who was elected in 1970 and only lost his seat by 203 votes in the October 1974 General Election.

The second reason I badly wanted to be selected was that I felt strongly that I could easily identify with the area. Not only my father, but my grandfather, had been born in the Rossendale Valley. In fact the Trippier family had fled France in the Hugenot Persecution of the Protestants in the 1700s and half of the family had settled in Newchurch-in-Rossendale, where they were employed in textiles. The other half became goldsmiths in London. Even my friends in textiles who knew this would crack the joke, 'Trust you to pick the wrong half, David.'

The first interview for what is commonly called the 'long list' was held at Haslingden Conservative Club, and, as usual, after my speech I had to answer questions which were very searching. I was to learn later that a lady on the interview panel called Kathleen Butterworth, who, like everyone else, had been primed to ask a certain question, had decided not to put her question to me because she thought it was unfair.

Apparently the question which I never heard was going to be, 'If you are selected to be our candidate, will you move house and come and live in the Valley?' I was certainly relieved that the question was never asked, because the whole of the interview panel was aware that I had only recently bought a house in the town next door and that I would be married within a few weeks. The question would certainly have embarrassed me at that particular time. The fact that in 1984 – without any pressure from anyone – we would move into the Valley never crossed my mind at that time.

Having been chosen by the panel to go on the short list, I found that the final interview would be held in Bacup Conservative Club only one week after I had returned from honeymoon. The agent was a Mrs Sheila Blaby, a delightful character, small and doll-like with a mass of curly hair. She was always ready for a laugh and of course a strong sense of humour is a vital prerequisite for any party agent. She told me that there were four potential candidates on the short list and those who were married would be expected to bring their wives, who might also be interviewed. In addition, we were to attend a short cocktail party before the interviews began. This was quite novel to me and I realised that we would be scrutinised to see whether we could socialise well and work a room. I also realised that I couldn't win when it came to ordering a drink. If I only asked for half a pint of bitter, I could be seen as a snob. If I ordered a full pint, they might think I was a raving alcoholic.

When Ruth and I arrived at the Conservative Club, we were introduced to the other candidates in the field. John Taylor, a solicitor in London, was a bachelor at that time and had fairly strong family ties with the Valley. He would eventually secure a safe seat in the Midlands, become a friend, and eventually be appointed a Minister. David Hodson, who was with his wife, was a barrister and had been born in the Valley. He later chose not to go into politics and became a circuit judge. The fourth candidate was Ronald Bray, Rossendale's former MP, who was prepared to throw his hat in the ring once again. His wife Margaret was also there.

As we were about to 'work the room', Ruth suggested we should split up. She said, 'You talk to the more senior people and I will talk to the Young Conservatives.' Ruth was getting good at tactics.

We were told that we would be interviewed in alphabetical order, which meant that I would be last. As there were about two hours to kill before we were summoned, it was suggested by Sheila Blaby that we might like to go home and come back. As we had not eaten that evening, we decided to go for a quick meal at the Old Mill in Ramsbottom. Since we had had our very first date there, we thought it might bring us luck once again. When we returned, we only had to wait for ten minutes and we were summoned into a huge room that was packed with Association Members. The ordeal was about to begin.

In introducing us to the audience, the Chairman of the meeting, David Irvine, chose to begin by congratulating us on getting married. The older ladies murmured 'Ahh – how nice' and the audience burst into spontaneous applause. We both thought that this was a good start. Having shared a number of platforms with me during the October 1974 Election in Oldham, Ruth was becoming a past master at looking up at me with adoring eyes when I was speaking. She had perfected this to such a fine art that she would look adoring even if she thought I was talking tripe.

When I sat down, the questions came thick and fast. One googly which I had not anticipated was, 'Are you a Freemason?' There were gasps of horror that the question had been asked by someone who was presumably hostile to Masons. I replied that I was – and proud of it. I threw in for good measure that both my father and father-in-law were too. I later discovered that two of the short list were and two weren't. The significance of the question was lost on me and apparently on everyone else.

After a few more questions the meeting came to a close. No-one had asked Ruth a question. We were excused, the members cast their votes in a secret ballot, then David Irvine came down to the bar – or sweat box – downstairs, where the seven of us were waiting for the result. He thanked all of us for applying and for our patience that evening. He said, 'The Association has decided to select Mr David Trippier as our candidate.' Turning to me, he went on, 'I would be most grateful if you and Mrs Trippier would come back into the room so that we can formally congratulate you.'

Standing ovations are very heart-warming and good for the soul; pity they haven't happened to me more regularly. It was a very emotional occasion and everyone wanted to shake our hands and wish us good luck. I said that I would do everything I could to win the seat. On the way home, we called in to see my father and break the news. He was tickled pink and he wanted us to stay the night with him, which we did.

The sitting Labour Member of Parliament was Mike Noble, who had undoubtedly worked hard to establish himself. Later, during the formal campaign at the next General Election, I was to get to know him better and liked him. Just prior to my selection as his Tory opponent, he had committed a gaff by opening a bazaar for *The Morning Star*, the Communist newspaper. He was also a member of the Tribune Group, whose left-wing policies seemed to reflect his own allegiance. I was bound to expose this.

Having been the candidate for Rossendale for a few weeks, I was beginning to realise that there were many effective officers and members of the Conservative Association who were prepared to work tirelessly to ensure we won the seat back. Amongst these were Graham Woodcock, who was the Association Chairman and a local solicitor, and who looked every inch a distinguished lawyer, and John Holt, a pipe-smoking local solicitor who was also the Leader of the Conservative Group on the Rossendale Borough Council. Graham was a gentleman and a wonderful chairman, whose personal support was particularly appreciated as he had initially indicated that he wished to be considered as the parliamentary candidate himself. To this day Graham realised that his principal contribution to the Party would be on the voluntary side. He was to become the North-West Area Chairman after Mary Tomlinson, my good friend and fellow Councillor from my Ward in Rochdale.

John Holt's great strength was in managing the General Election Campaign itself. He has very acute antennae for politics and is a dedicated and enthusiastic Councillor. He was a very popular Mayor of Rossendale. Sheila Blaby was my greatest support as my agent. She was unflinching in her loyalty to me and, in what is always a very special relationship between candidate and agent, she was my greatest ally and friend.

The Rossendale Free Press was to become very important to me, as its local coverage of the Valley remained unchallenged. Adrian Purslow was to take over the editorship from Bill Poucher shortly after my selection. The newspaper was owned by the Rochdale Observer

Group, which had always played such a significant part in our family's lives over many years. Adrian always made certain that political coverage in the paper was fair. As all my efforts had to be concentrated on Rossendale, I retired as Leader of the Conservative Group in Rochdale and in 1976 retired as a Councillor for my Ward.

A year later Ruth graduated with an honours degree in law from Manchester University and her parents, my father and I witnessed the degree ceremony in the University's magnificent Hall. Then the bombshell fell. Ruth received a letter from the Bar Council informing her that they had decided to change the system for those wishing to be called to the Bar. The letter stated that all those who wished to practice as barristers would have to become full-time students at the Bar School in London for twelve months. Prior to this, it had been possible to undertake a correspondence course. This was quite a shock. We had been married for only two years and we had never contemplated that Ruth would have to spend a year in London. Looking back at that period, it now seems that it passed quite quickly. At the time, however, it seemed like an age. Every weekend we managed to see each other and every other weekend I would travel to London and stay with her in a tiny flat in South Kensington. Every alternate weekend Ruth would come home to Bethany Farm and always get involved in constituency activities.

My expertise in cooking meals is renowned the world over. That's because I'm so bad at it. People seem to run and hide if I get anywhere near a grill or oven. Very sad really. On the other hand, during Ruth's year in London, I managed to turn my hand to cremating the odd steak here and there. Because of my inability to enjoy cooking, I would always be quick to accept any offer from close friends to have a meal during the mid-week period. Ruth's parents were superb as usual. Mary and Bill Tomlinson, Dennis and Kaye Everett and Eric and Jenny Taylor used also to entertain me regularly. I spent a lot of time moving from safe house to safe house, secure in the knowledge that their cooking was excellent and I had only to wait till the weekend, when the 7th Cavalry in the shape of Ruth would come and rescue me. Ruth realised that in the culinary field I was a great embarrassment to her. She would always say to those friends kind enough to sit me at their dining table, 'Ignore him. He only perfects this story of being a bad cook so that you will feel sorry for him. It's like people who break plates so that they can get out of washing up.' Fortunately they all kept feeling sorry for me.

One thing at which I became somewhat more proficient was building stone fireplaces. I built two at Bethany Farm which I thought were masterpieces. Most of our friends thought they were OK. I got slightly carried away with the first one I built in the sitting room. I was gripped with the challenge of copying a fireplace I had seen in an old copy of *Ideal Home.* It was going to be huge. I was happily cementing one course of stones on top of another when Ruth returned home from London for the weekend.

'Marvellous, darling,' she said. 'Don't you think you should check that this wooden floor will stand that weight that you are building on it?'

'Of course it can,' I said. But just to check, I went down to the cellar underneath the sitting room and, to my horror, saw that the ceiling was so badly bowed with the weight of the fireplace that it would only have taken one more layer of stones for the whole edifice to have come crashing through. I had to start work immediately building a mock fireplace in breeze blocks under the stone fireplace just to support it. It was a narrow escape!

In the summer of 1978 Ruth passed the Bar examinations and shortly afterwards was called to the Bar at Gray's Inn. It was a momentous occasion but she was only allowed to invite one guest. Ruth tentatively suggested that her guest should be her mother rather than I. It was obvious that Joan should attend the ceremony and I said so. She had supported and encouraged Ruth in all her academic work from the very beginning – long before I ever came on the scene. In addition to that, it was a very nice gesture and Joan was thrilled to go. Alec and I waited outside to add our congratulations afterwards.

Ruth was then very fortunate in being able to secure a pupillage with Stephen Grime, who was a rising star in Dean's Court Chambers in Manchester. The Head of Chambers was Norman Lees, who would later become a circuit judge. Stephen Grime would become a QC when he was only 39. To this day, Stephen and Ruth share a room in those chambers and Ruth is very proud to be a member of such a prestigious set.

Addressing a meeting during the 1979 election campaign. Eric Taylor is on the far left sitting next to Ruth. Sheila Blaby is third from the right.

Having secured her qualifications and now her career, Ruth was able to devote more time to supporting me in Rossendale. This was wonderful as we were better as a team. There was always a significant amount of work to do in Rossendale in order to become a successful candidate. This meant me travelling across to the Valley on most nights and certainly there was always a number of political or social events to attend at the weekend. What I had not realised, when I was appointed the prospective candidate, was that the Labour Government would last for as long as it did. When Harold Wilson handed over the premiership to Jim Callaghan in 1976, the Labour majority was already dwindling through the deaths of Labour Members. In by-election after by-election those seats would become either Tory or Liberal. Eventually Sunny Jim had to do a deal with the Liberals in 1978. The Lib-Lab pact, as it became known, was to guarantee a further extension of Labour rule, which was very frustrating for those of us who were dying to fight the fight in a General Election. How

Presenting clogs to Margaret Thatcher. Graham Woodcock is in the centre.

Ruth and I avoided being 'burnt out' before the Election in 1979 was a miracle.

The most significant political meeting which was to take place in the Valley during my candidature was when Margaret Thatcher came to speak in the Astoria at Rawtenstall in 1978. This was to be an Area meeting under the Chairmanship of Graham Woodcock, but I was asked to propose a vote of thanks to the Leader and present her with a fine pair of Lancashire clogs which had been made in the Valley. I was somewhat cynical as to whether she would ever wear them, although her reputation as a tough lady was such that she might have needed them to kick a few people up the backside. Instead it appeared that when she became the Prime Minister, she found a handbag to be perfectly adequate.

In the spring of 1979 Jim Callaghan lost a vote of no confidence which was tabled by the Opposition in the House of Commons, and he called an election to let the people decide. At last we were campaigning for real and this time the opinion polls were in our favour. Although the campaign in Rossendale could not enjoy the high national profile of the by-election in Rochdale in 1972, nonetheless we received considerable regional coverage as Rossendale was the seat in the north-west of England which had the most slender Labour majority. My party officials and workers threw everything into the campaign bar the kitchen sink and on polling day we knew we had a good chance. When the votes were counted, I had won by a majority of 1873 and became a Member of Parliament. It was a great victory and the campaign was won by excellent organisation and effective teamwork. It is always essential to remember the people who worked for you as well as those who supported you at the polls.

After all the celebrations and speeches of thanks in various Conservative Clubs up and down the Valley, Ruth and I arrived home just before dawn at Bethany Farm. We were alone at last. It certainly wasn't worth going to bed, however tired we were, so we stood arm in arm holding each other up and watching the sun come up. We were trying to absorb what had happened. Life had taken a new turn for both of us over the last twelve months and we had both realised our ambitions.

We never knew then, but the best was yet to come.

Celebrating success on election night.

CHAPTER XIII

Early Years at Westminster

'Aren't you lucky to be working for Kenneth Clarke?'

I HAD NEVER BEEN IN THE Palace of Westminster in my life before I became a Member of Parliament. I had consciously avoided visiting it because I was certain that I would be impressed, and then if I failed to become an MP, I would be miserable for the rest of my life. As it was, I was entering this distinguished building in my own right and I was looking forward to it.

I was more than impressed when I arrived – in fact I was overawed. It was everything I had imagined and more. I was captivated by the heritage as much as anything and that never left me for the thirteen years I was a Member.

When I arrived I was amazed that the policemen at the gates recognised me. They had received photographs of the new Members and had already begun to memorise our names and match them to our faces. Having been given a guided tour by Cyril Smith, I was handed over to the Conservative Whip for the north-west of England, Peter Morrison, the MP for Chester since 1974. I had obviously done him a great favour when I defeated him in the final selection for the candidature in the Rochdale by-election and he was selected for Chester. He was already on his way up the ladder and the fact that he had to look after a new brood of MPs elected in the north-west was a pleasure to him. The fact that one of that brood was myself, and I was just the new boy while he was the form prefect, must have thrilled him to bits. In the event, he could not have been kinder. He was concerned that I should be formally registered with the House of Commons Security Services, receive an official pass, a car park pass and then find an office somewhere. Perhaps most important of all, I was given a key for a locker on one of the House of Commons corridors. This was just like going to a new school on the first day. I was almost surprised that no-one gave me a gym kit and pumps.

There was one briefing after another. The Government Chief Whip, Michael Jopling, addressed all the new Conservative Members in a Committee Room. Although all the new faces were glowing as a result of their success in the election, there was also a feeling of apprehension that we should commit some major gaffe and make total fools of ourselves in the first few days.

Many of us had already made one mistake that day by greeting one another with the customary handshake. Apparently this was not on. MPs, by custom, don't shake hands with each other; they shouldn't need to. Even more surprising was that all MPs, whatever their rank and status, must address each other by their Christian names. The only exception was that the Prime Minister would always be referred to as 'Prime Minister'. Again by tradition, we were told that in the Members' Dining Room, the political parties sat for dinner in their own groupings and that it was customary for one table to be completely filled before starting to fill another. If there was an empty chair at a table on the Conservative Party side of the Dining Room, you had to sit in it.

I found this revelation to be rather interesting because it meant that if a Minister came into the Dining Room and took the remaining empty chair, it would certainly mean that you would get to know one another quite quickly. On the other hand, if you were on your third glass of wine and the Prime Minister was to walk in and pop herself down beside you, it could have a distinctly sobering effect. More to the point, it could have an amazing effect on your future political career – for better or worse.

My ruminations on this prospect were not too wide of the mark when I sat at a table in the Dining Room on the evening of the first day with two other new MPs. The remaining empty chair was soon occupied by Geoffrey Howe, the new Chancellor of the Exchequer. 'Hell's teeth,' I thought, 'This tradition obviously works.' He was delightful company and yet again I was quite overawed, but just about managed to call him Geoffrey. When I telephoned Ruth after dinner, there was a lot to talk about.

Although I stayed for the first few nights in the Army and Navy

Outside parliament.

Club, I was soon lucky enough to secure a small flat near Victoria, which would be my accommodation for eighteen months before I found something more suitable. I was not so lucky with securing an office because all the new members, whatever their party, were scrabbling around trying to get an office just for themselves. I found this to be impossible and initially had to share with four other colleagues. Worse still, this office was in Abbey Gardens, which is as far away from the House of Commons as it is possible to be. On the other hand, the view was delightful as it overlooked a lawn and gardens at the rear of Westminster School.

Having been sworn in and taken the oath at the Despatch Box, along with all the other Members of Parliament, I walked past the Speaker's chair and was congratulated by George Thomas, who by then had become a household name as a very popular and highly respected Speaker. He gave a reception for the new MPs within a few days of my taking my seat. I was impressed to find that as he welcomed each of us at the door of his State Rooms in the Palace, he was able to rattle off our names. Obviously he had had access to the same photographs as the police had used and must have spent an inordinate length of time committing to memory the faces and the names. That evening he made very few mistakes.

Once I had employed a secretary recommended by an employment agency, I was in business. The mail received was enormous and I thought that I would never get on top of it. After a few days, I slotted into a routine and by the time I returned home on the Friday, I was looking forward to the State Opening the following week and sharing my first impressions of my new career with Ruth.

I attended my first surgery in Rawtenstall Library on the Saturday morning. On my election, I had said to the press that I would make myself available for a surgery every two weeks in different locations in the Valley and that no appointments would be required. The surgeries started at ten-thirty in the morning and I found that over the years it was impossible to guess when they would end as they varied so much.

When I saw how many people were sitting in the waiting room for my first surgery, I was amazed. There were so many that I thought that it could last all day. There were two things which happened at that surgery which I remember well. The first was that quite a number of the constituents were expressing great interest in buying their council houses and wanted assurance that we would introduce legislation to enable them to do so. The second was verging on the unreal. A very small man walked into the office in a highly nervous state. When he sat down, he kept glancing furtively from side to side and for some reason looked persecuted. I was about to discover why. When he lowered his voice and told me that his wife kept beating him up on a regular basis, he had my full attention. I had heard about wife-beatings but husband-beatings were entirely new to me. When I had satisfied myself that he wasn't sending me up, I asked the critical question: 'Is she a big lady?'

'Massive!', he replied as fear shone through his eyes.

It was clear that he needed a solicitor, not an MP, and having photocopied a list of the solicitors in the Valley, I sent him on his way. I only saw him once again when he was out shopping with his wife about twelve months after this first meeting. I thought they must have reconciled their differences. Laden down with shopping bags, he beamed at me and I beamed back. Neither of us spoke or she would probably have given him the third degree as to how he knew me. She was enormous with a fierce look.

At the end of my first surgery, I left the library to walk over to my car and was approached by a gentleman who said, 'Mr Trippier, I'm so glad to have caught you. Whoever is the Member of Parliament for Rossendale normally accepts the position of President of the Bacup Flying Club. Would you be prepared to accept that office?'

I said I would be honoured and promised that I would attend their meeting at a well-known pub in Bacup the following Sunday.

I couldn't wait to get home to Ruth to tell her the good news. 'There's a Flying Club in Bacup and I'm going to be the President.'

'Good heavens,' said Ruth. 'I haven't seen many planes about in the Valley.'

'I've been thinking about that. There isn't much flat land in Bacup and I can't imagine where a plane could possibly land. However, apparently there is a Flying Club.'

When I went to the meeting, I dressed up in my blazer, trying to resemble 'Flying Officer Kite'. To my astonishment, as I walked into the pub and went through the bar area, I saw there were a lot of cloth

Presenting trophies to the Bacup 'Flying Club'.

caps about. I also saw the pigeons in the cages that were going to be auctioned. At that point I felt a complete idiot as I realised that the Bacup Flying Club was a pigeon fanciers' club. However, I enjoyed every minute of that afternoon and made some good friends. I was their president for many years and can never remember talking about politics – only pigeons.

On another occasion, and at a similar auction, I was in the company of Councillor John Holt, the Leader of the Council. He and I got totally carried away with the drama and put in a joint bid for a highly prized racing pigeon. When, to our amazement, no-one bid a higher amount, the enormity of our recklessness dawned on us both. As neither of us would dare go home with a pigeon for fear of what our wives would say, we bribed the Club Secretary to keep the bird in his loft for a reasonable fee. The pigeon would be a secret. We were certain we would make a lot of money with this pigeon, especially as his pedigree was so impressive. We decided to call him 'Concorde'.

Anyone who knows anything about male pigeons knows that the incentive to get the pigeon to fly back to the coop is to give him the smell of a hen pigeon, then – bingo – he tears back. When Concorde went on his maiden voyage, he never returned. We must have bought the only homosexual pigeon in the Rossendale Valley.

During my second week as an MP I witnessed the State Opening of Parliament and the debates which ensued on the Loyal Address.

This was the first time I had seen the new Prime Minister in action in the House of Commons and it was an historical moment. She was the first lady to become Prime Minister in the United Kingdom and her reception from the Conservatives when she entered the House was tumultuous. Her performance at the Despatch Box was brilliant and although the former Prime Minister, Jim Callaghan, was very gracious in complimenting her publicly on her appointment, it was clear that he did not wish to remain Leader of the Opposition for very long.

There are relatively few reserved seats in the chamber. On the Government side, the ministerial team sit on the front bench. The bench behind is occupied by the Parliamentary Private Secretaries and the seat immediately to the side of the gangway is reserved, by convention, for former Prime Ministers, in this case Edward Heath.

At that time there were approximately 650 MPs who were expected to sit on benches which only accommodated 450. So when the House was full, people were standing or sitting in the aisles and galleries or near to the bar of the House next to the Sergeant-at-Arms' chair. This was a totally new experience for me and in complete contrast to the more conventional but much smaller Council Chamber in Rochdale, where everyone had their own seat. Sir Winston Churchill once likened addressing the House to speaking in the middle of a huge crowd. So it is.

I managed to squeeze myself on to the very last bench at the top of the gangway and for the period that I remained a backbencher, I always occupied that seat. At his reception for new members, the Speaker had politely requested that we should stay in the same seat so that he could more easily identify us when he wished to call us to ask a question or make a speech.

As the weeks unfolded in my first Parliament, the new entry settled down and slowly but surely we got to know each other quite well and to become friendly with many of the MPs who had served for some time.

Although I foolishly thought that I was relatively young to become an MP, as I was only 32, I found that there were quite a few who were younger. It was also clear that the new intake of Conservative MPs was dramatically different to previous intakes. For example, there were more of us elected in 1979 who had been to Grammar School than Public School. Although I had thought that there would be many Conservative Members from my own profession, there were only four of us who were stockbrokers. The vast majority of professionals were lawyers and most of them were barristers. There was a paucity of Members with industrial experience.

In any event, I was proud to be there and initially happy with my new environment. It certainly helped that I had known a number of new MPs when they were only candidates. Out of these, John Lee, was to become the closest friend, and it was fortuitous that his seat, Pendle, was very near to Rossendale and in many ways similar. Our political paths were to run almost in tandem throughout our Parliamentary Careers. Ruth was also very friendly with John's wife Monique and that enabled them to share the pleasures and the pain of being Parliamentary wives. Later on, John became godfather to our middle son Edward and we all remain close friends to this day.

There were a number of so-called select Dining Clubs limited to about 20 members who would meet on a regular basis once a month and chew the political fat over an evening meal in one of the smaller Dining Rooms in the House. John Lee and I were invited to join the Guy Fawkes Group. We had no secret designs to burn Parliament to the ground, but had simply convened for the first dinner on November 5th. John Watson, the MP for Skipton, was the convener of this group and its members were an interesting bunch. To begin with there were John Major, Stephen Dorrell, David Mellor, Matthew Parris, Brian Mawhinney, Robin Squire, Graham Bright, John Lee and myself. Interestingly, most of us became Ministers and obviously one became Prime Minister, but looking back at its formation by John Watson, it is surprising that he was the first to decide that Parliament was not for him and voluntarily left to pursue his business career. It is even more interesting that out of 140 new Tory members, he would approach those of us whom he thought were like-minded and were comfortable in the centre of Conservative Party thinking. There were other Dining Clubs who were to the far right and others still who were on the left. I was happy to be with the Guy Fawkes Group.

There was always an element of competition between colleagues. It would be demonstrably daft to imagine that it did not exist. I have never believed any MP who says that he or she is not competitive or that he or she lacks ambition. It has to be a lie because every Member of Parliament has to have ambition and be competitive to get elected in the first place. The idea that all ambition would vanish away once you became an MP is clearly ridiculous. More to the point, there is far more competition in politics than in any other walk of life. If it isn't transparent, it will be just beneath the surface, bubbling away, ready to erupt at a moment's notice.

My opportunity to meet with and secure new friends was obviously enhanced by the Guy Fawkes Group, but I had an additional advantage in having my very own political godfather. Walter Clegg was a very senior backbencher who was the MP for North Fylde – soon to become Wyre – in Lancashire. He had been a Whip but not a Minister. I don't know who adopted whom and I don't think it matters, but it was wonderful to be able to run to someone for advice, knowing that Wally would have no ulterior motive in anything he

The author's political 'godfather' Sir Walter Clegg (right) with Henry Purcell and Lady Clegg.

said other than to help me. At the time he was the Chairman of the North-West of England Conservative MPs and Treasurer of the 1922 Committee. He would later be knighted and become the President of the North-West Area Conservative Party. He and his wife Elise were regarded as the backbone of the Tory Party in the North-West and to this day I have never heard anyone speak ill of him. As they had no family, Wally lived for Lancashire cricket and politics. Elise lived for Wally. He had a distinguished War career in the Royal Artillery and, like my father, was captured in the North African desert. Unlike my father, he was not repatriated and remained a prisoner of war till 1945. He then qualified and practised as a solicitor. He would constantly pull my leg about the Royal Marines, saying that we were more likely to start a war than finish one, while I would constantly refer to him as a 'nine-mile sniper'. All good humoured stuff. Despite our age gap, we had two other things in common apart from our interest in politics and matters military. He had been born in Rossendale, where his father had had a pub in Rawtenstall, and until his father and mother moved to Blackpool, he was a pupil at Bury Grammar School. When he died in 1994, I spoke at the funeral, which was packed with his many friends. Many of those who attended were not Conservatives at all, but nonetheless liked and respected Wally. It was a great tribute to him.

As the rules of the House of Commons make clear, a new Member of Parliament cannot ask questions of Ministers at the Despatch Box until he or she has made their maiden speech. Some were inclined to rush at it and get it over with as quickly as possible. Others took a long time and it was sometimes years before they spoke. I decided not to be first in the queue but to deliver my speech after a few weeks. Again convention dictates that the new Member should say complimentary things about his seat, which was easy for me because there are so many parts of the Valley which are outstandingly attractive. It was also expected that the Member would compliment his predecessor, which again was easy because I liked Mike Noble. After that you can say whatever you wish, provided it is relevant to the subject being debated on that day. All of this had to be contained in a speech lasting no longer than ten minutes. If you spoke for longer, it could well be that the Speaker would not call you again for ten years. Custom decreed that you would not be interrupted by another Member, and if you were lucky, the Minister replying to the debate would give you an honourable mention in his wind-up speech and, if you were very lucky, would wish you well in your parliamentary career.

Successful speechmakers will confirm that as a rule of thumb, it takes half an hour of preparation for every minute of delivery. Having heard this maxim, I was certainly going to take at least five hours preparing my ten-minute maiden speech. In the event, I decided to speak in a debate on employment which was to feature Jim Prior. He would be winding up for the Government as he was the Secretary of State for Employment. In addition to complying with the established customs of the House, I spoke up for the footwear and textile industries which employed approximately fifty per cent of the workforce in my industrial constituency. Looking back at my first speech in Parliament – which is recorded, like everything else, in Hansard – it was hardly the crowning moment of my career. It was fine, it may even be considered quite good, but when I heard other maidens delivered by Chris Patten and Matthew Parris, I considered mine to be average.

After a few months as an MP, I had settled into a routine and was able to take stock of where my parliamentary career was leading. It was not all plusses by a long way. Although I enjoyed the cut and thrust of debate and was becoming a regular participant in the Ministerial Question Time which was held every day in the House, I was becoming somewhat disenchanted. The dreadful realisation that I had little or no power was beginning to dawn on me. Here I was, having achieved a lifetime's ambition, and yet I was politically neutered. Having previously been a Leader of a Council, with enormous power, I had thrown that away and become little more than lobby fodder. I had been a big duck on a little pond and sacrificed that to become a little duck on a very big pond. The frustration of not getting on was beginning to get through to me. The only power in Parliament was in the hands of Ministers and it seemed that a single Member of Parliament who was a backbencher was unable to change the course of history.

If anyone felt that proposed legislation which was to be debated in Parliament was flawed in some way, the only hope of making an impact was to gather a number of colleagues together and try to persuade a Minister to change the Bill before it became an Act of Parliament. At this time I didn't seem to be making any headway with my own political career. I had singularly failed to get elected as the Secretary of the Backbench Defence Committee, which would have been the first step up the political ladder. I was not well known enough to secure the support I needed.

In this critical analysis of my personal situation, the most worrying aspect of all was that I was lonely. London can be the most vibrant place on earth, but it can also be a very lonely place. Despite the friendships I had made in Parliament, there were long periods of isolation when I seriously wondered whether I had made the right decision in going into Parliament at all. I was relatively newly married, with a wife who was my closest friend, yet I only saw her at weekends. I was particularly sensitive to the impact of the recession on my constituents, many of whom were losing their jobs. The surgeries were getting longer and the letters in the mail were horrific.

Despite the revolutionary changes which the Thatcher administration was introducing, it was against the backdrop of a deep and painful recession in the economy. On the one hand, the Government had enormous courage in curtailing the abuse of power by the trade unions, making industry stand on its own feet by deregulation, and giving infinitely more power to the individual. On the other hand, unemployment was rising rapidly and the impact on my constituency was increasing dramatically, with factories closing down at an alarming rate.

The unexpected downturn in my fortunes was beginning to have a deleterious effect on me and my performance. The telephone calls to Ruth in the evenings were getting longer and longer and despite the comfort they gave me, I realised that the only way I was going to snap out of this spiral of self-pity was to get a grip on myself. The answer, which Ruth and I came up with, was very clear: I must get my head down and work, work and work. I would fill every working hour with constituency business or parliamentary speeches in the House. I visited the House of Commons Library more frequently and became more efficient at carrying out extensive research. Above all else I wanted to become a House of Commons man.

This hard work paid off. Twelve months after I became an MP, I was elected as the Secretary of the Defence Committee and resolved to shine in that role. If there was any respite from this treadmill, it was occasionally popping into the Strangers' Bar, which was known as the Kremlin because it was largely frequented by Labour MPs, with only a few exceptions. Amongst the few of us who dared to make regular appearances there were Marcus Fox, Sir George Young, Kenneth Clarke and myself. Apart from anything else, it was one of the few places where one could get a decent pint of 'Wallop'.

Kenneth Clarke interested me a great deal. He was then a Parliamentary Under Secretary of State for Transport. His performances at the Despatch Box were unrivalled and he was already building up an excellent reputation as a considerate and caring Minister, who was liked and respected by Members on both sides of the House. He was sharp, scruffy and baby-faced.

He was already a hero in my book after I visited him in his Ministry to argue for more motorway signs describing different towns in the Rossendale Valley. I never realised it before, but just as Rossendale is not named on the map because it is a conglomeration of a number of towns, Ken Clarke's constituency, Rushcliffe, near to Nottingham, is exactly the same. When I asked for the largest town, Rawtenstall, to be signed on the motorway, the civil servants sitting on either side of him at the meeting objected because they said it would take very expensive signs as there were too many letters in the name Rawtenstall. Ken laughed and agreed to let me have my signs.

Within the first two years of my parliamentary career I had voted against the Government on two critical issues. The first was in a debate on the textile industry in which I believed the Government was not taking enough notice of the industry's lobby to strengthen the Multi-Fibre Arrangement. This was an international agreement to curtail cheap textile imports. The second was in a debate on the disabled in which I believed that more should have been done for the handicapped and said so in one of my more impassioned speeches.

On this second occasion, Peter Morrison as my area Whip was beside himself with anger at the embarrassment I caused the Government, and spent a great deal of time trying to talk me out of rebelling. Shortly after the vote, when I came out of the 'No' lobby where I had been somewhat conspicuous as the only Tory amongst all the Socialists who were voting against the Government, I had to go to a cocktail party on the terrace. Willie Whitelaw was at the bar and offered to get me a drink. Peter Morrison loomed behind me and said 'I can't see how David can get a drink out of the Deputy Prime Minister when he's just supported the Socialists.'

Willie turned to me and said, 'Don't make a habit of it – there's a dear chap,' and got me a drink. Peter Morrison, hoping that Willie would have given me a rollicking, was crestfallen.

Having kicked up such a fuss on these two issues, it was clear to my constituents that at least I was my own man and not lobby fodder. At the same time, I was determined that on every other issue I would be loyal and supportive. I also realised that the real secret of success was to persuade a Minister to change legislation before it found its way on to the statute book, and with the help of a number of friends, I managed to do precisely that during the passage of the Housing Bill, giving the right to tenants to buy their council houses.

This came about after Miss Hannah Law visited me at a surgery. She was a former Matron of the Rossendale General Hospital, a member of the Conservative Association, and a friend. Hannah pointed out a flaw in the proposed Housing legislation which I had not thought of. A generous discount was given on the price of the house to those whose name appeared on the rent book. The longer the person had been a tenant, the more generous the discount.

Hannah Law and thousands like her up and down the country did not have their names on the rent book. Instead the rent book was in her mother's name, and as she lived with her, Hannah had paid the rent for countless years. Sadly her mother died shortly before Hannah came to see me and the proposed law did not allow her to receive any discount at all because her name had only been exchanged for her mother's on the rent book for a few weeks.

Having rehearsed the arguments for changing the law with my friends in the Guy Fawkes Dining Group, who agreed that this was an anomaly, I felt confident enough to approach the Housing Minister, John Stanley, to try and persuade him to change the Bill. He said that he would give it serious consideration and during the Report Stage of the Bill, when I delivered a speech covering the main points of my argument, he agreed to change the Bill and give the discount rights to those who had been paying the rent, whether they were named in the rent book or not. I was delighted and so was Hannah Law. This was progress and I felt I had achieved something important.

Things were now beginning to look up and, to cap everything, our first son, Alexander, was born on 10th August 1981. Ruth had had a relatively easy pregnancy and throughout had looked wonderful. Alex was a few weeks premature and was delivered in St Mary's Hospital in Manchester. Amongst the first letters of congratulation we received was one from George Thomas, the Speaker of the House of Commons. I was amazed that he knew, but news travels fast. George also promised that if Alexander was christened in the Crypt in the Palace of Westminster, he would gladly make available his State Rooms for the reception afterwards. Needless to say, we took advantage of his kind offer and the Speaker's Chaplain, John Austin Baker, christened Alexander Austin in the Crypt. Our family and friends travelled to London for this great event.

The following year Kenneth Clarke was promoted to become the Minister for Health and approached me to become his Parliamentary Private Secretary. I could not have been more delighted and it was a great honour to be chosen by him. Instead of people coming up to congratulate me on my appointment, all of them said, 'Aren't you lucky to be working for Kenneth Clarke?'

I knew I was.

CHAPTER XIV

The Importance of Entrepreneurship

'Welcome to the Valley of Enterprise'

I WAS SOON TO LEARN that the role of a Parliamentary Private Secretary to a Minister is a demanding one, which requires a wider variety of skills than most people would think. For certain, it is much more than being a bag-carrier. In the first place, the PPS is the eyes and ears of the Minister in the House of Commons. He is expected to relay back to the Minister any concerns that the backbenchers have concerning the area of his brief and as Ken Clarke had a very great responsibility as Minister for Health, it was clear that I would be kept very busy. Everyone had an opinion on health matters. There was also the daunting prospect of impending legislation in the shape of the Mental Health Amendment Bill, for which I was expected to be at his beck and call, not least during the passage of the Bill through the Committee stage, which would take countless hours. I would sit immediately behind him both in Committee and in the Chamber when he was making a speech or answering questions.

I was also expected to attend the Ministerial meetings which took place in the Department of Health and Social Security every Monday morning – sometimes at a moment's notice. These meetings were chaired by Norman Fowler, who was the Secretary of State. Those meetings gave me my first insight into the internal workings of a Government Department and I found that discussion would range over a wide field, including policy making, political awareness and the inevitable problems that would beset any or all of the subject areas. There was no doubt that I had been plunged into the front line of politics, but however difficult his brief might be, Ken was certainly up to the task.

Ken Clarke has a very agile mind and his ability to think on his feet is stunning. I realised very quickly that I was 'sitting at the feet' of someone who would teach me more about politics than anyone before or since. His capacity to absorb facts after only reading them once was perhaps his most outstanding characteristic. He could cut through the butter and get to the heart of the matter faster than anyone I have ever met. My difficulty was keeping up with him.

Although Ken was seen by many of our colleagues as being on the moderate side of the Conservative Party, and thus dubbed 'a wet', he could also be very tough in many areas where he was as dry as the Sahara Desert. I instinctively believed that he had a natural capacity for 'greatness'. I knew he would go far and everyone agreed with me.

His bonhomie and somewhat unkempt appearance could easily lull people into believing that he was over-relaxed and too laid back. His hush puppies, which were to become his trade mark, sent out similar signals. The truth was exactly the opposite and he was conscientious, ambitious and a 'workaholic'. He loved the House of Commons and particularly the Chamber, where his performances at the despatch box were vintage stuff. He preferred speaking without notes and his debating style was so sparkling that he could always hold the attention of the House without any difficulty. His command of the English Language and grasp of a very wide vocabulary were one secret of his success.

Despite his pugnacious debating style, he was, and remains, one of the most popular MPs in the House. Michael English, who was a Labour MP for one of the Nottingham seats and like me a Rochdalian, once told me that Ken Clarke was the most honest politician he had ever met. Knowing Ken as well as I do, I would agree. Unlike most politicians I have known, he would never court publicity, and yet his media coverage was always considerable. Journalists were attracted to him like moths to a flame. He was a reporter's dream because his soundbites were always pithy and often amusing. He was also very easy to work with. He hardly ever lost his temper and seemed happiest when he was under great pressure. Often we would pop in to the Kremlin for a pint together and if he had been speaking in a late night debate, we would sometimes go afterwards to Ronnie Scott's Jazz Club, where he was well known by the regulars.

When we got to know each other well, I politely suggested that he

With Ken Clarke.

might get his hair cut if he was appearing on television. There was also a period when I noticed that he had lost a little weight, which was a very rare happening, and he started to tug at his trousers to hitch them up from time to time. It was funny enough seeing him standing at the despatch box and sweeping his hair back with his right hand, but it was all too much if he was at the same time hitching up his pants with the other hand. I bought him a belt, which I don't think he ever wore.

One of Ken's closest friends in the House was Jim Lestor, the MP for Beeston. Jim suggested that the three of us should lose some weight over two months and organised a slimming competition, in which the one who lost the least weight would take the other two out for a lunch at the Ritz. As I had never been to the Ritz, I was an enthusiastic competitor.

When the two months had elapsed, Jim had lost a stone, I had lost half a stone and Ken had put on a stone, and so he took us to the Ritz. After tucking into the heavy puddings and waiting for the coffee, Ken disappeared to go to the toilet. In his absence, Jim and I decided we felt sorry for Ken as he had to pick up the bill, and we decided we would pay for the wine, which Ken reluctantly agreed to. When eventually the separate bills arrived, the wines that we had enjoyed cost more than the food by a huge margin. That would teach us!

Like my mother, Ken has a frustrating habit of very rarely criticising anyone or gossiping behind their backs. Again, I believe it is one of the reasons that he is so popular. I once criticised John Prescott, who was Ken's shadow spokesman, for behaving like a thug in a particular debate. Ken immediately sprang to his defence and said nice things about him, rounding off with the comment, 'He's also very knowledgeable about jazz', as if that should exonerate him from blame of any kind. Very wearing!

Apart from being Ken's number one fan, I was also to become a fan of his wife Gillian. They had originally met each other at Cambridge, where they were both students. Had they not married, Gillian would undoubtedly have gone on to become a Don. She was not only Ken's greatest supporter, but also his most valued friend. Gillian is clever and perceptive with a dry, sharp sense of humour which she has often used to defend Ken and occasionally to keep his feet on the ground. She is politically astute, caring, and sufficiently confident to ignore many of the petty comments that prevail amongst some MP's wives. Ruth admires her greatly.

During the first few months that I was Ken's PPS, I paid a visit to St Helen's on Merseyside to meet a man called Bill Humphrey. He, rather like Ken Clarke, was to have a dramatic effect on my life. With his habitually granite expression, and wearing reading glasses, as he did, almost permanently, he was seldom seen without a pipe nearby, if not between his teeth. The reason for my visit was a deep sense of frustration with the rising unemployment in my constituency, which was causing me grave concern. At times it seemed that there was a textile mill closing every month and a footwear factory closing down every other month. I felt powerless and to make matters worse, I realised from the very beginning of the recession that many of the unemployed had been working since they were sixteen and that, having been made redundant at a critical age, they would have enormous difficulty in finding alternative employment.

A Main Board Director of National Westminster Bank heard me expressing my concern at a lunch in the Bank's headquarters in London and recommended that I should visit an organisation run by Bill Humphrey called the Community of St Helen's Trust. It turned out to be a revelation.

Despite the fact that widespread unemployment had been a feature of St Helen's in the past due to large redundancies at glass companies like Pilkingtons and Rockware, unemployment was beginning to fall as a result of a greater emphasis being placed on small businesses, some of which were new start-ups. In other words, there was now a new drive for enterprise in St Helens, encouraging people who had perhaps never considered becoming self-employed to start up their own company and become the employers of tomorrow. The catalyst for making this happen was Bill Humphrey; and the St Helen's Enterprise Trust was the engine which encouraged and helped these new entrepreneurs to succeed.

The idea had originally come from Pilkingtons. To their eternal credit, they had recognised that they had a responsibility to the community and, as with many traditional industries, they foresaw that with modern technology and higher productivity per man, they were unlikely to increase their share of the labour market. At the same time they recognised that in the past they had enjoyed the finest asset that any community could provide, namely the very people they employed. The time had come for them to put something back into the local area and so they set up the Community of St Helen's Enterprise Trust and asked one of their former senior executives, Bill Humphrey, to become its Managing Director.

Bill Humphrey was an amazing man. He had served in the Royal Air Force during the War as a pilot in Bomber Command and had two Distinguished Flying Crosses to his credit, but yet constantly refused to talk about his wartime exploits. He had wide industrial experience and showed a fearsome determination in stimulating enterprise at every turn.

The success of this man and his Trust was later to be faithfully recorded in a splendid book entitled *The Pathfinder.* It was written by a very good friend of mine called Ian Hamilton-Fazey, who was the northern editor of *The Financial Times* until 1997. The title of the book expresses the fact that the St Helen's Trust was the first Local Enterprise Agency in the country, whilst at the same time drawing on Bill Humphrey's wartime service, where he was primarily a 'Pathfinder' in the RAF.

My first impression of Bill Humphrey will remain with me for ever. He was quite a dour sort of chap who would stomach no nonsense, and was quite outlandish in his views and tenacious in sticking to them. He was also quick to shoot down any alternative philosophy to job creation and was very convincing as to what was required. I had planned to stay in St Helen's for an hour. In the event, I spent most of the day there. As it was a Friday, I could return home for the weekend and share my revelation with Ruth. 'I have the solution to our problems in the Valley,' I said to her. 'I'm going to start the Rossendale Enterprise Trust and it will be grafted on to Bill Humphrey's experience in St Helen's.'

Within a week, I had arranged for senior Councillors from the Rossendale Borough Council to pay a visit to St Helen's. They were Conservatives, Liberal and Socialist Councillors as it was imperative to get cross-party support for the initiative. Then I persuaded Sir William Mather, the Chairman of the Regional Board of National Westminster Bank, and Ezra Forrest, the Director of the Bank's South-East Lancashire Area, to let me have a secondee for two years who would become the Director of the Trust. Roger Pearson, who had previously worked at Nat. West in Bury, was an inspired choice and became one of the most successful Directors of any Local Enterprise Agency in the country. I persuaded local industry to sponsor the Agency, and in no time this new creation was offering a hand-holding service to small firms and encouraging people to start their own businesses. Everyone I met gave the initiative their solid backing. The local authority were magnificent and twelve months after we were formed, thanks to the support of Stephen Hartley, the

Ruth and Alex on the campaign trail.

Chief Executive of the Council, we were offered new premises in the centre of Rawtenstall, as we had clearly outgrown our original home in small offices in a Mill in Haslingden.

I had learnt from Bill Humphrey that whilst it was essential to get the local authority to become a key partner, the private sector should be in the lead and have the majority of the seats on the Board. Neville Cormack, who was a very successful local carpet manufacturer, became the Chairman and successfully steered the Rossendale Enterprise Agency through a multitude of changes to the great success it still is today. Far from objecting to the private sector being in the lead, the Rossendale Borough Council accepted it readily. In no time at all they were erecting signs at the side of all the major thoroughfares leading into Rossendale saying 'Welcome to the Valley of Enterprise'.

Through a collective decision to fight back, and with people working together in partnership, the unemployment figures in Rossendale began to fall. Having been at the terrifying level of 18.1% in the depths of the recession, by 1983 unemployment had fallen to 6.4%. It was, perhaps, the most dramatic fall in such a short time scale anywhere in the United Kingdom.

In the Spring of 1983 I was informed by 10 Downing Street that the Prime Minister was thinking of visiting Lancashire and asked whether I had any suggestions as to where she might go. It was perfect timing as we were anxious to have an official opening for the Trust's new headquarters. When she came to Rawtenstall in May 1983 to open our offices, I was able to show Margaret Thatcher a video commissioned by National Westminster Bank on the Rossendale Enterprise Trust which told its own tale. She was clearly impressed and needed no persuading of the importance of entrepreneurship.

Immediately after the General Election in that same year, Ken Clarke and I were on the telephone congratulating each other on being re-elected. Towards the end of the conversation he said, 'If I were you, I would stand by to receive a special telephone call offering you a job.'

'I already have a job working for you.'

'No, you clot. I think you may become a Minister.'

CHAPTER XV

Minister of the Crown

'The Prime Minister is going to telephone me.
It's either a rollicking or a job.'

THE GENERAL ELECTION IN 1983 was to be very successful for the Conservatives, giving Margaret Thatcher an increased overall majority of 142. Many of us had seen changes in our parliamentary boundaries and I had lost a valuable part of the old Rossendale seat, namely Ramsbottom, which had been merged into an entirely new seat called Bury North. At the same time I had seen the remainder of my old constituency merged with Darwen, which had previously had its own Conservative Member, Sir Charles Fletcher Cooke, who had retired. This was a very welcome addition to the constituency and Darwen had a solid core of Conservative voters and an enthusiastic and vibrant Conservative Association. I was therefore returned to Parliament as the Member for Rossendale and Darwen with an increased majority of 8,821.

Throughout my first Parliament as an MP I was allowed to practise as a stockbroker and partner in Pilling, Trippier and Co, Manchester, and I would look after my own personal clients from our offices in St Ann's Square. It was whilst I was in those offices, the day after my evening telephone conversation with Ken Clarke, that the special telephone call which he had predicted came through.

Sadly I did not take it. We had engaged a new young telephonist called Susan only a few weeks earlier and she was beginning to show signs that she was on top of the job. On the day of the call I was sitting at my desk talking to a client on the telephone. At that time my desk boasted two telephones – you can see that it was a 'high tech.' office. When my conversation with the client was at an end, I replaced the receiver. The other telephone rang immediately.

Susan said in awe, 'Mr Trippier, the Prime Minister has just been on the telephone.'

'What! Are you certain it was the Prime Minister?'

'Oh yes Mr Trippier', she said in hushed tones. 'It was definitely Mrs Thatcher. She said who she was and anyway, I clearly recognised her voice.'

'Then why didn't you interrupt me or ring me on my other telephone?' I practically screamed down the receiver.

Susan pondered this for a few seconds. 'But Mr Trippier, when you interviewed me for this job you told me that *the client* must always come first.'

I was now becoming hysterical, 'Yes, yes – but there must be exceptions like – er the Queen or the Prime Minister, for goodness sake! Anyway – what on earth did you say to her?'

'I said you were busy.'

'Oh my God! What exactly did she say to that?'

'She said she would ring back in two hours' time when she sincerely hoped you would not be busy.'

Because all men are but little boys grown up, I immediately rang Ruth in her Chambers. 'You won't believe this,' I said, 'But the Prime Minister is going to telephone me at about noon. It's either a rollicking or a job.'

'I can pop round about then,' said Ruth excitedly, 'This is high drama.'

When Margaret Thatcher telephoned at 12 o'clock, I made sure that this time the lines were clear. When she spoke to me, I instinctively stood to attention. After the initial exchanges of congratulations which were called for following her victory, she said, 'David, I would like you to join the Government and become a Minister in the Department of Trade and Industry. Having seen what you have done in your own constituency with the Enterprise Trust, you will be the Minister for Small Firms. Try to replicate your experience in the rest of the country.'

'Thank you, Prime Minister. I will do everything I can.'

'The good news is that you should report to Cecil Parkinson at the Department tomorrow. The bad news is that you must resign as a partner or director of any business you are in by midnight tonight.'

When I eventually replaced the receiver, Ruth asked what she had said.

'It was good news and bad. The good news is that I will be the Minister for Small Firms and the bad news is that I have to leave this firm, so you will have to work harder to keep me in the standard of living I have become accustomed to.'

She beamed at me. 'Wonderful. Now telephone your father.'

When I did, he couldn't speak as he was so full of emotion, and had to ring me back. When I told Peter Gartside and the other partners in Pilling, Trippier and Co, they were very kind, but in order to comply with the Prime Minister's edict, they sent someone out to buy a rubber stamp which erased my name from all the letter-headed notepaper and contract notes leaving the firm's offices that day. It was as if I had died.

That afternoon, I travelled to London by car and went into the Department of Trade and Industry. I was met by Dr Tom Cassidy, a well built Welshman with a fringe of black hair and his own special brand of dry humour, who was to be my Private Secretary, and he introduced me to the staff in the Ministerial Office. I was to have my formal meeting with Cecil Parkinson the following morning.

On the evening of the famous telephone call, Ken Clarke and Jim Lestor took me out for dinner to a Greek Restaurant in the West End. On meeting me, Ken said, 'Welcome to the greasy pole.' Later on he said, 'Never forget, all political careers end in tears.' He handed me a book which he had suitably inscribed called *How to be a Minister* written by Gerald Kaufman, who had served in Harold Wilson's Government.

The following morning I met Cecil Parkinson and the rest of the Ministerial team. The three Ministers of State were Kenneth Baker as Minister for Technology, Norman Lamont, whose brief covered many of the responsibilities for the Department's sponsorship of industry, and Paul Channon, who was the Minister for Trade. The three junior Ministers were John Butcher, Alex Fletcher and myself. My responsibility was to sponsor all those companies who employed numbers ranging from one to two hundred employees, which covered ninety-six per cent of all firms in the United Kingdom. Although I respected the enormous responsibilities of my colleagues, there was no

At 10 Downing Street the day after the author was made a Minister. Left to right: Lord Jellicoe, Dennis, the author, Margaret, the Duke of Kent.

doubt in my mind that if we were to make a dramatic impact on unemployment, my brief was going to become increasingly important.

At the end of the Ministers' meeting, Cecil asked me to attend the reception at No. 10 Downing Street that evening, to which the Prime Minister had invited a whole host of entrepreneurs who had been successful in the export field. This was my first official engagement as a Minister and I had a marvellous opportunity to speak to Lord Jellicoe, the Chairman of the British Overseas Trade Board, and the Duke of Kent, who was his Vice Chairman. Their advice as to what should be done to encourage small businesses was to prove invaluable as I formulated the policy which should be introduced to ensure success.

After a few days in the Department, I quickly recognised the

Alex with his own red box.

importance of the Minister's Red Box. The papers contained in that box would have to be read and certainly absorbed. More often than not, an opinion would be sought and I was expected to mark the papers accordingly. It was clear that the boxes would become the bane of my life, often ensuring that I would work through them until the early hours of the morning. I established a routine whereby I would arrive at the Department at 8.00 am and rarely leave before 7.00 in the evening. There were many meetings with civil servants and Members of Parliament, Ministerial visits to various parts of the country and, of course, regular meetings with other Ministerial colleagues in the same Department. I was loving every minute of it. Perhaps best of all, I was covering a subject area I knew something about, and which filled me with a passion I had seldom felt for anything else.

I made the dreadful mistake of asking my private secretary, Tom Cassidy, to furnish me with the biographical details of all of the five staff who were in my private office, including himself. When the sheets of paper were handed to me describing his Ph.D. from Cambridge and the rather impressive qualifications of the civil servants under him, I realised that I was only slightly more qualified than the typist – and that was a close run thing.

After a few months as a Minister, I was encouraged to watch on television the serial entitled *Yes Minister.* Halfway through the programme, Ruth reminded me that it was a comedy – I thought it was a documentary. It was unbelievably near to the bone and horribly accurate. I loved it and always referred to the series as a long-distance training programme for members of the Government.

The very first official Ministerial visit I made in the regions was to St Helen's. It was important to me that I should say thank you to Bill Humphrey for teaching me how to stimulate enterprise. Bill had organised a buffet lunch with the invaluable assistance of Pilkingtons and their Chairman, Anthony Pilkington. When Bill met me at the door, he was like the cat who had swallowed the cream. He had not only had an enormous influence on me and, soon after, on the Rossendale Valley, but along with National Westminster Bank, had played a significant role in me being appointed a Minister and was now able to assume that the new enterprise culture would be spread even wider and the growth in Enterprise Agencies would accelerate. I was determined that he should be proved right on both counts.

One of the most significant meetings I had in the early stages of my Ministerial career was with Steve O'Brien, who was the Chief Executive of Business in the Community – BIC as they were to become known. Steve, tall, good-looking, with a pleasant manner, had been ordained as a priest in the Church of England in 1971, but had subsequently left the Church for the voluntary sector. BIC was an umbrella organisation, whose President and guiding influence was the Prince of Wales. It had the responsibility of encouraging the development of Local Enterprise Agencies throughout the land. At the time of my meeting with Steve O'Brien, there were about ten LEAs then up and running. All of them were based on the solid template set out in St Helen's, and although it was clear that Rossendale was the third to be established, I was genuinely surprised to find that some other people had spotted the enormous potential of private sector-led partnerships offering an effective hand-holding service to help the strategic development of small firms.

The meeting with Business in the Community was a huge success. First of all, I was very impressed with Steve O'Brien, whose commitment to the cause was total. Secondly I think he saw the advantage in working closely with a new Minister who had the personal experience of setting up an Agency from scratch. Thirdly, we both wanted to see Her Majesty's Government as a serious and effective partner in this huge undertaking. The fourth significant matter discussed at the meeting was the bombshell I dropped on Steve's desk, and which had him gasping for breath. I said that I wanted to see three hundred Local Enterprise Agencies within three years. I set this out as a target and although Ministers are well known for setting targets without a clear vision as to how they are to be achieved, I genuinely believed that this target was attainable.

Like many of my more dramatic ambitions, I had first thought of this figure in the bath, but there was a logical thought-process that led me to that figure. My first thought was to have an Agency in every constituency, which would have meant 650. This clearly wouldn't work, as even in St Helen's there were two MPs and so two constituencies. On the other hand, there were some constituencies that were geographically spread out and could require two, sometimes three, agencies. It was obvious that the figure set had to be attainable, otherwise I would lose credibility and they would lack quality and effectiveness. The number was one question – the other question was: could this number be achieved in three years?

In the event, it was proved that it could be done for in 1986 there were three hundred and twenty Agencies in the UK, all beavering away to help small firms. None of this could have been achieved without the magnificent support of Business in the Community, who had set up regional centres to support the initiative. Looking back at our initial meeting, I don't think that either Steve O'Brien or myself realised the enormity of the work which we would both have to put in. For him it meant tearing around the country encouraging the formation of these Agencies, persuading the private sector and the local authorities to get their act together and achieve something on the ground that was not only tangible but made good common sense.

For me it also meant tearing around the country preaching to the unconverted, sometimes the sceptical, and occasionally to the converted – speaking at regional meetings and national conferences, to say nothing of officially opening the Agencies when they were up and running. I think my record was four official openings in one day.

In the very early days of this great crusade, I had to persuade some very influential people in the Department of the Environment that the sponsorship of LEAs should rest with the Department of Trade and Industry. Initially it had been the responsibility of the Department of the Environment, for no better reason than the fact that Michael Heseltine, who had been the Secretary of State for the Environment between 1979 and 1983, had also visited St Helen's and met Bill Humphrey. When I learnt of this, I suppose I should have guessed it. Although other Ministers and MPs had passed through Bill Humphrey's hands, not everyone could grasp the significance of what they had seen or been told. Michael, with his immense vision, spotted it immediately.

In the event, Lord Bellwin, the Minister of State in the Department of the Environment, and his boss Patrick Jenkin as Secretary of State, recognised that the future development of Enterprise Agencies should move to me at the DTI and I have good reason to be grateful to both of them for their decision.

My immediate predecessors as Small Firms Ministers were David Mitchell from 1979 to 1981, and John McGregor from 1981 to 1983. Both of them had achieved much during their respective tenures of office. Although there were many successes recorded to their credit, their principal one was the establishment and growth of the Small Firms Service, which was a wholly-owned Government facility whereby there was a Government Office established in every region, staffed by civil servants. In addition to the core service, there was an impressive team of industrial advisers whose private sector experience ranged over a very wide area. They were undoubtedly successful in tackling many of the problems which beset small businesses.

At my first meeting with the key people in the Small Firms Service and the private sector counselling teams, I detected that they were very wary of me. Knowing that I had come to my new post with a background in Local Enterprise Agencies, and that the national press had reported this again and again, they thought that I had plans to scrap them. Nothing was further from my mind. To improve the service for the important people – the entrepreneurs – I told them I needed both the Small Firms Service at a regional level and Local Enterprise Agencies working in the communities. I was also very keen to see the Enterprise Agencies use the expertise of the SFS and call on their services, which would often be very specialised. I gave them a specific example: an Agency could not be expected to have an expert on patents, for example, but the SFS certainly did. The Agency would be expected to use that individual to give his assistance either in the Agency's offices or at the premises of the company concerned. I know that at the end of the meeting, the Small Firms Service went away a lot happier than when they came.

After the Tory Party Conference in 1983, I was sad to see my boss Cecil Parkinson resign as Secretary of State. Although his leaving the Government at that time was well documented, and the reasons surrounding the resignation are well known, it was a particular blow because he had given me his personal support and backing for those initiatives which I had instigated.

His successor was Norman Tebbit, who came to the Department having been the Secretary of State for Employment. He was also to be very supportive and encouraging in those policies I put before him. To my intense relief, he was happy to let me get on with the job and very rarely interfered. He was more concerned with de-regulating the City and privatising just about everything that moved, and especially those things that didn't.

There was no doubt that by the end of 1984, the 'Enterprise Band Wagon' was well and truly on the move and I was a very happy man. Even Cabinet Ministers like Peter Walker and Tom King asked me to speak in their constituencies to launch Local Enterprise Agencies and to promote the small firms ethos.

In the run up to the Conservative Party Conference in Brighton, the economy was looking more stable and all the statistics were pointing to the success of small firms and the antidote they had provided to the levels of unemployment. Although everyone was turning out to be a expert on small firms, and insistent on sharing their innermost thoughts with me either verbally or by letter, at least

The Director of the Small Business Bureau, Alan Cleverley, (in the centre) shares a joke with Ruth.

most people were convinced that we needed to encourage a more buoyant risk-taking culture, with the rewards matching the risks. The Treasury was more responsive than ever before and the Chancellor's Budget, which some of us were keen to influence, was helpful to small businesses and in some cases positively discriminated in their favour.

There was a multitude of organisations who would lobby me on every small firms issue, including the Chambers of Commerce, Institute of Directors, CBI, Small Firms Council, Forum of Private Business and Federation of Self Employed, as well as several others. The one organisation which was my closest ally and from which I drew my greatest strength was the Small Business Bureau. Originally it had been formed by David Mitchell when he was an Opposition spokesman, and long before he was Minister for Small Firms. Although it was an arm of the Conservative Party, that never stopped any of its members being tenacious in their lobbying techniques. At the beginning and at the end, the SBB would remain loyal supporters of a Conservative administration, but in the middle it would expect a clear and constructive response to the cases it brought before me. Its chairman was Michael Grylls, who was the MP for North-West Surrey, and the SBB Director was Alan Cleverley, who was also Micky Grylls' constituency agent. Michael was a persistent but gentlemanly advocate for small businesses. Alan was a great character, who worked harder than any Tory agent I have ever known.

During the Party Conference in 1984, the Small Business Bureau successfully lobbied delegates to vote for their balloted motion, which was put to the Conference on the Thursday afternoon before the Prime Minister addressed it on the Friday. I was to wind up the debate and had to prepare most of my speech at relatively short notice, as we all had to wait for the result of the ballot to see whether the debate was indeed going to be on Small Businesses.

We won the ballot and the debate on Small Businesses was a great success. Speaker after speaker had prepared well and spoke passionately. Sitting on the platform with me was Norman Tebbit, Lord Young, who had recently been appointed to the Cabinet, Kenneth Clarke and all the Ministers from the Department of Trade and Industry. Ruth sat immediately behind me on the stage with her fingers and toes crossed as I stood up to reply to the debate. I couldn't allow this to be anything other than a smash-hit success. There could be no excuse for delivering something as average as my maiden speech in Parliament, since apart from the packed Conference Hall, the debate was being televised and I had a lot of promises to deliver. Fortunately it was a huge success and I received a standing ovation.

That evening Ruth and I went with a group of friends for a celebration dinner, never dreaming that later that night the Grand Hotel was to be bombed by the IRA and that the consequences were to have a direct and tragic effect on our lives and the lives of our closest friends.

CHAPTER XVI

The Brighton Bomb

'I had never felt more useless in my life.'

I DON'T THINK THAT ANYONE in the country could take in the fact that the IRA had tried to wipe out the vast majority of the Government who were staying in the Grand Hotel in Brighton. Having seen the aftermath of the effects of the bomb, which had ripped through the central part of the hotel, I am convinced it was a miracle that more were not killed or injured. That said, the impact was still very bad.

Ruth and I were not staying in the Grand, but in an hotel a short distance away. The effect on both of us was dramatic, but particularly so on Ruth who was seven months pregnant with our second child. I was still working on a red box when the bomb went off. I recognised the sound for what it was and woke Ruth. We dressed hurriedly and ran to the Grand Hotel. When we arrived, it was already being cordoned off by the emergency services. We stood outside the taped-off area shivering in the cold, not knowing who had survived and who had not. We heard that the Prime Minister and Dennis Thatcher had escaped but it was clear that John Wakeham had been seriously injured and Tony Berry, who was an MP, had been killed.

Relieved as we were that the Prime Minister and her husband had escaped unscathed, our main concerns were for three of our closest friends, Eric and Jenny Taylor and Mary Tomlinson. Our spirits rose when Mary Tomlinson came through the rubble and dust and although she, along with everyone else, was in a state of shock, at least she was safe. We heard that Jenny Taylor was injured and had been rushed to hospital. There was no news of Eric. Nobody had seen him emerge from the hotel; you couldn't miss him even in a chaotic crowd like that, for he was six foot two and everyone knew him. I knew that he must still be in there. Rather than wait around feeling useless,

Ruth and I shot off to the hospital to see Jenny. We were relieved to see her alive, although her leg had been badly injured. She wasn't concerned about that at all – her concern was for Eric. Standing at Jenny's bedside, I had never felt more useless in my life.

The news was filtering through bit by bit. We heard that Norman Tebbit and his wife Anne were injured, but we didn't know how badly. Then I heard in the hospital that my political godfather, Wally Clegg, had been brought in. Leaving Jenny, I rushed from ward to ward trying to find him. When I was on the point of giving up, I found him covered in blood, waiting to go into the operating theatre. I couldn't speak but he grasped my hand and said faintly, 'If the Germans couldn't get me, I'm damned if the IRA will.'

Knowing he would be alright, I returned to Ruth, who was sitting by Jenny's bedside trying to comfort her. There was still no news of Eric; he certainly hadn't come out and it was rumoured that he was still in the hotel buried under the rubble. It looked bleak but Ruth and I tried not to show it in front of Jenny. By lunchtime on the Friday, we had still heard nothing of Eric.

That day the Prime Minister came round the hospital to talk to those who were injured and I admired her courage. Despite what had happened, she had delivered her speech in the Conference Hall, denounced the IRA, and was now tearing round the wards trying to comfort everyone. She sat and talked to Jenny for ages. She must have heard that the chances of Eric being found alive were slim.

Mary Tomlinson, who was certainly unwell, displayed great courage throughout. Ruth was also becoming ill with the dawning realisation that we were in danger of losing our closest friend. Mary persuaded Ruth to go with her and fly back to Manchester as quickly as possible. Graham Elliott, who was a friend and a Director of British Midland Airways, arranged the transport for them and others in a similar condition.

I certainly couldn't leave and stayed behind comforting Jenny. I stayed another night in my hotel, unable to sleep until the police rang me after midnight. They had found Eric's body buried under the rubble and the Fire Brigade had cleared debris and cut through beams to find him. As I suspected, he was dead. The police asked me to go with them to the mortuary and identify the body, which I did. That was bad enough but it was even harder returning to the hospital shortly afterwards to tell Jenny.

Those of us who witnessed the trauma of the Brighton Bomb were reeling from the horror of the event. Our emotions ranged from anger on the one hand to despair on the other. My feelings were a mixture of both. I had lost one of my closest friends and still couldn't believe it. For Jenny the impact was unimaginable and the nightmare persisted for many years. Ruth was more devastated than I had ever seen her. She loved Eric, and his humour, advice and friendship had meant a great deal to her over many years.

It was not surprising that very soon after the Brighton Bomb, on 19th November, Ruth was rushed into St Mary's Hospital in Manchester to give birth to our second son. Edward should have been born on 1st January and for many weeks he was in an incubator.

At the time that Edward was born, I was about to rise at the Despatch Box to reply to the debate on the Films Bill, for which I was expected to assist Norman Lamont in ensuring its safe passage through Parliament.

A note was passed by a policeman to a doorkeeper standing behind the Speaker's chair. Then the doorkeeper passed it via the Whips sitting on the front bench to me. It simply read, 'You have a new son. Mother and baby both well!' I was staggered and then delighted. The last man who was to speak from the back benches was Jeremy Hanley, who was well qualified to speak on films as his mother, Diana Sheridan, was a well known film star. The grinning Whips had whispered the news to Jeremy. Always quick on his feet, Jeremy, who had been speaking about the latest *Superman* film, said that the whole House would be delighted to hear that there was a potential new superman born today to the Minister's wife. It was well over the top. The House cheered and I was very moved but desperate to deliver my speech and travel back to Manchester through the night to be with Ruth and the new baby.

I rose at the Despatch Box and thanked Jeremy for his congratulations and the House for its reception of the news. I then said, 'Whilst I do appreciate that it is your prerogative, Mr Speaker, to name people in this House (which in fact meant that they were to be thrown out), with your indulgence, sir, I name my son Edward David Trippier.'

Edward's Christening by Canon Trevor Beeson in the Chapel of St Mary Undercroft at the Palace of Westminster.

More cheering and the Speaker, Bernard Wetherill, was laughing and slapping his thighs. (The following day he sent me a signed copy of Hansard recording what he insisted was a unique occasion in the history of Parliament.) I wound up the debate and dashed out of the Chamber.

Eventually I escaped about midnight and drove to Manchester. Ruth was fine and much relieved that the baby was safe. When I visited Edward in his incubator, he looked so helpless, and had so many wires attached to him, that I could hardly see his face. The nursing sister said, 'Don't worry, he will be fine.' I'd always thought that St Mary's Hospital in Manchester is the finest children's hospital in the land. Our experience in November 1984 confirmed this.

After the Brighton bombing, those of us who were members of the Government threw ourselves into our work. If nothing else, we had to show that the turbulent events of the week before had not dimmed our spirit in any way. MPs from the Labour and Liberal Parties behaved in an impeccable way and their concern and sympathy were clearly genuine. As for those of us who were Ministers in the DTI, we were acutely conscious that we were without a Secretary of State for months until Norman Tebbit had recovered sufficiently to return to the Department. We also realised that Anne had suffered even more than Norman and would be a paraplegic for the rest of her life.

During this period, I had been concentrating my efforts on reducing red tape and unnecessary burdens on small firms. I started the initiative because I was appalled at the answers I received to two specific questions I asked my civil servants to research. The first was, 'How many regulations have to be met and complied with by someone starting up a business from scratch?' The second question was, 'How many regulations have to be met and complied with by those businesses employing just one person?'

It took approximately two weeks for the civil servants to find the answers, but having checked their facts, they were shocked and I was horrified. There were fifty-four regulations which would have to be checked, and in most cases complied with, if a person was starting a business. If that business then wished to employ one other person, there were forty-five more regulations which had to be met. There were ninety-nine regulations in all. The facts were incredible and utterly ridiculous.

I drew up charts of these regulations in my office and wrote to the Prime Minister. I also spoke to Lord Young who, although he was a Cabinet Minister Without Portfolio, had a particular interest in small businesses. The upshot of all this was that I was asked by Margaret Thatcher to make a presentation on this matter to the full Cabinet.

The faces of the Cabinet Ministers round the table mirrored the shock which I had felt on first hearing the news. The Prime Minister was superb in rattling everyone's cage and making clear that these regulations should be reviewed by such Departments as the Home Office, the Department of Employment and the Department of the Environment. She then asked David Young to chair a Cabinet Committee on Deregulation, on which I would serve as the lead Minister. I left the Cabinet Meeting delighted with the result, but acutely conscious of the fact that I had made myself unpopular with those Ministers who would now be expected to remove certain regulations or at the very least justify retaining them.

This whole exercise was to produce not just one White Paper on Deregulation but two. It ultimately led to a reduction of a third of the regulations and a much more flexible and user-friendly approach to start-ups. Nonetheless it was clear that this successful exercise in slashing red tape must become a permanent feature on the landscape. There would always be Government Departments who would dream up new regulations, and they would need to be scrutinised more carefully to ensure they did not act as a deterrent to the enterprise we were trying to create. Quite apart from the red tape imposed nationally, there would always be new European Directives flying across the water from Brussels which could increase the burden. A Deregulation Committee was set up, chaired by Sir Nigel Mobbs, empowered to review all such measures.

Eventually Norman Tebbit returned to the Department and although he had lost a considerable amount of weight, it was clear that he had not lost his fire. Only a few months after his return, the Prime Minister had a Government re-shuffle and Norman was appointed Chairman of the Party. David Young was appointed Secretary of State for Employment and Ken Clarke was appointed his Deputy in the same Department with the title of Chancellor of the Duchy of Lancaster and a seat in the Cabinet. I was pleased for David and delighted that Ken was in the Cabinet.

To my amazement, Margaret Thatcher telephoned me to say that she wanted me to transfer to the Department of Employment and work for David and Ken, but retaining my role as Minister for Small Firms and assuming additional responsibilities for Tourism, Deregulation and Training. Apparently David had made it clear to the Prime Minister that if he was expected to make a significant impact on the level of unemployment, which by then was reaching the dreadful figure of three million, he needed to take the responsibility for Small Firms and Tourism – the strongest growth areas in the economy – out of the hands of the Department of Trade and Industry. He and Ken had also said that they would want me to have responsibility for both. The Prime Minister agreed on both counts. I was delighted with the proposal and thrilled to be working with Ken once again.

The Department of Employment welcomed us with open arms. Previously they had felt the strain of announcing monthly unemployment figures without having the responsibility of announcing what was going to be done to tackle the problem. This was now to change and although the challenge was considerable, the three of us knew where the answer lay.

For my part, I insisted on bringing the civil servant teams in the Small Firms Division and Tourism Division over to my new Department intact. I also insisted on keeping my Government driver, Margaret Narroway, with me. This attractive girl, with her good figure and reddish hair, was a star, a confidante and friend. Like many of the Government drivers, she seemed to know what was going to happen in a re-shuffle before it happened. This was because of the close network of drivers and their strong links with the drivers at Number 10. It was amusing to find that one of the *Yes Minister* episodes on television featured James Hacker's driver, who always knew 'what was going on' more than the Minister. How that programme got its inside information remained a mystery to me.

During my early days in the new Department, I was to get to know my fellow Junior Minister, Alan Clarke, quite well. Alan, of the famous *Diaries* fame, had the office next door to me and his brief was far less exciting than mine. He was clever, autocratic and also remarkably laid back. I can't remember him ever taking more than one Red Box home in the evening, whereas I would invariably have two. Worse still, I was unaware that he was such a womaniser in the Department, which speaks volumes about my naivety. Contrary to what most people would have predicted, Alan and I worked very well together, despite our very different backgrounds.

The additional responsibility I now carried as Minister for Tourism was a godsend. It had been a sector of the economy which had been underrated for too long. It certainly needed a higher profile and my initial task was to improve its image. The British had always had a hang-up about those hard-working individuals who are employed in hotels and restaurants. We were bedevilled by the 'upstairs-downstairs' image of their profession and got terribly mixed up between service and servility. David Young and I secured a significant increase in the Department's funding for tourism, and over a few months we had persuaded the national press into supporting our initiatives and writing positive messages about good practice and significant employment opportunities in the sector.

John Prescott was Ken Clarke's Opposition spokesman in the Commons and was constantly sniping at our attempts to encourage employment growth in tourism. He was insinuating that the jobs we were promoting weren't real jobs but 'candy floss' ones. Knowing how easy it was to wind up John Prescott, and how he burned off a very short fuse, I decided to ambush him during our Ministerial Question Time. I had primed Nicholas Soames to goad John with some well-timed interventions from the back benches, but always from the sedentary position. John was hurling abuse at me across the despatch boxes and denouncing the jobs in tourism as nothing more than 'ice cream salesman' jobs. When I sprang to my feet and accused John of insulting the hundreds of thousands of people who worked in the tourism economy, Nick struck like an exocet. He shouted out, 'Can you get me a gin and tonic, steward?' – a reference to the time when John Prescott had been a steward on board a passenger liner.

On hearing the remark, he turned puce. 'Shut up you,' he shouted to Nicholas.

Unabashed, Nick pressed on. 'Can you add just a sliver of lemon and a few chunks of ice?'

John was red-faced and beside himself with anger. 'You shut up now – you public school prig,' he roared.

Everyone was falling about laughing, including the Socialists. The House was in chaos and the Speaker was shouting, 'Order, Order' to try to restore calm.

John Prescott decided after that to lay off attacking jobs in tourism and I decided to buy Nicholas Soames a large gin-and-tonic in the Smoking Room that evening.

There was to be another gin-and-tonic story when I paid an official visit to Manchester and attended a lunch organised by the Chairman of Granada Television, David Plowright. I should have known that David would have something specific to ask me to do. He is a man of immense energy and vision. Before we went into the lunch, he took me on to the roof of the Granada building and, as we looked over the vista of that part of the city, he revealed his plans for turning a lot of disused warehouses into a Granada Studios tour. His ambition was to encourage the general public to visit the site and discover what went on behind the scenes in producing films and television serials such as *Coronation Street*. He certainly captured my imagination and I was convinced he would make it work. 'There's only one problem,' he told me. 'Having completed the business plan, there is a shortfall and I need a Government Grant of about half a million pounds from you to make it work.'

As I looked a little pale, he said, 'Have a gin and tonic.' When I had seen the formal proposals and the business plan, I agreed to the grant.

When the work on the site was eventually finished, many months later, David Plowright was kind enough to invite me to open the tour officially, despite the fact I had by then moved to a different Department. He also invited my old friend John Lee from the Guy Fawkes Group, who was my successor as Minister for Tourism, and we both made speeches. I couldn't fail to make the point that the drink that David had given me was the most expensive gin and tonic I had ever had.

My time as Minister for Tourism was a very enjoyable one, primarily because I met so many happy people who were engaged in

Outside the Rover's Return with David Plowright.

it. Due to their success, we were seeing a net increase of fifty thousand jobs a year and to this day it remains the second largest employer in the economy.

The success of small firms in the economy was also coming through. When I first became the Small Firms Minister, the failure rate in that sector had been unacceptable, although the statistics were still more favourable than they were in America. In the USA approximately half of small firms went into liquidation over a period of three years. Over that same period, in the United Kingdom, one out of every three would go to the wall. However, if those entrepreneurs took advantage of the advice and hand-holding service provided by the Local Enterprise Agencies and the Small Firms Service, the rate of failure dropped to one in five over a period of three years. The message was very simple. Everyone needed some assistance in securing a viable company; they only had to realise it.

As I was responsible for the Enterprise Allowance Scheme, I insisted that no-one could draw the forty pounds a week available for a year to start-ups until they had been on a management course. This in turn reduced the fatality rate. The failure rate of companies who had taken advantage of the Small Firms Loan Guarantee Scheme was also beginning to drop and slowly but surely the percentage of people employed in the small firms sector grew and grew. It was a cultural revolution. Ken Clarke became as enthusiastic about small firms as David Young and I were, and together we were quite a team. David came to the Department every morning with ten new ideas he'd thought of in the bath. He would then bounce them off the Ministerial team and we would find perhaps only one which would work very well. Nonetheless he had immense vision and he was a first-class Secretary of State. He also worked very well with Ken and admired his intellect and public performances in the House and the country. Once Ken had bought into an idea, he would run with the ball and no-one could stop him.

The training programmes were also going well. Although we had experienced problems initially with the bureaucracy of the Youth Training Scheme, we had cut out a lot of the red tape and more and more youngsters were finding full-time employment at the end of their training. David introduced a programme called 'Action for Jobs', which was a huge undertaking with regular advertising on television spelling out the various programmes we were responsible for and encouraging people to take advantage of them. We were also involved in a road show where the various Ministers in the Department would deliver a very sophisticated presentation with videos, slides and just about every electrical form of support to huge audiences, who were prepared to go to a breakfast meeting. They were a great success and very enjoyable.

As the unemployment figures were constantly coming down and the economy was on the up and up, it seemed inevitable that Margaret Thatcher would call a General Election late in 1987. When she fired the starting gun in October, once again the campaign was to be a huge success for the Tories. Apart from her unrivalled leadership skills, Margaret Thatcher had always been fortunate in the choice of her principle enemies. First it was Michael Foot, then General Galtieri, then Arthur Scargill and soon it would be Neil Kinnock.

The campaign in Rossendale and Darwen went well and it was certain that the higher profile I had enjoyed in the country was of advantage. I was returned with a majority of 4,982.

Having been told by David Young and Ken Clarke that it was time for the Prime Minister to recognise what I had done in the Government and give me a leg up to Minister of State, I was secretly confident that it would happen. Even when the telephone call came through to our home from Number Ten and the Prime Minister spoke to me, I was certain that she was going to promote me.

Alas, she didn't.

CHAPTER XVII

Inner Cities

'Watch out for the Minister.'

ALTHOUGH I WAS DISAPPOINTED not to have been promoted, I slowly realised that Margaret Thatcher had moved very few people in the re-shuffle after the 1987 General Election. However, I did have a new job in the Department of the Environment. I was to become Minister for Inner Cities, which was going to be a high profile and front-line responsibility.

On the night of the Election, when it was clear that the Tories had won, the Prime Minister had announced from Conservative Party Headquarters at Smith Square that the Government would concentrate more of its efforts on the inner cities. Although I was delighted to have this role in a Department that was the largest spender in Inner Urban Areas, I was also realistic enough to know that my close association with Ken Clarke had typecast me in the eyes of Margaret Thatcher as 'not one of us'. No matter. My past experience had taught me to get my head down and work my back off.

My first meeting in the D.O.E. was under the chairmanship of Nick Ridley, who was the Secretary of State. The Ministers of State were William Waldegrave, who was responsible for Local Government, Michael Howard, who was one of the few junior Ministers to have been promoted to Minister of State and covered the Water Industry, and the Earl of Caithness, who had responsibility for Housing and the Environment. The Junior Ministers were Marion Roe, Christopher Chope, Colin Moynihan and myself.

Although the other Parliamentary Under-Secretaries of State were to assist the Ministers of State with their portfolios, I had my own totally separate brief – Inner Cities, Urban Affairs and the Construction Industry. I would assist Malcolm Caithness with Housing, but would be expected to concentrate on the new policy for the inner cities.

I was bound to be a little wary of Nick Ridley, as his credentials were very far to the right of the Party. I was also conscious that his public appearances and television interviews left a great deal to be desired. I was to find that – contrary to my initial reservations about working for him – he was a superb Secretary of State with a fine mind and sensitive soul. His chain smoking and scruffy appearance belied his great charm and fine talent as a painter.

He became my closest ally and friend in the Department. Although there were many differences between Ken Clarke and Nick Ridley on the political front, Nick shared a talent with Ken for writing beautifully scribed personal messages of thanks or praise. The text would be kind and witty, so that one instinctively stored them away in one's personal archives as they meant so much.

The only serious mistake that I ever made with Nick Ridley concerned his military experience in the armed forces. My father told me that Nick had been a captain in his old regiment, the Northumberland Hussars, for a period. Because his elder brother, the Viscount Ridley, was the Honorary Colonel of the regiment, I presumed that Nick was as keen on the forces as I was. He wasn't. In fact the only reason he was in the Northumberland Hussars was that after going up to Oxford and serving in an infantry battalion during National Service, like everyone else, he had to complete a period of service in the Territorial Army. Nick, over a few whiskies in the House of Commons smoking room, made clear to me that he found the whole business of military training to be perfectly ghastly.

Eventually he secured the best job in the officers' mess, and one that fitted his talents to a 'T'. His Colonel appointed him as mess secretary charged to organise the social side of the mess and arrange mess dinners, ladies nights etc. Being a man of impeccable culinary rectitude and proficient in the art of wine tasting, he was not content to acquire all the principal ingredients for the recipe of success from Newcastle, but was moved to travel to London and visit Fortnum and Masons to buy the best vintage port and the finest cheese that money could buy.

On one occasion, having made his purchases at Fortnums, he travelled back to Newcastle on the sleeper. In those days, there was a luggage rack consisting of a string hammock above the bunks. Nick lovingly placed the sizeable cuts of brie in this string netting and happily climbed into bed. The cabin was very hot and during the night the cheese melted and dripped through the netting and on to him. In the morning, as the train was parked in a siding near to Newcastle Station, Nick awoke to find himself encased in cheese, rather like Tutankhamen. He cracked the now dried cheese by beating his chest and other parts of his body to escape from the cast which had mummified him. This was too much. It was the end. He walked down the platform carrying the cases of port – sat in the cafeteria in the station and penned a letter to his Commanding Officer resigning his commission. It was accepted.

Within the first few weeks in my new role, there was to be a slight contretemps which could have been nasty but fortunately was happily resolved. The Prime Minister was determined that there should be an overarching committee which could draw together the Departments of State which had some responsibility for Inner Cities. This would include ourselves, the Home Office, the Department of Trade and Industry, the DHSS and the Department of Employment. The press was speculating as to who the supremo would be who would chair this initiative. Clearly it would have to be a Cabinet Minister.

In the recent re-shuffle Ken Clarke had been moved with David Young to the Department of Trade and Industry. Ken had still not got his own Department, although he obviously remained in the Cabinet. As Ken had already displayed great enthusiasm for Inner Cities when he was in the Department of Employment, he was the obvious choice. Nick Ridley did not agree and apart from his cynicism about Ken's political leanings, thought that the lead Department should be the D.O.E. In the event Margaret Thatcher appointed Ken Clarke to the post and Nick had to accept it. This was the third time that fate had played a part in bringing Ken Clarke and myself together and it was now clear that we would achieve success on a number of fronts.

By this time there was already a number of Urban Development Corporations which had been set up to stimulate private sector investment in areas of dereliction or decay. Michael Heseltine had set up the first two in London Docklands and in Merseyside. Nick had added to the list, which brought on stream new U.D.C.s in Trafford

Park in Manchester, in the Black Country, in Tyne and Wear and on Teesside. The Welsh Office had also started one in Cardiff Bay. As enormous powers were given to the boards of these Development Corporations, one didn't have to be a genius to work out that some of them would be unpopular with the local authorities in those areas who believed that they and they alone could encourage the necessary private sector funding essential to transforming the appearance and economic activity of the areas concerned. The fact that they had not been able to do it in the past seemed to escape them.

My immediate task was to work up proposals for four more U.D.C.s, and we decided that they should centre on Leeds, Bristol, the Don Valley in Sheffield and Central Manchester. Once the firm proposals had been made, it would require legislation to give them the necessary powers and the Chairman and Board Members would be appointed by Ministers. They would all have planning powers, including Compulsory Purchase Order powers, and the huge sums of money injected into the areas would initially assist with land clearance and land assembly.

The money for setting up another four U.D.C.s was seen as an investment, not a cost. When development was under way, I was looking for a leverage of four to one, which meant that for every pound of taxpayer's money invested in the U.D.C.s, we would expect at least four times that figure to be invested by the private sector. More important than anything would be the economic regeneration leading to significant increases in employment.

Once the official announcements were made on the location of these new U.D.C.s, it was easy to gauge the reaction. The City Councils of Leeds and Sheffield were reasonable in commenting on the Government's proposals. Bristol City Council was vehemently against the Government interfering in their territory, and despite my visiting that city on a number of occasions to calm fears, they continued to oppose the plans and eventually took the Department of the Environment to the House of Lords sitting as a court. Apart from one minor change to the boundaries of the U.D.C. area at Temple Meads, they lost the case and we were able to proceed.

My experience in dealing with Manchester City Council was altogether different. The information concerning our proposals had leaked in the press so that it was a foregone conclusion that I would shortly announce that the Government would create the Central Manchester Development Corporation and detail the boundaries of it. Prior to this announcement, I decided that I would meet with Graham Stringer, the Leader of the City Council, to discuss the matter. I had met him on previous occasions and been impressed by his grasp of issues, and although our politics were poles apart, I respected his opinions on several important matters. When we met together, he made clear to me that he was very unhappy with the Government stepping in and wanted to try to influence me on setting the boundaries of the U.D.C. Area. I thought that his alternative proposals were soundly based and I readily agreed to them. I also said that I would be happier if we could work as closely as possible with the City Council and was prepared to allow his Planning Department to do most of the work on planning issues. I also said I was prepared to appoint some Labour Councillors to the Board and thought that he would be a very valuable member of it. He said he would think about it but warned me that when I made the announcement, he would attack the Government, and indeed me, in the press. I understood that and respected his position. Eventually he did go on the Board, primarily to safeguard the Council's position, but I learned a lot about Graham Stringer during that time and recognised that although he had an amazingly quiet manner, he had enormous leadership powers. Certainly his commitment to Manchester was absolute and he was then, and remains to this day, a very consummate politician whom one could easily admire.

During this period, I went to Liverpool on an official visit. I was the first Minister to do so for several years. Derek Hatton had declared Liverpool to be a no-go area for Conservative Ministers, but as he had now been removed from centre stage, I wanted to convey the clear message that the Government would be pleased to work in partnership with the City Council if they could face such a prospect. Although I was uncertain as to what would happen, my visit was to be a success and was carried in the national newspapers and the national media. Knowing the area very well, having spent so much time in Merseyside with the Royal Marines Reserve, I was keen to get involved with a number of joint projects to stimulate the economy there, as it had taken such a hammering during the Hatton era.

At around this time, I was keen to streamline a number of grant schemes which were confusing to those who might benefit from them. I decided to introduce a new grant régime with a single scheme known as City Grant, which would be available in each of the fifty-seven inner urban areas in the country. This replaced four different grant schemes and is still in existence to this day.

Ken and I had learnt a great deal from our experience in the Department of Employment and from the Action for Jobs roadshow. We decided to do exactly the same high profile presentation on Inner Cities. It was called 'Action for Cities' and, like its predecessor, was to be a huge success. Towards the end of this campaign, in April of 1988, Ruth gave birth to our third son, George. As usual Ruth delivered prematurely, but thankfully nowhere near as prematurely as Edward after the bombing in Brighton. George was a robust and energetic child from the very beginning. Ken Clarke was to be one of the godfathers, along with Keith Walker, whom I had first met in the Young Conservatives. Jenny Taylor was the godmother and everyone seemed genuinely delighted to be involved in what became our third christening in the Crypt of the Palace of Westminster. Just before the christening, Ken Clarke was appointed Secretary of State for Education. At long last he had his own Department and I was delighted for him.

Although it was obvious that Action for Cities was working very well and the attention we gave to the Inner City areas was beginning to bear fruit, there was another Departmental initiative which was to be a complete failure. This time it was an initiative in housing.

In the Conservative Manifesto issued during the 1987 General Election, it was promised that if elected, we would introduce Housing Action Trusts. These would attract substantial Government funding and the purpose of the Trusts was to target some of the most difficult Council Estates in the country, temporarily decant the residents, dramatically improve the properties and then give them the opportunity to remain as tenants of the Local Authority or come under a private landlord or a Housing Association.

The policy was doomed from the start because whichever estate we

Sandy Bishop.

named as a target area, the residents were understandably aggrieved because in the naming of them, we had blighted not only the estate but also the people living there.

One of the proposed areas was the Gipton Council House Estate in Leeds. I had travelled to Leeds by train with my Private Secretary, Sandy Bishop, a lively, intelligent girl, and an ideal assistant for the sort of project we were engaged in. The visit turned out to be a fiasco. There were demonstrations on the estate and at times it looked as if the demonstrators were going to turn nasty. Although it may have been clear that the Council tenants didn't trust their own Council to deal with their problems, they trusted the Government even less, and they said so.

At one time, as I stepped off the mini-coach carting myself and the team of civil servants from the Regional Office around the area, the crowd of anti-HAT protesters surged forward and I remember thinking if I go down on the ground, I might never get up. Sandy was calling out to the other civil servants to 'watch out for the Minister'. Fortunately I managed to stay upright and survived.

Shortly after this we travelled to the school where I was to address the residents in a huge hall. It was packed and heaving. The crowd were baying for my blood. In the front row on one side of the hall sat the local vicar, the Roman Catholic priest and a few Non-Conformist ministers – more dog collars than you could shake a stick at. On the other side, the front row was occupied by some evil looking representatives of the Socialist Workers Party, who all seemed to wear similar clothes. The S.W.P. uniform seemed to be black jeans, black sweaters and black boots. The men wore national health round spectacles and had hair so short that it must have been cut an eighth off the wood.

When I was allowed to get a word in, I made it clear that I had come to hear what they had to say and I assured them that I was anxious to take everything down in order to gauge the situation.

After the meeting, an enormous lady stormed up to me to perform her own personal demonstration before my very eyes. By this time I'd had enough. It had been a very tough day. The lady opened her handbag, pulled out an enormous pair of knickers, and stretched them out in front of my face. They bore the legend, 'Knickers to you'. Unknown to me, the regional and national press picked up my reply. I simply said, 'Yes, madam, as I've said throughout, I've come here to take everything down.' This line, reproduced in some of the national newspapers the following day, was to be a source of great amusement in the Department, not least to Nick Ridley.

If I thought that my experience in Leeds was difficult, much worse was to come when I visited Tower Hamlets and spoke to a packed meeting of approximately 950 people jammed into a public hall. The BBC was even going to film this one for their *Panorama* programme. It must have been good television. It took twelve policemen to protect me going into the hall and twenty to protect me leaving it.

The decibel level was as high as it ever gets as I tried to speak above the chanting and screaming crowd. When I was about to leave the stage at the end, Vivian White from the *Panorama* programme stuck a microphone under my nose and asked, 'What do you hope to get out of a meeting like this, Minister?'

I shrugged my shoulders and said, 'What about the Victoria Cross?'

This was also reported in the national newspapers, but as with the first report of my visit to Leeds, the journalists wrote the story in a humorous vein. Fortunately Nick Ridley appreciated my warped humour and thanked me for being prepared to be in the front line. It wouldn't have been appropriate for him to go to these meetings, and although Malcolm Caithness was very supportive of me, I suspect the reception for the 20th Earl of Caithness on a council estate could have made my experiences look like a Teddy Bear's Picnic.

When the *Panorama* programme was shown the following Monday, it led to most of our friends telephoning me or Ruth in concern for my life. When Ruth went into the chemists in Haslingden the following Saturday, the lady pharmacist, who knew us well, said, 'I was so concerned to see *Panorama* with all those people baying for David's blood, I found myself talking to the television set and saying, 'Oh David, David – come home to Rossendale, lad, we don't treat you like that up here.'

Although the HAT policy was eventually to be a success, it only became so because the policy was changed to precisely what it should have been from the very beginning. That is to say that Local Authorities were asked to bid for a Housing Action Trust if they thought it could help them. This was significantly better than Central Government trying to impose a HAT on an area whether the people wanted it or not.

From 1987 to 1989, my experience as the Minister for Construction was very satisfying. I was lucky to be doing the job at a time when the industry was very busy. Needless to say, my other responsibilities in the redevelopment of inner cities was to fuel a great deal of activity for the Construction Industry. My relationship with the various bodies who represented the industry was excellent and I learnt a great deal and enjoyed the portfolio immensely. I led several Trade Missions abroad, always taking a significant number of Construction Company representatives with me.

In the re-shuffle which the Prime Minister carried out in the summer of 1989, the telephone call came from Number Ten and Sandy Bishop ran along the corridor to pull me out of a meeting I was having with Malcolm Caithness. This time there was to be no disappointment. I was to be promoted to Minister of State.

CHAPTER XVIII

The Green Minister

'I've never seen myself as an environmentally friendly person.'

HAVING RECOVERED FROM THE exultation of being promoted, I invited all my former private secretaries to dinner to celebrate. They were a wonderful bunch of people, whose assistance and wise counsel I had appreciated over six years: Tom Cassidy, who had looked after me in the DTI, Steve Palmer and Kathryn Jendon in the Department of Employment and Teresa Vokes, and now Sandy Bishop in the DOE. For obvious reasons, Sandy was the most ecstatic about the promotion, as she was in office when it happened and I genuinely believed that she did as much as anyone to ensure that I got a leg up the ladder.

The following morning I read the newspapers to see the extent of the re-shuffle. Again there were not that many changes, but Nick Ridley had been moved to the Department of Trade and Industry and Chris Patten had become the new Secretary of State for the Environment. Although I was very sorry to see Nick move, having been told during the telephone call from the Prime Minister that she wanted me to stay in the DOE, I was delighted to be working with Chris Patten, for whom I had always had a genuine admiration.

Our first meeting on the day after the re-shuffle was to be a complete surprise to me. I had assumed that he would want me to take the lead in Housing – possibly Planning – and I hoped he would allow me to keep Inner Cities, where we were making significant headway across a broad front. My assumptions turned out to be completely wrong. Having exchanged congratulations on our respective promotions, we sat down alone in his office. Chris Patten said that he believed that the top priority for the Department was for us to increase our credibility on environmental issues. He admitted that he was unnerved by the significant support which the Green

Chris Patten visiting Rossendale Groundwork Trust.
Left to right: the author, Chris Patten, Peter Wilmers and John Davidson, National Chief Executive for the Groundwork Trust.

Party had secured in the recent European Elections and the fact that they had secured fifteen percent of the total vote sent a clear signal to the Government that we needed to do much more. He then said that he wanted me to become the Green Minister and recapture this lost support.

Astonished, I said, 'Whilst I'm very flattered, Chris, I've never seen myself as an environmentally friendly person. I don't pretend to know a great deal about the subject. I'm essentially a street fighter.'

'That's exactly right and what we need is a street fighter to expose all the myths that are flying about and promote the positive.' Then he was especially kind and said, 'David, have a think about it and come back to me during the day.'

'I don't need to think about it. If you want me to do the job, I will do it.'

When I returned to my own office and told Sandy Bishop that I was taking on the 'green portfolio', she was delighted. 'It's the number one issue in the country at the moment, Minister, you must be very pleased.'

I gave her a silly grin and telephoned Ruth about my new appointment.

She thought it was fantastic: 'It's the hot spot in politics at the moment.'

'I thought it was supposed to be Inner Cities.'

'It was, but the spotlight is now on the Environment. You lucky devil. First the spotlight was on Small Firms – then Inner Cities – now the Environment. You seem to have a nose for trouble. Once again you are at the sharp end. I think you'll love it.'

Within a matter of weeks I was indeed loving it. With briefing after briefing in my office, I was slowly climbing up the vertical learning curve and getting to grips with the issues. There were many of them, including: global warming, the hole in the ozone layer, pollution of the air and water, litter on the streets, protecting endangered species, policy on the countryside. Everything from the street corner to the stratosphere but no clear direction. No clear goals were set to achieve what was needed – a drive towards sustainability.

I was clearly going to need considerable help with this new role and now I was entitled to a Parliamentary Private Secretary of my own who sat in the Commons. In much the same way that Ken Clarke appointed me to be his P.P.S. from a short list of names submitted by the Government Whip's Office, I too was sent a list. I chose Timothy Kirkhope, who was the Member of Parliament for Leeds North East, and who seemed delighted to be offered the job. He became a good friend and was invaluable to me as a P.P.S. until he was promoted to become a Government Whip in 1990. In 1995, after I had left Parliament, he became a Junior Minister in the Home Office. When he left me to go into the Whip's Office, I appointed another M.P. to take on the role, who was Dr Ian Twinn, the Member for Edmonton. He too was highly competent.

When Tim Kirkhope joined me in 1989, there was much to do and not much time in which to do it. The very best news was that Chris Patten was totally committed to the Environment. For a long time he had been concerned that most of the electorate did not expect a Tory Government to care about sustainability, and his experience in his last job as Minister for Overseas Development had confirmed his worst fears.

We embarked on a rapid expansion of the various divisions which made up the Environmental Directorate in the Department. Civil servants who were working in these divisions and thought they were committed to a life of penury in the twilight zone suddenly took on a new lease of life. First of all, we were committed to producing a White Paper which would spell out our aims and ambitions up to the year 2000 and beyond. Secondly we would introduce an Environmental Protection Bill which would address the problems in the waste disposal industry, pollution of the air, litter laws and genetically modified organisms. Thirdly our stance on Europe must change. Previously other Environment Ministers sitting in the Council of Ministers had never taken the United Kingdom seriously when it came to major decisions such as reducing carbon dioxide emissions or volatile organic compounds. Now we would work with the Commission to help write the agenda for the Council of Ministers. I wanted us to be in the vanguard – not guarding the last van.

I introduced a fundamental shift in our relationships with the Environmental Lobby Groups. Collectively these were known as N.G.O.s, or Non-Governmental Organisations and ranged from Friends of the Earth on the more extreme level to the C.P.R.E. (the Council for the Protection of Rural England), who smiled at me a little more but were still just as tenacious and effective. There were so many of them and it was clear to me that the Government had spent too much time in hand-to-hand combat with them all. This had to change so I started an 'Open Door Policy' and invited them into the Department either for collective meetings or for bi-lateral exchanges. I was perfectly sincere in explaining that we would need their help in framing the forthcoming legislation and in writing the White Paper. We certainly didn't know all the answers, but with their assistance we stood a better chance of getting things right. I knew I couldn't compromise their rights to criticise and occasionally 'kick up hell', nor would I have dared to try, but whenever I could, I would try to work alongside them to achieve the best results for delivering sustainability.

It was during this time that I got to know Jonathan Porritt of Friends of the Earth very well. It was always impossible to persuade him to compromise his position or his strongly-felt views on so many matters, but we developed a mutual respect and common understanding of the problems that we faced. I learnt a great deal from him and to this day he is kind enough to say that 'Trippier's Open Door' policy marked a significant turn-round in the Government's relationships with the N.G.O.s

At the same time it was essential to have the Open Door Policy available to Industry, and there were as many meetings with the various Trade Associations as there were with the N.G.O.s. The carpet on the floor of the Minister's corridor was worn out by the Chemical Industries Association, the CBI, the Association of Chambers of Commerce et al. All of this was to achieve the best balance between 'licence' and 'liberty' whilst still achieving improved sustainability.

This intense learning process led to me being able to distinguish between what was sound environmental thinking and what was 'guff'. I was sending out clear signals that I was prepared to listen to constructive thinking and well argued cases, but when it came to the impractical virtues expounded by some of the long-haired sandal brigade who would like all of us to travel everywhere by bicycle and sit at home knitting woolly socks, I reverted to my 'street fighter' mode and denounced them.

The others who got my goat were the 'BANANAS' (Build Absolutely Nothing Anywhere Near Anyone). As with all things, some balance needed to be brought into the equation, but with extremists there would be no balance at all. Nonetheless, the vast majority of lobbyists and environmental protagonists were prepared to be constructive and I attributed the success of the White Paper and the eventual Environmental Protection Act in 1990 to partnership. I failed miserably to bring Greenpeace into that partnership and they remained the only N.G.O. who not only avoided any contact with the Government, but were constantly guilty of misrepresentation and exaggeration.

I received more letters than any other Minister in the Government, including the Prime Minister. The letters could cover every environmental subject under the sun, and many of them would be sent by children of a very young age. Sometimes a letter would be written by one child on behalf of all the children in his or her class at school, while sometimes every child in the class would write. I had to reply to every one I received and it was worth wearing out my right wrist signing them. What was encouraging was that children knew a darn sight more about the environment than my generation knew when we were their age. The new generation also had very high expectations and in the main looked to the Government to deliver. Chris Patten and I believed that we had to hand down to them a better quality of life than the one we had inherited. If I wasn't being told what to do through my mail, I was hearing it from meetings in my office. If I wasn't getting it there, I could never escape the advice which my own children chose to give me in 'quiet moments' at the weekend.

It was clear that I was enjoying this role immensely. I particularly enjoyed the Council of Ministers in Europe, where I was determined to initiate measures which would benefit the UK. For long enough we had been reacting to measures introduced by the Germans or the French. Now we were on the front foot and determined to scotch the myth that Britain was 'the dirty man of Europe'. Most of the time I would attend the meetings and on other occasions Chris Patten would go, but no-one could get a razor blade between us.

My job entailed a great deal of travel. The Ministerial meetings of the United Nations Environmental Programme were invariably held at their headquarters in Nairobi, Kenya. These would invariably end with a Ministerial Agreement and I particularly enjoyed acting as honest broker between the Americans, who were reluctant to alienate the pro-Oil and Transport lobbyists on Capitol Hill, and our fellow European colleagues, who wanted the Americans to do more and move more quickly. On one occasion I had the opportunity to attend a major International Conference at the White House. I genuinely believe that in a lone discussion with George Bush, who was then the President, I persuaded him to be more Environmentally Friendly in the speech he delivered at the end of the Conference.

At this time Chris Patten was becoming increasingly embroiled in

George Bush.

the ongoing rows about the Community Charge, for which he had responsibility. The pressure on him was immense and whilst the attention we were paying to the Environment was going well and we were slowly turning the tide of public opinion in our favour, the opposition to the Poll Tax was going in exactly the opposite direction.

In 1989, we were determined that there would be a new regulatory body set up called the Environment Agency, which would be an amalgamation of the National Rivers Authority and Her Majesty's Inspectorate of Pollution. This would be a very popular move and I was anxious to ensure that H.M.I.P. would merge with the N.R.A. without widespread acrimony. To achieve this, I had to stem the outward flow of inspectors, who were being offered attractive salaries by the private sector, and I persuaded the Treasury to give three increases in pay to them over an eighteen-month period. It was a recognition of their status and the additional responsibilities they had been given in policing the Environmental Protection Act, but the cynic in me also realised that without matching the salaries of the private sector, much of the talent and knowledge would be lost to the gamekeepers and be in the hands of potential poachers.

I recognised the importance of tackling environmental problems at a local level. I had been one of the founders of the Groundwork Trust in Rossendale and had seen the success of their environmental work in the local community. I had also seen many improvements in Darwen in the other part of my constituency, which was covered by the Blackburn Groundwork Trust. So, rather like the Local Enterprise Agency movement, I was determined to spread the Groundwork Trust movement throughout the country.

The Groundwork Trust was already a success in those areas where it had established itself in the community. It was a practical organisation which would tackle eyesores, clean up rivers, plant trees, repair footpaths and bridleways, as well as running environmental education in some schools. It was becoming the outward and visible sign of environmental partnership in action. The Department of the Environment made money available to the National Groundwork Foundation via the Countryside Commission. They would then dispense whatever money they thought appropriate to stimulate a new Groundwork Trust in an area or to support an existing one. As with many other Government initiatives, the private sector was prepared to sponsor the trusts and they would also receive assistance from the Local Authority in the Groundwork Area.

Much of Rossendale and Darwen had been transformed by their work and even prior to me becoming the 'Green Minister', Ruth and I and our boys had been involved in working on local initiatives to improve the landscape. The local Director was a 'workaholic' named Peter Wilmers, and although I was able to replicate the Rossendale and Darwen experience throughout much of the country, I knew that I owed Peter Wilmers an enormous debt of gratitude for showing me how local conservation could be not only effective but enjoyable.

The National Chairman of the movement was Christopher Chataway, the well known Olympic runner and former Tory Minister, and the Director General was Jim Davidson, whose enthusiasm I found to be infectious. When Chris Chataway paid a visit to the Groundwork Trust in Rossendale and stayed with Ruth and me in Helmshore, I was mad enough to agree to do a sponsored run with him which nearly killed me. There were shades of the green beret course at Lympstone

The other Environmental Group with which I had a very close association was the Tidy Britain Group. They had a significant impact on my thinking and more specifically on the way I tightened up the litter laws in the relevant part of the Environmental Protection Act. Although I recognised the importance of driving the environmental agenda in Europe, and sometimes on a wider international stage, the basic truth was that the vast majority of people relate more closely to the built environment or the landscape with which they are surrounded, either where they live or where they work. Many of them were unhappy at what they actually saw, and although litter may be viewed as being small beer when weighed against global warming or the hole in the ozone layer, it was clear that a clean and tidy environment was seen as a hallmark of a decent, civilised society. In many ways our society failed this simple test. If it was unacceptable to many of us who lived in Britain, I dreaded to think of the impression we gave to foreign visitors coming to this country for the first time.

For many years the Tidy Britain Group, which was so ably led by its Director General, Professor Graham Ashworth, had not only led the crusade for a cleaner Britain, but had argued for tighter legislation to act as a deterrent to those who couldn't care less about the state of our streets or countryside. I was now about to give them the chance they richly deserved, and Graham and his team from the Tidy Britain Group were superb in rising to the challenge.

There were essentially two problems. The first problem was the people who indiscriminately dropped the litter in the first place. The second problem was the failure on the part of local authorities to pick it up. I introduced a fixed penalty for dropping litter of £25 and gave powers to local authorities to take shops or companies to court if they did not keep their shop frontages clear of litter or keep the land surrounding their companies' premises litter free. I also made governors of schools legally responsible for keeping clean their school grounds. I finally gave powers to the individual to take the local authority to court if they had been dilatory in cleaning up any area. Although the fine of £2,000 was bad enough, I thought that the adverse publicity which the local Council would attract in the local or regional press would turn out to be the more effective deterrent. Even so, there were howls of anguish from certain quarters, where it was thought my measures were too severe. Contrary to their views, I did not want to clog up the courts with these cases; I simply wanted people to stop behaving in such a filthy and irresponsible way.

In the summer of 1989 a wonderful and amusing event took place in our private life which was a welcome relief from my hectic time as a Minister. Jenny Taylor was married. Long after Eric Taylor was killed in the IRA bomb attack on the Grand Hotel in Brighton, Jenny had been very fortunate in meeting Hugh Broadbent, who was a successful businessman in Saddleworth and who, by coincidence, had been to Manchester Grammar School with Eric. He is tall and white-haired with a markedly pleasant expression. We had seen much of Jenny since the bomb and were delighted to meet Hugh, who is a true gentleman with a dry wit. He too has become a very good friend. When they told us they were to be married, we could not have been more pleased but the best was yet to come. At a party at our home, Dowry Head, Jenny took me to one side: 'David – you

Ruth, Jenny Taylor and Mary Tomlinson.

Dowry Head – the author's home.

know that the wedding is to take place at Christ Church in Saddleworth?'

'I do. I couldn't be more pleased.'

'Well, my father is dead, my stepfather is dead and I have no brother. Would you be kind enough to give me away?' I was so emotional I could hardly speak. This was true friendship on a grand scale.

'What an honour, Jenny! You can imagine that it would mean a great deal to me to give you away and as I have no daughters, only sons, it will be a unique occasion which I never dreamt would come my way.' I was tickled pink.

That was that, and on the 3rd June 1989 Jenny and Hugh were married on a perfect day. The aftermath, two days later, was to be a source of great amusement to the four of us.

The wedding had received some national press coverage because Jenny had been the widow of a bomb victim, and when Jenny and I arrived at the church, I was amazed by the number of photographers who were there. Photographs were taken of Jenny and me prior to entering the church and obviously photographs were taken of Hugh and Jenny coming out. Copies of these photographs were transmitted to the London office of a well known and respectable tabloid newspaper with a massive circulation.

However, a huge mistake was made by the picture editor, who, on looking at the two photographs, had assumed that Hugh had given Jenny away and I had married her! The picture editor recognised who I was and that was going to be the story in the newspaper's gossip column.

In the middle of that morning I was back in London in the Department of the Environment, chairing an important meeting in my office. I had said to Sandy Bishop, my Private Secretary, that I should not be disturbed. When Sandy came into the meeting saying that my wife was on the telephone and it was very urgent, I realised it must be and took the call. Never short of witticisms in a crisis, Ruth started the conversation by saying, 'If you are going to leave me and the children, David, I think it reasonable that at least we should discuss it first.' When I said I hadn't a clue what she was talking about, she referred me to the offending newspaper article, which Sandy Bishop produced for me. The headline ran, 'Bomb Victim's Widow Marries Minister'. The story then went on to explain who Jenny was and then who I was and so on and so on. I collapsed in my chair and slowly it dawned on me that a mistake had been made by the picture editor. Ruth thought that the matter would have to be put right. What on earth would all my constituents think? She also suggested that although it wasn't her line of legal work, I should contact John Kay, our family solicitor, to see what redress might be forthcoming.

The first telephone call was to Jenny and Hugh to see whether they were upset by the article. They weren't and in fact they couldn't stop laughing. I then telephoned John Kay, who couldn't stop laughing either, but pointed out that as the article was not malicious but written as a good news story, I would certainly get a fulsome apology in the paper, but not damages. John said I should leave the matter with him and he would sort it out. Within an hour, I had the editor of the gossip column on the line positively writhing with embarrassment over the matter. 'I cannot tell you how embarrassed I am,' he told me. 'We will certainly print a full apology in the paper tomorrow, but in case the idea has crossed your mind – we will not pay.' John had obviously broached the subject.

The day after, I read the very generous apology in the paper and thought no more of the affair. Returning home on the Friday, I couldn't get into our kitchen for the number of bouquets for Ruth and me which covered the floor. On all the cards attached to the various bouquets was the same message from the picture editor and the gossip column editor: 'We are so glad you are still together.'

A few months later Chris Patten came bouncing into my office. 'You know that I was supposed to be joining the Prince and Princess of Wales for a major international environment conference on board the Royal Yacht when it visits Brazil?'

'Yes, I remember you being invited by Prince Charles. I thought your wife Lavender was expected to go too.'

'Well, now we can't go. The Prime Minister needs me to attend two important Cabinet Meetings and the Prince has asked if you and Ruth can go instead.'

The wedding of Jenny Taylor and Hugh Broadbent.

I smiled at him ruefully: 'Oh damn. What bad news – for *you*, I mean.'

Laughing, he said, 'I knew you'd say that.' Then he stalked out of the room.

I telephoned Ruth immediately: 'We are going on the Royal Yacht to Brazil with the Prince of Wales.'

There was a long pause at the other end of the telephone. 'Very funny,' she said, 'For half a second I almost believed you.'

When I convinced her that I was perfectly serious, Ruth started laughing and screaming down the phone. There was a long silence, then: 'My God, I've got nothing to wear.'

CHAPTER XIX

The Prince of Wales

'Halfway through our meeting, Prince Harry crashed through the door.'

WITH THE NOTABLE EXCEPTION of the Prince of Wales, I have never pretended to know any member of the Royal Family well. There have been occasions when, like many other people, I have met some of them briefly or, in most cases, fleetingly, but I would be very surprised if they remembered me at all.

On the other hand, it is equally true to say that Prince Charles and I know each other well and that is entirely due to the fact that the three subject areas for which, over nine years, I had Ministerial responsibility – small firms, inner cities and the environment – were of considerable interest to him.

I must admit that the Prince developed his passion for these areas before I was appointed to have a Government responsibility for them. Nonetheless it was an amazing coincidence that as I was moved from Department to Department in my Ministerial career, I would find that once again I was deeply involved in a field where the Prince wished to see great progress and where I would be expected to brief him on a regular basis.

In many ways it was an amusing coincidence which had not escaped him. When I was appointed Minister for the Environment, Prince Charles said to me, 'This is the third time this has happened, David. It is amazing. You must tell me what subject area you are going to cover next so that I can develop an interest in the subject before you are made Minister for it.'

Long before Ruth and I flew out to Brazil to join the Royal Yacht, I had got to know him well and was a great fan of his. I was constantly amazed at the depth of his knowledge in whatever area we were discussing and his feel for the subject showed a remarkable sensitivity and clear understanding of the real issues.

In 1983, when I first became Minister for Small Firms, it was fairly obvious that we would have to meet soon. His presidency of Business in the Community was more than a gesture of Royal Patronage, but a position he held as the founder of a wonderful initiative which was to help me spread the gospel of entrepreneurship and accelerate the growth of Local Enterprise Agencies throughout the land. In addition, he had also started the Prince's Youth Business Trust, which was to support many young people who would become self-employed or start their own small firms. It was, and still remains, a huge success.

At the first meeting we had at Kensington Palace it was important that we should share our thoughts on what more could be done for small firms. I was particularly interested in his views on Business in the Community and what his ambitions were for that organisation. At this meeting, as at many others, Steve O'Brien, the Chief Executive of B.I.C., was present. I was not only delighted that our views coincided but that he was very easy to talk to, relaxed, charming and very witty. It was clear that he recognised the enormous strengths of small businesses and their employment potential. At times he was quite passionate about the subject, which suited me well as I shared his convictions. I told him of my ambitions to secure funds from the Treasury to support Local Enterprise Agencies so that the Government could be seen to be an active partner in this great initiative. Not surprisingly he wished me luck with that. In fact it wasn't long after the meeting that the Treasury – God bless them – gave permission for such a scheme, which became known as LEAGS (Local Enterprise Agency Grant Scheme). It made funds available, providing the private sector could sponsor the agencies with matching funds.

At the end of the meeting it was clear to me that we were going to get on very well together and that he would be a very valuable ally. Given his important position, it was certainly possible for him to promote the small firms cause better than any politician ever could.

Apart from meeting the Prince at several functions up and down the country, there were other opportunities to brief him on what the Government was doing and, more importantly, what we might be thinking of doing. One such meeting will remain in my memory forever; again, it was at Kensington Palace. I was driven there by my new Government driver, Mick Burke, who always had a bland,

Prince Charles.

untroubled expression, which disguised his dry wit. Margaret Narroway, my former driver, had been promoted to being an organiser with the Government's Ministerial Car Fleet. On the journey to Kensington Mick reminded me that it was Prince Harry's fifth birthday.

As I stepped into Kensington Palace, I saw what was the aftermath of a children's birthday party, with wrapping paper strewn about the floor. Prince Harry had obviously had a rare old time unwrapping presents downstairs. I was ushered into Prince Charles' sitting room, met the Prince and my old friend Steve O'Brien, and the three of us sat down.

Halfway through our meeting, Prince Harry crashed through the door and ran into the room carrying a book. I instinctively stood up. I think Prince Harry thought his father was alone, so he was clearly surprised to find anyone else there and stood looking up at me. Prince Charles laughed and said, 'Now Harry, you know you shouldn't be in here because I'm having a meeting. This is Mr Trippier and he's a Government Minister.' Prince Harry didn't seem in the least phased by the occasion but I was. I stood there thinking, 'What on earth do I call him?' He looked so small. After a couple of seconds, I gave a small bow, stuck out my hand and said, 'Your Royal Highness – Happy Birthday.'

Prince Harry smiled and said, 'Thank you very much.' He then ran over to his father and climbed on his knee.

Prince Charles said to him, 'Now you've already had an exciting day and you should be doing your homework.'

'I have done it,' said Prince Harry. 'Have a look.' He then showed his father his homework and Prince Charles studied the book for a few minutes. Meanwhile, I sat down.

I thought that this was miraculous. I was privileged to witness a perfectly normal scene which could have taken place in any family. The conversation between father and son clearly showed the great affection they had for each other, which was emphasised by Prince Harry jumping on to his father's knee. It was a wonderful vignette which many people would envy me for witnessing.

Prince Charles handed the book back and said, 'That's very good. Well done. Now off you go.'

As he left the room, I stood up again. 'Goodbye', he said to me.

I smiled and said, 'Goodbye.'

'I'm very sorry about that, David.' said Prince Charles.

'Not at all, Sir. I enjoyed it. I have a son of a similar age. I just think it's a tragedy they have to grow up.'

He laughed and said he agreed with me. We then got on with the meeting.

When the meeting was over, I left the Prince and Steve together and walked into the corridor, closing the door behind me. I nearly jumped out of my skin because there was Prince Harry again. 'Do you want to see my new bicycle?' he asked me.

'Yes, I'd love to.' This birthday present was standing against the wall a little further down the corridor. It was blue and had 'Police signs' all over it and a small siren.

'It doesn't work,' he said. 'It won't move.'

'Wait a minute – I think the brakes are stuck.' I got down on my knees and released some more sticky tape and wire round the brakes and the bike moved quite easily. While I was doing this I was thinking, 'Ruth isn't going to believe this story.' I also thought, 'This is going to look pretty damn funny if Prince Charles comes out of that room with me on my knees.' Needless to say, the Prince of Wales chose that exact moment to come into the corridor and when he saw me, he certainly looked puzzled.

Fortunately Prince Harry saved my embarrassment by explaining that I had repaired his bike. Prince Charles laughed and said, 'I didn't know that Royal Marines were technically minded.'

'We're not. This is about the limit of my skill.'

I went outside and climbed in the Government car. As we drove away I said to Mick, 'That was one of the most entertaining meetings I've ever had.'

'It can't be as good as my experience, Minister.'

'What do you mean?' I asked.

'Prince Harry came out to talk with me with that Jack Russell dog his dad has. He must have chatted to me for at least ten minutes.'

'Crikey. What did you call him, Mick?'

'I didn't call him anything as I couldn't think how to address him.'

'I know. I had the same problem. Did you get out of the car?'

'No way! I've read in the newspapers about how bad tempered that dog is, and I wasn't getting out of this car to have that little bugger sticking his teeth in my ankles.'

I couldn't stop laughing. 'I'll tell you what: Prince Harry is a great character; he will do very well.' Mick agreed.

Throughout the period that I was the Minister for Inner Cities, I continued to see Prince Charles at several events and for an occasional briefing, but it was when I was the Minister for the Environment that I saw him most frequently.

I remember being asked by Commander Richard Aylard, who was the Prince's Private Secretary, if I would travel to Highgrove with my Private Secretary for a meeting on countryside matters. I readily agreed and Sandy Bishop and I turned up on the doorstep at the appointed time to be greeted by the Prince, who had one arm in a sling. He was recovering from a serious polo accident and had had to have a steel pin put through his elbow. Not surprisingly, he was suffering some pain. The Jack Russell eyed me suspiciously.

There were about ten people at the meeting and it went very well. When we went into the dining room for lunch, I found I was sitting on the Prince's right. We had fish and as the Prince had only one useful hand, I saw that he was having some difficulty cutting it up with his fork. Food was flying everywhere and I offered to help him. The Prince said, 'It's perfectly alright, David, when any food slips off the table, I try to catch it in the turn-ups of my trousers. That way I can save some for dinner.' I cracked up as did the rest of the table. In the event the Jack Russell was doing a marvellous job hoovering up the food which had slipped on to the floor.

The trip to Brazil in 1991 turned out to be a huge success. The Prince of Wales had wanted to explore the possibilities of influencing industry to become more environmentally responsible in the run-up to the Rio Summit, which would be held twelve months hence.

There were to be two British Ministers – myself and Lynda Chalker, who would be joining us later on. She was the Minister for Overseas Development. Amongst the industrialists, there was the Chairman of British Petroleum, the Chairman of Shell Oil and the Chairman of Lloyds Bank, who was also Chairman of Business in the Community. There was the European Commissioner for the Environment, Carlo Ripa De Meana and the Director of Environmental Protection Agency in the U.S.A., who represented the American President at all the international meetings I attended. The rest of the group were international big hitters either in the private sector or the environment. Most of the preparatory work had been carried out by Jonathan Porritt, the Prince's Private Office and the British Ministers.

The Conference was only part of an official visit to Brazil by the Prince and Princess of Wales. They were the guests of the President of Brazil, President Coller, who would give a State Banquet for the Prince and Princess and in turn would be invited to dinner on board the Royal Yacht at the end of the Conference on board that ship.

Apart from the advance party, and those who were to join us later in the week, most of the official party, including Ruth and myself, accompanied the Prince and Princess on the Queen's Flight, which flew from Heathrow to Brasilia, the capital city of Brazil. As with all Ministerial visits, the Department paid for me while Ruth had to pay for herself.

The flight to Brazil was an experience in itself. The Prince and Princess could not have been more charming or relaxed. Ruth had not met either of them before, and was soon at ease with them both. I had never met the Princess and was totally mesmerised by her beauty and her friendliness. During the long flight, I went into the private part of the plane to brief the Prince on the Government's perspective on the forthcoming Conference and Princess Diana asked Ruth to accompany her to go and watch the in-flight movie which was being shown at the rear of the plane.

When we landed at Brasilia Airport in the late evening, we were driven to the Hilton Hotel, which apparently offered the best security protection for the Royal couple. When Ruth and I went to our room, we were both astonished at the small size of the bath in the bathroom. When I got in it, my knees were almost up to my chin. I made some daft remark to Ruth to the effect that I hoped that the Royal couple had better facilities in their room on the floor immediately above.

In the morning some of us were to fly to the heart of the Amazon Rain Forest, which I had never visited before. As we walked out of the hotel to be driven to the airport, Prince Charles pulled me on one side and said, 'David, is your bath very small?' When I said it was, he said, 'So is mine. Incredible.'

On that day, there were only eight of us who were to travel to the rain forest and that was certainly the maximum number which could be comfortably accommodated in the small plane that transported us. Ruth and many others in the party were unable to come with us. As I wedged myself into my seat, to my surprise Prince Charles announced that he was going to pilot the plane on take-off and landing so that he could get his flying hours in. He was clearly going to do this, but made something of a joke of it by saying to me, 'Is that alright with you, David?' I replied that the Government could ill afford a by-election in my constituency. He laughed and still carried on.

During the journey, which lasted an hour, we flew over the

Amazon Rain Forest and I was enthralled by its magnificence. I have often made speeches about the importance of preserving it, but actually to see it and realise the sheer scale of it was breathtaking.

The Princess sat next to me and in our conversation informed me that President Coller's Private Secretary had telephoned the Prince's Private Secretary to ask how many miniature medals the Prince of Wales was going to wear on his dinner jacket that night at the State Banquet. 'Don't you think that's a hoot?' she said.

'I can just imagine President Coller tearing down to the Military Museum in Brasilia, smashing the glass on top of a medal exhibition, and awarding himself a few extra decorations to keep up appearances tonight. One way or another, I bet he will have more medals up than the Prince.'

'I'll take the bet,' she said. 'Five pounds says he won't have as many medals as the Prince.'

I roared with laughter. 'O.K., your Royal Highness – I bet you five pounds that he will have more than the Prince.' We shook hands on the bet.

Later on during the flight she confided in me that she did have a slight problem with the banquet that evening. She explained that she and the Prince were very concerned that they shouldn't be seen to upstage President Coller and his wife and so she was fairly certain that she shouldn't wear her tiara at the banquet.

I couldn't resist a crack by saying, 'This is obviously a common problem that faces most of the housewives in Britain.' She giggled. I saw the problem but I didn't know how thin-skinned the President and his wife would be about these matters. I did know that Mrs Coller was a former belly dancer, so I suppose it could be a little tricky.

'I think you have got to wear the tiara. A tenth of the dinner guests tonight will be British and we would expect our Princess to look the bee's knees. I don't think that it matters that Mrs Coller will not be wearing a tiara. She's not a Princess like you.'

She threw up her hands in a gesture of mock surrender. 'O.K., O.K.,' she said. 'I can see you feel strongly about it.'

'Good. I'm glad that's settled.'

When we arrived at our destination, the Prince left us to go to the cockpit and land the plane on what was a very small runway. We then travelled by coach into the heart of the rain forest and visited a small village. It was wonderful to watch all the Brazilians, and particularly the children, lining the route cheering and waving at the royal couple. Later we visited a conservation area where previously mining had taken place and the landscape had been restored to its former splendour.

After a few hours we returned to the plane to fly back to Brasilia. As with the outward journey, everyone was very relaxed. Myself, Prince Charles and Princess Diana read each other's horoscopes from the back of a magazine. I recall they were fairly bland, as they often are. After landing at Brasilia, we were driven back to the hotel, where I couldn't wait to tell Ruth about the visit.

Having changed into a dinner jacket, and with Ruth looking lovely in a long dress, we went down to the hotel lobby. I was convinced Ruth's dress was new but she played my mother's old trick in telling me I'd seen it before.

When the royal couple came down to the lobby, Prince Charles looked resplendent with his medals on his chest and 'sharp bits' below them, and the Princess looked magnificent in her evening gown and – surprise surprise! – she was wearing her tiara. She walked up to Ruth and pointed to her tiara; then she gestured to me and said, 'He's made me wear this. It's so heavy it's killing me and it has been lacquered in with my hair style. If I nod my head, its perfectly possible that my head will crack open.' We all laughed.

At the reception before the banquet in a magnificent building in the centre of the city, I saw President Coller in the distance with his wife. To my amazement, he had fewer medals than the Prince of Wales.

All the guests were to file past the Prince and Princess and the President and Mrs Coller, who were standing in a line. The British Ambassador asked the British contingent to hang back until the Brazilians had walked down the reception line and asked me if I would lead them up. Having been with the Prince all day long, I bowed and couldn't resist saying, 'I know we've never met, Sir, I'm Trippier.'

'You don't say,' said the Prince laughing. 'I'm Charles. Haven't I seen you somewhere before?'

On board the Royal Yacht.

He then turned to the President to introduce me and explain who I was. President Coller was very young and looked like a film star. The only trouble with him was he was short in the medal department. I shook hands with him and then Mrs Coller. When I came to the Princess, I bowed as low as I could get and before I could say anything she said, 'You owe me five pounds.'

'Sadly I do,' I said. Later that evening I offered her a five pound note. She laughed and put it in her handbag.

CHAPTER XX

Deputy Chairman of the Party

'Dying for Britain, albeit slowly.'

IN THE SPRING OF 1990 I was sitting on the front bench in the Commons, having just completed a Ministerial Question Time, when Kenneth Baker, who was the Chairman of the Conservative Party, walked into the Chamber and signalled that he would like a private word with me. When we were alone, he said that the Prime Minister wished to appoint me as the Deputy Chairman of the Party, with specific responsibilities for the marginal seats in the country. I had to smile at that as I had a marginal seat. His purpose in approaching me in this informal way was because he wished to prepare me for the shock. 'What shock is that, Ken?' I asked.

'The shock is that she wants you to remain as Minister of State and do both jobs.'

'As well as looking after my marginal seat?' After a pause I went on, 'Please don't misunderstand me, Ken. I'm very flattered, but to become Deputy Chairman is a very serious role and I would want to do the job in a serious way. Anyway – why me?'

'The Party needs to have a higher profile up and down the country. More regional television and radio interviews with someone who already has a high profile, but will get the Party's message across. You fit the bill. I have asked the PM's permission and she thinks it's a good idea. Will you do it?'

'Ken, its always nice to be wanted and I will certainly do it. I just have to think how I'm going to divide my time between Conservative Central Office, the Environment Department, the constituency and my family.' Ken Baker told me to expect a phone call from Number Ten. As always, I telephoned Ruth immediately to see what she thought.

'Wow,' she said. 'It's certainly good that the Party Machine want you to have a higher profile and I accept that it will be better for that profile if you remain a Minister. I'm just thinking how you will fit everything in.'

'I know, but as there will have to be a General Election within the next two years, this is a job which will have to be done and completed within that period. I certainly wouldn't be doing the job for longer than that. The main point is that I've got to play my role in helping the Party to get re-elected next time.'

'Absolutely right. Anyway, I'm so thrilled that people are wanting you down there. Don't forget that this family want you occasionally up here.'

I laughed. 'Only occasionally though.'

Later that day the PM's office was on the phone and I went to see Margaret Thatcher in her study at Number Ten. Having confirmed my appointment and told me how she wanted me to do the job, which simply entailed me dying for Britain, albeit slowly and certainly not before the General Election, we spent a good half hour together simply preparing the Press Release announcing my appointment. I was impressed that she wanted to spend so much of her valuable time on a Press Release rather than handing it over to someone else to complete. She wrote most of it right there in front of me and I only altered it slightly. Brave man!

After leaving the Prime Minister, I went over to Conservative Central Office in Smith Square to meet all the staff and find out where my office was going to be. I knew quite a few of the staff, many I didn't, but they were enthusiastic, cheerful and totally dedicated. In my new role as Deputy Chairman of the Party I had succeeded Lord Young, who had in turn succeeded Jeffrey Archer. David Young had by now left the Government and was spending more time with Cable and Wireless PLC. As we were old chums, it was easy to deal with the hand-over and I took his former office, which was furnished in art deco. Not my normal style, but it was about time for me to get 'with it' a little more.

My office was very near to the Chairman's office. There were four Vice Chairmen of the Party under me: Tom Arnold MP, who was Vice Chairman responsible for candidates; Dame Joan Seccombe, who was responsible for Women; Geoffrey Pattie, responsible for

Lord Young.

emancipation affairs in Central and Eastern Europe; and Jim Spicer MP, who was responsible for overseas support. I was delighted to be working so closely with the Conservative Research Department, whose work I had always admired.

Having settled into my office, I walked back over to the DOE to have a natter with Chris Patten. I knew that Chris had supported my appointment as Deputy Chairman, but as I was still one of his Ministers in the Department, I wanted to know what he really thought about me having this dual role. In the event, Chris was delighted that it was one of his Ministers who had been selected and promised his support whenever it was required.

The fact that I was able to handle the dual role was due entirely to the support teams in Central Office, the Private Office in the DOE, and Ruth and the children at the weekends. Once again I was tearing around the country addressing Party Meetings, supporting MPs in marginal seats or prospective candidates who hoped they would become MPs. At the same time, the additional job meant that I was always shooting off somewhere at the weekends to events organised by the Party faithful. In addition, I would normally have to attend meetings with the senior officers of the Party, which took place between Tuesday and Friday at eight o'clock in the morning under Kenneth Baker's chairmanship. I would then just manage to make the 9.30 meetings of Ministers in the DOE under Chris Patten's chairmanship.

The most important meetings of all were every Monday morning at 9 am, when Ken Baker and I would have a private meeting with the Prime Minister in the Cabinet Room at Number Ten. This 'start the week' meeting was to concentrate on the political aspects of the Government's work. The most difficult thing about the Monday morning meetings was to ensure I got on the first flight from Manchester Airport to Heathrow in order to arrive on time. I didn't think it fair to Ruth and the boys for me to leave home on Sunday. Fortunately I was always able to make the meetings on time.

The most dramatic of these 'start the week' meetings with the Prime Minister took place on the Monday immediately following the local elections in May 1990. In most areas the Conservatives had done very badly, with many Conservative Councillors losing their seats, primarily because of the adverse effect of the Community Charge, which was already becoming widely known as the Poll Tax. In Rossendale and Darwen we were particularly badly hit and lost many seats and some first-class councillors. During the meeting, the Prime Minister came out with an astonishing statement: 'I think the people will like the Community Charge when they begin to understand it.'

I was aghast and could not resist saying, 'With great respect, Prime Minister, that is like saying "turkeys would enjoy Christmas if we could just explain it to them".'

There was a dreadful silence and Ken Baker started to study an invisible spot on the ceiling. 'What do you mean, David?' Margaret Thatcher snapped at me.

'Last Thursday the Tory Party was virtually wiped out in the local elections. In my own constituency we lost an excellent Tory Mayor, the Leader of the Conservative Group and even in the safer wards we didn't win a single seat. However equitable the community charge may appear in theory, it is a disaster in practice. There are some things you cannot sell and we cannot sell this policy to people who have been paying between £80 and £100 in rates for their cottages in my constituency, and are now having to pay more than £300 for every person in that house who is over eighteen years of age. It is totally impractical.'

Again there was a stony silence. Ken Baker had perfected a feat which I had hitherto thought impossible, which was to move his chair away from me by waggling his bottom from side to side in the seat, and by the end of my outburst seemed far away from me in the Cabinet Room.

The Prime Minister then turned on Ken. 'What do you think, Kenneth?' Instead of saying something supportive to help me – such as reminding her that she appointed me and that I had a marginal seat, and that perhaps she should listen to what I was saying – he simply said, 'It's obviously less popular in certain areas than it is in others.'

I simply sat there thinking, 'You can say that again.' We continued with the rest of the agenda and it was clear that Margaret Thatcher was very annoyed with me.

As we climbed into the car outside Number Ten to go to Central Office, Ken exhaled and said, 'If you are still in a job by the end of this day, David, it will be a miracle.'

'I thought you were the one who kept reminding me that she couldn't stand sycophants,' I retorted.

'Yes, that is true, but – hell's teeth – there is a balance.'

When I went into my office I telephoned Ruth: 'Don't get upset but I might be for the chop.'

When I explained what had happened at Downing Street, Ruth was as supportive as usual: 'It would be grossly unfair to be given the order of the boot because you spoke the truth.'

'I know, but I think we should stand by.'

The whole event was very sad for me. I greatly admired Margaret Thatcher as a formidable leader who had done so much for the nation and restored the people's confidence in themselves. However, on this one issue, she didn't seem to want to listen. Worse still, there was no-one who was particularly close to her who could influence her on the matter. Peter Carrington and Willie Whitelaw, who had been her closest confidantes, were no longer on the scene and she had a strained relationship with her Deputy Prime Minister, Geoffrey Howe, who couldn't get through on this issue.

However, the day came and went and to my relief I was not sacked. Tragically, only a matter of six months later, she was no longer Prime Minister.

CHAPTER XXI

The Leadership Battle

'Do you think you will be sacked Mr Trippier?'

IT WAS CLEAR TO EVERYONE that Margaret Thatcher was in serious trouble when Geoffrey Howe, the Deputy Prime Minister, resigned from the Government on the 1st November 1990. As is the custom, he was given the opportunity to address the House of Commons to explain why he felt it necessary to go. That speech, delivered on the 13th November, sounded the death knell for the Prime Minister. In many ways it was very untypical of Geoffrey to speak in such a vindictive manner. The body of the speech, which was heard in silence, was certainly well crafted, but we were all waiting for his peroration at the end and he was anxious not to disappoint. He threw buckets of poison on the carpet and ended with the words, 'The time has come for others to consider their own response to the tragic conflict of loyalties with which I have myself wrestled for perhaps too long.'

When Ken Baker and I spoke in private after the debate, we both felt that it was inevitable that there would now be a challenge for Margaret's leadership and it was glaringly obvious that the challenge would come from Michael Heseltine. With all the speculation in the media over the weeks preceding Geoffrey Howe's departure, the Prime Minister, when referring to Michael Heseltine, had goaded him with the now famous phrase, 'Let him put up or shut up'.

Michael had rejected the idea of taking on Margaret for some time. Primarily his instincts told him that he could not win but now events had changed dramatically. The situation for the Government was deteriorating so rapidly that the Labour Party were ahead of us in the opinion polls by double figures. Twelve months before Geoffrey resigned, Nigel Lawson, a well known disciple of the Right, had resigned – unable to stand it any more. The Government was certainly in a crisis and growing numbers of Ministers and backbenchers believed that it would be impossible to win the next election if Margaret remained as Prime Minister. I was one of them. Then Michael threw his cap in the ring.

The first ballot for the leadership was to be held on the 20th November, and although Margaret refused to canvas for herself, there were many prepared to do it on her behalf. There were equally many canvassing for Michael, and although no Minister was prepared to come out of the closet to give him public support, there were scores of former Ministers who did.

Although much was said at the time about the deep division within the Party on Europe, it was crystal clear to me that the Poll Tax had become an albatross round the PM's neck. Michael Heseltine had pledged to rid us of it. Like me, he never believed we could sell it. Like everyone else in Central Office, I remained neutral and gave no comment to the press or anyone else for that matter. Michael was clearly attracting increasing support and from unlikely quarters, including Nigel Lawson.

The result of the ballot was announced, with Margaret having polled 204, Michael 152 and 16 abstentions. Under the rules of the ballot, Margaret was four votes short of a majority for an outright win and there would have to be a second ballot.

I had supported Michael for the sake of the Party. There is little point in writing a book like this if you don't tell the truth and the truth is that at the first ballot I allowed a relatively small number of my constituency party, who were still behind Margaret Thatcher, as well as others, to believe that I had voted for her. For the first and only time in my life my father's words haunted me: 'Tell the truth, then you can remember what you said.' It made me feel extremely uncomfortable and I quietly resolved that whatever the consequences, I would declare my position in the next ballot.

Two days later Margaret Thatcher decided not to stand in the second ballot. It was a traumatic decision and it was unbelievably sad that she had not decided to retire at the peak of her career, some two years before. It was in many ways historic because with the notable exception of Neville Chamberlain, who left office in 1940 in very special circumstances, all other Prime Ministers in this century had left office at the behest of the electorate or the doctor. The tragedy was that by pressing on and ceasing to listen, she had become the author of her own misfortune. No-one with any decency could deny that during her premiership she was courageous, formidable and that certainly in the earlier years at Number Ten, she had played the most significant role in reversing Britain's fortunes and restoring our prestige on the world stage.

It was clear to most of us that Douglas Hurd would now become a candidate in the second ballot and rumour suggested that there was an increasing likelihood that John Major would stand. John was Margaret's Crown Prince. In the past she had genuinely believed he would succeed her when eventually she decided to retire. Now that she was forced to retire, she threw all her weight behind his nomination, which was registered, and she campaigned vigorously for his election.

After two days of campaigning by the three candidates, both John Major and Douglas Hurd had attracted numerous Ministers, who had pledged their support and were prepared to campaign for one or the other. No Minister had stepped forward publicly to support Michael Heseltine.

The vast majority of my colleagues were hedging their bets. There were four reasons why I believed that Michael Heseltine would be an admirable Prime Minister. First of all he had immense charisma. Secondly he had enormous vision and I had myself worked in three separate areas where he had pioneered great initiatives long before I came on the scene – Urban Development Corporations, Local Enterprise Agencies and the Groundwork Trusts. Thirdly he had achieved significant success in many strategic developments in the north of England, and I was first and foremost a northerner. Lastly, I guessed that the Labour Party would hate to have him as their principal opponent. That opinion was easily confirmed in my mind by a few discreet enquiries amongst Labour MPs whom I knew well. They would prefer the Conservative Parliamentary Party to support John Major or Douglas Hurd – anyone but Heseltine.

In the middle of the week, with eight days to go to the second ballot, I telephoned the Chairman of my Conservative Association in the constituency and every one of the Branch Chairmen in

Rossendale and Darwen. This was my own straw poll and it was not clear cut. The majority wanted me to support Heseltine but the others were equally divided between Major and Hurd. I then decided to make a move. I told Ken Baker that I intended to go public in supporting Michael and intended to campaign for him. He was not surprised; although he never declared himself, I knew that in the ballot he would support John Major.

When I then telephoned the Press Association with the prepared text of a statement declaring my support for Michael, all hell broke loose. As I was the first Minister publicly to support Michael, that was a story in itself. The fact that I was also the Deputy Chairman of the Party added lustre to the coverage. During that day I went through umpteen television and radio interviews as well as bi-laterals with hoards of reporters. Within an hour of me going public, Michael Heseltine had telephoned me to show his appreciation of both my support and my courage in declaring it. I firmly believed that because I had stood up to be counted, other Ministers would follow suit. They certainly did, but only after another two days had elapsed.

During those first two days I felt like an infantry officer in the First World War who clutches his pistol, jumps out of the trench urging everyone on, and finds himself in 'no mans land' with no-one having followed him. After those two days, David Hunt, who was the Secretary of State for Wales, went public and supported Michael. Then, every day, we saw more and more Ministers declare for Michael.

From the moment everyone was aware of my position in the campaign, I seemed to appear as the Heseltine representative on most of the television programmes that went out, unless the candidates themselves were appearing. The Labour Party could only sit on the side lines until the election was over. They were totally eclipsed because this was a Tory Party Show.

It was without doubt the cleanest campaign I had ever been involved in and no-one made any cutting or disparaging remarks about anyone else. Everyone treated opponents with dignity and those of us who appeared regularly on television would say generous things about the other two candidates. To be fair, there was no hypocrisy in this. I greatly respected Douglas Hurd and John Major. Douglas was always an outstanding Minister and in my view would always have been rated as a potential Prime Minister. John Major I knew well from the Guy Fawkes Group, and recognised his amazing capacity for seizing on the principle in any discussion or argument to get to the main issue at hand. I simply believed that Michael was the man with the best leadership qualities.

There were regular meetings of Michael's campaign team, of which I was now an active member. There were also long conversations with fellow MPs, especially those who could not make up their minds whom to support. I had endless telephone calls with colleagues and although I thought by the weekend prior to the ballot that we were at least holding Michael's vote, John Major's campaign was gathering momentum and he was also attracting increased support. There were basically two reasons for this. First of all, he had not been around long enough to make many enemies, and secondly he had made public that one of his policy objectives was to create a 'classless society'. This struck a chord with many of the waverers.

The classless society fitted well with the fact that – as many of his campaign team repeatedly made clear – John had come from the wrong side of the tracks, having had a relatively humble background. It was extremely difficult for those of us in the Heseltine camp to counter this. Michael was never perceived as having a humble background, despite the fact that his mother had virtually bankrupted herself in paying for his school fees. That didn't seem to cut much ice when people's attention was continually focused on photographs in the national press of Michael, his wife and children appearing in front of what was clearly their stately home. In retrospect this should have been avoided. In truth it should have been acknowledged that Michael's financial success in publishing was entirely due to his entrepreneurial skill, he having started the business from scratch.

It was becoming clear by the Monday morning, with only a few days left before we cast our votes, that the campaign was moving away from us and that John Major was the favourite. In the run-up to the ballot there was frenetic lobbying going on, more television and radio interviews, and then the day of the ballot was upon us. We waited for the results, which showed that John Major had won with a huge majority. Michael was second and Douglas third.

Although I secretly felt towards the end that John Major would win, I had anticipated that the result would have been closer. I telephoned Ruth to chew the fat and was surprised and moved to hear her crying down the phone. It was a particular surprise because Ruth has never been a weepy person. Even to this day, I could count on one hand the times that she has cried. Although I was unbelievably sad for Michael, she felt the anguish even more keenly than I did. We had to pull ourselves up by our bootstraps and get on with life. After receiving a very kind telephone call from my constituency Chairman, Geoffrey Law, who was brilliant in comforting me, I had to perform in front of the cameras once again as the media circus was determined to drag the event out to the bitter end.

One interview stuck in my mind. Interviewed by Jim Hancock from Granada on the lawn across the road from Parliament, he put the question that was obvious to many people, including me. I knew that Jim hated putting the question because we were friends and I had great respect for his ability and integrity. Nonetheless he was honour bound to ask, 'Do you think you will be sacked, Mr Trippier?'

'That is a decision for the new Prime Minister,' I said.

Two days later I received a telephone call from John Major. I knew that this time I would have to go and had steeled myself for the axe to fall. 'Congratulations, Prime Minister,' I said to John.

'Thank you, David. I would be grateful if you would remain in the Government. It has been a trying time for all of us over the last few weeks, but what is past is past. I need a Government of all the talents.'

It was the last thing I was expecting.

CHAPTER XXII

The Council of Ministers

'Get them on their feet.'

JOHN MAJOR'S RESHUFFLE had many surprises in it. Certainly there were a number of people who were told to pack their bags and clear their desks, but the fact that Michael Heseltine was invited by John to return to the Government and become once again the Secretary of State for the Environment was the most welcome news to me. Ken Baker became Home Secretary and Chris Patten became Chairman of the Party.

Michael Heseltine had already thanked those of us in his campaign team for our efforts and I was pleased to receive a personal letter of thanks from him, which naturally I have kept. As soon as he arrived in the Department of the Environment, he sent for me and in a private meeting we had a long discussion. He ended the conversation by saying, 'David, John Major has asked me to reform the Community Charge and that is an enormous job. I can't possibly attend the meetings in Europe and the United Nations on the Environment, as Chris sometimes did. You will have to cover the Environment brief entirely by yourself until I can see my way through sorting out the Poll Tax. This means that I would be most grateful if you would leave Central Office; I need you here.'

When I asked him what John Major had said about this, he replied, 'He is happy to support me and simply wants you and me to sort it out. If you decide to leave this Department and stay as Deputy Chairman, I will of course support your decision, but I would much rather we worked together here.'

I replied that I understood completely and recognised the work that he would have to undertake with the Poll Tax. I said I would speak to him later that day. I then had to go over to Central Office, where Chris Patten was being welcomed by the staff.

After making a brief speech from the staircase in Central Office, Chris had a private chat with me in his new office.

'Do you know that Michael Heseltine has told John Major that he needs you to be full time in the DOE?' Chris asked.

I told him I did.

'If you decide to stay here, I would be delighted to work with you once again. It's entirely your decision.'

I was already certain that I should stay as a Minister and relinquish being Deputy Chairman when, on my way out of Central Office, I bumped into Kenneth Clarke, who was also leaving, having attended a separate meeting. I told Ken what had transpired that morning and asked his opinion. 'I don't think there's a decision to be made, David. You should stay as a Minister of State and leave here. Michael needs you badly and anyway you will work very well together.' Ruth had said exactly the same thing that morning.

I had made my decision and I informed Michael and later Chris that I wished to remain in the DOE. Chris was charming about the matter and I then attended my first meeting of the new Ministerial Team.

Michael had ordered that the boardroom table in his office should be removed and replaced with armchairs and sofas. The Ministers sat around eyeing each other up. Michael Portillo was Minister of State for Local Government. Sir George Young, who had been brought back into the Government by John Major (having been dropped by Margaret Thatcher many years before), was now Minister of State for Housing and Planning, which was a very welcome appointment to me as we were old friends. With me still covering the Environment, that completed the line up of Ministers of State. The Junior Ministers were Tony Baldry, who was an excellent second-in-command to me, Baroness Blatch, who covered Heritage and the Departments brief in the House of Lords, Robert Key, who assisted Michael Portillo, and Tim Yeo, who assisted George Young. It was going to be interesting to see how Michael Portillo and Michael Heseltine were going to get on.

The following day it was announced that John Cope would become Deputy Chairman of the Party, taking over from me. To my intense disappointment, one of the tabloid newspapers said that John

Major had sacked me from that position because I had supported Michael Heseltine in the leadership contest. The newspaper journalist who wrote that article would have been mesmerised by the truth of the matter, which was that my good friend Michael Heseltine had been instrumental in me leaving Central Office, not John Major. The article still grated because it was unfair to me and to John Major, who had behaved impeccably.

My secretary in Central Office, Sophie Fryer, wished to leave Central Office and work in the House of Commons alongside Barbara Womford, who was my constituency secretary in Westminster. I was flattered that she wished to remain with me and Barbara was delighted to have some help. They both got on very well together. In truth I needed two secretaries because the constituency workload was colossal. No MP could have had two secretaries whose background and approach was so different. Barbara was a chirpy and cheerful cockney with a tremendous sense of humour. Any constituent who had to speak to her on the phone found her delightful. In complete contrast, Sophie had been to Cheltenham Ladies College, had a Master of Arts degree from St Andrews University, and had a beautiful speaking voice. In fact she was so 'far back' she was coming out the other side. She was also very cheerful, had a rich sense of humour, and was always charming with everyone. They were a wonderful pair. They also worked very well with Sandy Bishop in my Ministerial Office.

Prior to Barbara Womford working for me, I had been blessed with a secretary called Liz Dean, who was superb. She was very efficient and good fun. When I employed her, she was had been going out with Philip Hacking, who was Ruth's cousin and had been a groom at our wedding. She eventually left to marry Philip and live in Norwich – so I lost a secretary but gained a new member of the family.

Back in the Department, the civil servants who worked under me seemed relieved that I had relinquished my job as Party Deputy Chairman; so too were my Conservative Association officers and members in Rossendale and Darwen. It had been an enormous workload and looking back on that period, I'm not entirely sure how we all got through, not least Ruth and the boys. Living in the constituency made life and work at the weekends much easier, but even then I was acutely aware that for me to retain my seat, the Party's standing in the country would have to improve dramatically.

I had always attended most of the Council of Ministers' meetings in Brussels when Chris Patten had been Secretary of State, but now I was attending them all. I loved every minute of that and felt that on so many fronts we were managing the agenda well and moving it forward. It was usual for the Member State occupying the Presidency for a six-month period to host an informal Ministerial meeting in their own country. When Ireland held the Presidency, Padraig Flynn, the Minister for the Environment in that country, was the Chairman of the Environment Council of Ministers. Padraig is tall and angular. He is always laughing and often, without any prompting from anyone, breaks into song. He did a brilliant job in getting us to work together in achieving consensus on a wide variety of issues. For his informal Council of Ministers meeting, he chose to host the event at Ashford Castle in County Mayo in the West of Ireland, and it was a huge success. All the Ministers brought their spouses and Ruth was able to go as it was held over a weekend. All of us flew to Dublin from all over Europe to meet a chartered plane which was to fly us to Knock Airport. That was an experience in itself as the tarmac only covered part of the runway at that time. When we landed and the aircraft was taxiing to the terminal, we trundled past a row of gleaming black limousines with their drivers all standing to attention beside the cars. Every one of them was a Mercedes with the exception of a black Jaguar, which was in the middle of the row and stood out like a sore thumb.

As we unfastened our safety belts, the Irish senior civil servant who worked for Padraig Flynn came up to us and said, 'As you know, Minister, you have to have special security cover as the British Minister. You and Mrs Trippier have two bodyguards who will stay with you throughout the weekend and you have to travel in a bullet-proof car, which we hope will be as inconspicuous as possible.'

'Don't tell me that the inconspicuous car is the Jaguar that stands out a mile in the midst of all those Mercedes?'

'You guessed it, Minister.'

When all the Ministers had piled into the separate cars with their spouses, we set off like the bats out of hell with police outriders on motorbikes at the front and rear. The speed was astonishing. As we tore through village after village, the children were coming out of school and stood on the pavement in amazement as the cavalcade swept past them. It was amusing to imagine what they must have been thinking. This was not an everyday occurrence and most of them thought that the couple sitting in the back of the black Jaguar were the nobs. They started waving madly at us. I sat there feeling embarrassed and Ruth started waving madly back.

When we arrived at Ashford Castle, we were both enthralled by the sheer beauty of the countryside and the hotel. The Irish are the most hospitable people in the world and they went to enormous lengths to make us feel welcome. Nothing was too much trouble for Padraig Flynn, who was determined to see that Ruth and I were well looked

Environment Ministers outside Ashford Castle. Left to right: Dr Klaus Topfer (Germany), Padraig Flynn (Ireland), Lone Dibker (Denmark), Mit Smet (Belgium), Alex Bodry (Luxembourg), the author.

after, and although he was always courteous to all the other European Ministers, we were to receive special treatment. He showed us to our room, which was the principal guest room where umpteen Presidents of the United States had slept when they visited Ireland. There were scores of photographs of past American Presidents dotted around the room and hung on the walls. Even in the bathroom, when one sat on the loo, there was a photograph of Ronald Reagan hung on the back of the door laughing at me. Not surprisingly!

Padraig said proudly that President Reagan was the last President to have slept in the enormous bed. I'd never seen a bigger bed in my life and said to Padraig, 'Have you checked he's not still in there. Because it would take half an hour to find him.'

We were told that a security guard from the Garda would be sleeping in a chair outside our room all night. Terrific! Then we went to meet Padraig's wife Dorothy, whom we instantly liked, and with her warm, friendly expression, lovely lilt and strawberry blond hair, she was an enormous hit on the weekend. At one time she had completed some training as a nurse in England.

The evening meal was followed by a delightful concert of the very best of Irish folk songs and dancing. The following morning the Ministers went off to our meeting. Once again Padraig handled all the controversial agenda items with aplomb and there was no major dispute. In the afternoon we all went our separate ways to have a break from the long meeting that morning. Some of the Ministers went to play golf, some went clay pigeon shooting, some went for a walk and Ruth and I went riding.

We were driven to the stables in the nearby village, which had featured in the famous film *The Quiet Man*, starring John Wayne and Maureen O'Hara. Once again we had to have protection. There was a sergeant from the Garda who rode with us and two other policemen riding in a Range Rover which followed us everywhere. Ruth's horse was highly spirited and later in the ride, when we broke into a gallop through a forest, it was clear to me that he was completely out of control. The horse suddenly came to a grinding halt and Ruth was thrown through the air, did a somersault and landed on her back. I was close behind and hurriedly dismounted and ran over to her. Although I was terrified that she might be seriously injured, the Garda officers were white with fear. It was as if they were already reading the headlines in the *Irish Times*, 'British Minister's wife Killed in Riding Accident.'

'Oh God, darling, are you alright?' I asked. She couldn't speak. She was winded or perhaps worse. 'Can you stand up?'

'No,' she whispered.

I was now frantic. 'Why can't you stand up, why can't you stand?' I spluttered.

'Because you're standing on my damn jacket.'

There were sighs of relief and laughter broke through. To her eternal credit, Ruth mounted the horse once again and we trotted back to the stables.

In the evening after the meal we went down to the nightclub, which had originally been the dungeons and was now tastefully decorated and had a medieval theme. Everyone was in a good mood. Padraig Flynn stepped on to the stage and started to sing well known Irish songs, including *Danny Boy* and *The Mountains of Mourne.* He had a very good voice. I accompanied him on the piano and the German Minister, Dr Klaus Topfer, played the spoons.

Then the professional entertainment began and two excellent guitarists came on the stage and insisted that I accompany them, which was great fun. Everyone was dancing and singing. Ruth was asked to dance by a tall, good looking German civil servant who obviously fancied his chances. He assumed that Ruth was one of the team of British civil servants and with his hand on her back, cooed into her ear, 'I can see that you are alone.'

Smiling, Ruth said, 'No, I'm with the piano player.'

The German shot a glance at me on the 'Johanna' and his hand flew off Ruth's back as if it were charged with electricity. 'Oh,' he said. 'I think you are Minister Trippier's wife.'

Correct,' said Ruth and burst out laughing.

Derek Osborne, who was the senior British civil servant accompanying me and an excellent man, overheard this and roared with laughter. The German saw the funny side and started to laugh too. Then everyone laughed as the story went round like wildfire. I was completely oblivious to all this until much later in the night, when I retired from the piano, my fingers worn to the bone.

Ruth dancing with an admiring German Civil Servant at Ashford Castle.

The success of Ashford Castle was to have a lasting effect on all the Ministers who attended the Council Meeting. For a long time after the Irish Presidency, those of us who thought we might have little in common with each other were able to work together more comfortably as a result of enjoying each other's company on that weekend. Many of us remain friends to this day, including Padraig and Dorothy. Perhaps most important of all for me, I actually realised that we had more that united us than divided us and for the first time, I really felt that the European alliance could be a success.

The most significant event which took place whilst I was a Minister under John Major was my speech at the last Party Conference at

Blackpool before the General Election the following year. I had to reply to a major debate which would take place on the Environment and it was the first debate of the Conference. It had to be not only good; it had to be excellent. I spent countless hours in preparing it and although I would certainly have to respond to some of the specific points made by speakers from the floor, I had been doing the job as Green Minister for two years and there could be no excuse for not knowing the answers to the questions that would be raised.

It was John Major's first Conference as Prime Minister. It was also Michael Heseltine's first appearance on the rostrum after so long a period in the political wilderness, and we didn't know how the bulk of the Conference would respond to all this. Added to this drama, I wasn't so sure how some of the Conference delegates would react to me, as it was so widely known that I had been a Heseltine supporter. There were a lot of unknowns and a lot at stake.

In the retiring room behind the stage, and just before I was to walk up the steps to face the Conference, John Major came up to me, put his hand on my shoulder and said, 'Get them on their feet, David. This has got to be a great Conference.'

After all the speeches from the floor, I rose to reply flanked by Chris Patten, Michael Heseltine, all the Ministers from the DOE, Willie Whitelaw, John Wakeham and David Waddington.

I spoke as I had never spoken before. I felt such passion that at times there was a serious danger I would fall forward over the lectern and drop into the front seats. I ranged over all our achievements, cracked the jokes and spoke with the conviction I felt so deeply.

I then sat down and, God bless 'em, they all stood up.

CHAPTER XXIII

An Honourable Discharge

'I think we should prepare ourselves for a defeat.'

AFTER THE CONSERVATIVE PARTY CONFERENCE in October 1991, it was clear that at long last the Party was beginning to get its act together. John Major had made a magnificent speech at the Conference in which he appealed for unity, and it had struck the necessary chord. Michael Heseltine's oration restored him to his rightful place as the darling of the Conference, a position he had always held before going into the political wilderness. My old chum, Ken Clarke, made a wonderful barn-storming speech in his new position as Secretary of State for Health and life for the Tories was beginning to settle down. There was a glimmer of light at the end of the tunnel. Nonetheless it was going to be a long and hard fight back if we were to recapture the lost ground we had foolishly sacrificed over the last few years.

Michael Heseltine had completely overhauled the Community Charge and replaced it with the Council Tax. Despite the fact that the vast majority of the population welcomed the change, there was still intense bitterness about the old Poll Tax, which was to linger on for some time.

Morale in the Department of the Environment was quite high and improving month by month. Michael Heseltine was a superb leader and the rest of the Ministerial team were very happy to rally round him. He held a very successful 'away day' at his home, where the Ministerial team had a brain-storming meeting lasting all day, with dinner in the evening. It was refreshing to get away from the Department and to engage in a 'no holds barred' discussion on future policy.

Back in the constituency, the mood was swinging away from outright opposition to the Government, but we still had a long way to

Michael Heseltine's Environment team outside his home.
Left to right: Tim Boswell (Environment Whip), Tim Yeo, Robert Key, the author, special adviser, Michael Heseltine, Lady Blatch, Tony Baldry, Michael Portillo, Lords' Whip, Sir George Young.

go before becoming remotely popular. My Labour Party opponent was Janet Anderson, and there could have been no doubt in her mind that I would be unseated at the next election. I had fought Janet in 1987 and won. It wouldn't be so easy this next time. On the occasions when we had met, we had always got on very well together. Certainly she believed in a clean fight during a General Election and between elections she campaigned in the same way. I never doubted her integrity.

My own Conservative Association was strong, despite all of us being somewhat battle scarred, as was to be expected when the Party had been in power for thirteen years. My constituency chairman, Geoff Law, was a huge success and a delight to work with. I can picture him now as I write: a somewhat weather-beaten face that

With John Major on the campaign trail during the 1992 election.

radiated good health, thinning hair and a melodious voice – and above all that wonderful charm of his. We were also firm friends which helped enormously. I had a relatively new agent, Stephen Frost, who was working his socks off in the constituency, Sheila Blaby having recently retired after a lifetime's distinguished service to the Party. I also had the comfort of knowing that when John Major fired the starting gun for the General Election, Councillor John Holt would once again be Chairman of the Campaign Committee and his experience had always proved invaluable to me.

On the national front, it was pretty clear that Neil Kinnock as Leader of the Opposition was proving to be a liability rather than an asset, whereas John Major was seen as a decent and honourable man.

As time went on, it was fairly obvious that John was not going to call an election until the end of that Parliament. The one clear advantage of that was that everyone could prepare for it, including the candidates. The disadvantage for the Government was that as time ran out, we were slowly being backed into a corner. When eventually the Prime Minister announced to the House of Commons that he was

A rally in Rossendale attended by Michael Heseltine and his wife Ann. Standing (next to the author and Ruth) is Geoff Law.

calling a General Election for April 1992, it was clear from the ecstatic cheering on the Opposition benches that they were certain they would win.

All the MPs left Westminster to get down to the hard grind of the Election campaign. As usual the Rossendale and Darwen Conservative Association rolled into action like a well oiled machine. Most of the election literature was in draft form and the battle plan had been worked up for weeks in preparation for this moment. My instincts told me that it would be difficult to win, but in line with Ruth's philosophy, it was imperative that I get my head down and fight the fight. A lot could happen in three and a half weeks and despite the opinion polls which pointed to a decisive Labour victory, we had never been swayed by the opinion polls in the past and refused to be now.

Michael Heseltine had kindly offered to come and speak on my behalf at a huge rally which was held in the Astoria in Rossendale. The meeting was packed and it was a great success, with Michael at his very best. Shortly after our rally Neil Kinnock held an even bigger one in Sheffield, when history will record that he 'blew it' and destroyed Labour's chances of winning the election. He was over-confident and overbearing. It was glitzy, it was in bad taste, but more importantly, it was bad politics.

In the third week of the campaign Ruth and I were together with a team of canvassers on a housing estate in Darwen. It had become increasingly clear as the campaign unfolded that there were many who had not forgiven the Tories for introducing the Poll Tax, despite the fact that it had been scrapped. It had been a difficult night on the door knocker and when for a moment Ruth and I were alone, I shared my fears with her. 'I don't want you to be upset, but I think you and I should prepare ourselves for a defeat.'

Ruth looked me straight in the eye and said, 'I know. Don't worry, we are tough and will have to learn to live with it. How many votes do you think you will lose by?'

'It's difficult to judge, but maybe 2500.'

'I was thinking along similar lines – probably 2000.'

During polling day itself it was very clear that a number of Conservative supporters had stayed away and the Labour Party was packing them in. Ruth and I walked from our headquarters to the Astoria for the count, accompanied by Geoff Law and John Holt. The atmosphere was electric. Television cameras seemed to be everywhere and it was clearly a nail-biting finish. After two recounts, I was out by 120 votes.

I remember thinking, 'Well at least it's an honourable discharge.' I would have hated to have been annihilated. Janet Anderson thanked her opponents for a clean fight, but to my surprise never said a single thing about me serving the constituency for thirteen years. This wasn't sour grapes, nor was it the way that Janet would normally behave. It was abundantly clear that had she said anything remotely kind to me, she would later have been 'carved up' by some of her more fanatical supporters. I suppose that is why I will always be a Conservative, because I have never known a time when my own party supporters have criticised me for being generous to members of an opposing political party. In fact they would expect me to behave in that way. Most, but not all, of the Labour Party don't play by those rules.

Ruth and I returned to the Conservative Club in Haslingden to thank our helpers and supporters, who had been marvellous throughout. We arrived at the Club just in time to see on the television that a panel drawn from the three Parties was reviewing the results announced so far. One of the panel was Ken Clarke, and when he was told that I had lost my seat, he was visibly shocked and was kind enough to say nice things about me.

Ruth was very tough about it all and it wasn't difficult for either of us to put a brave face on it, particularly as it became increasingly clear that John Major was going to win through and once again the Conservative Party would form the Government.

My father, Bunty and Roddy then made a surprise entrance. Bunty, who was pushing my father in his wheelchair, said, 'We've always come after you have won in the past, we just wanted to come to be with you when life doesn't seem too good.' I thought that was a marvellous gesture and my father hugged me but couldn't speak, as he was full of emotion.

We returned home and saw Ruth's parents, Joan and Alec, who had been babysitting for us. They too were very kind and supportive as always, and Alexander, who was only ten, had stayed up just to give us comfort.

'We must be realistic about all this,' I said. 'I thought I was going to lose by a much bigger majority and have been expecting this for at least a week. I think "it's fate". It was meant to happen and I accept it. Please don't worry about it. I'm very happy to be home with my family and – just think – I've got rid of all those red boxes.'

The next few days were crowded, with the telephone ringing non-stop. Everyone was very kind and letters started pouring in. Michael Heseltine wanted me to go and work for him as a special adviser when he moved to the Department of Trade and Industry. Chris Patten, who had also lost his seat, telephoned and we agreed we had been clobbered by the aftermath of the Poll Tax.

On the Sunday night following Polling Day, John Major telephoned me from Downing Street. He could not have been kinder. I was very impressed that he had taken the time and trouble to ring when he had so many other things to do. Here was the man whom I had not supported in the Leadership contest but who had saved my

Ministerial skin when he could have hung it out to dry. Later in the conversation he said, 'David, I'm certain you will get a safe seat. You have been a very successful Minister and I know you will be back.'

I knew he was shocked by my reply. 'It's very kind of you to say that, but I've had time to reflect on what has happened and I don't want to go back. I've had a wonderful career in Parliament and I wouldn't have missed it for the world, but I've now been there, read the book and got the tee-shirt. I am forty-five years old and I've got a chance to prove to myself that I can do something else in life. Most importantly, Ruth has carried this family on her back for the last thirteen years and that includes me. I'm looking forward to spending more time with the family. I don't think the children know me and that can't be right.'

John then said that he couldn't believe that I could get politics out of my system, but if that was going to be my decision, he would have to accept it. He ended the conversation by saying that if I ever needed his help, I had only to ask. Days later, I thought that I should have asked him for a reference just in case I couldn't get a job. Truth is, I wouldn't have dared.

I guessed that he must have read my thoughts, for a few weeks later I received a letter from him offering me something much better than a reference. He said he was making a recommendation to the Queen that I should become a knight.

CHAPTER XXIV

Business Matters

'Arise, Sir David.'

WHEN LIFE WAS BEGINNING to settle down after the General Election, Ruth and I discussed whether we should remain in the Valley, as I was no longer the MP for the constituency. Our oldest friends were in Rochdale but we had made new friends in the constituency with whom we wanted to remain in close touch. From a practical point of view, although ostensibly we lived in the countryside, we were only four minutes from the motorway so communications were very good, and of course we loved the house. The discussion gave Ruth the perfect opportunity to push her case for a few alterations and an extension. 'Cheap', she assured me, 'compared to moving.'

However, there was one practical difficulty which we had to address. Alexander had passed the two entrance examinations for Manchester Grammar School and as neither side of our families had ever had anyone clever enough to get there, we were determined he should go in September that year. As we lived on the north side of Manchester, the 'school run' was going to be difficult, but as the only move Ruth would contemplate was north, not south, our decision to remain was easily made and Ruth got her extension!

Edward was attending Bury Grammar School, which was far less of a problem as it was relatively easy to get to from Helmshore, and George would go there in September. George, who was only four years old, would neither climb on my knee nor cuddle me. The awful truth was that I had never been there for him and he hardly knew me, because I had been away so much. The fact that he soon became as affectionate towards me as his elder brothers owes everything to the fact that I was then able to spend so much time with him. In fact he has substantially over-corrected in the 'affection department', and it's now difficult to get him from round my neck. That, however, is a wonderful problem to deal with.

Within a few days of me losing my seat, the telephone had started to ring, with old friends offering me serious jobs. Stan Clarke, the Chairman of St Modwen Properties PLC, wanted me to become a non-executive director of the company. Stan was a brilliant self-made man, whom I had met when as Minister for Construction I had opened a new development for St Modwen on the Festival Park site in Stoke. We got on very well and hopefully I would have something to offer. Another offer I received was from Jim Shaw, the Chief Executive of Dunlop Heywood, the Consultant Surveyors in Manchester, whom I had also befriended when I was a Minister. They too wished me to become a non-executive director.

Although it looked as if life might become a little rosier, there were two jobs I had to decline. The first was the offer from Michael Heseltine to become a special adviser in the Department of Trade and Industry. It was a serious and responsible role but returning to the Department would have crippled me because I would have had no executive power, which, of course, I had once had as a DTI Minister. It hurt me to turn down Michael's offer because we were such good friends. He took my decision well and knew that I wished to succeed in the private sector.

The other role that I rejected was a much bigger job. The highly distinguished Executive Director of the United Nations Environment Programme, Mostaffa Tolba, was shortly to retire and nominations were being sought from the developed countries for a name most of the delegates could support. I was approached by the hierarchy in UNEP's headquarters in Nairobi and also by my successor in the Department of the Environment, David MacLean. I had been officially approached for the role when I was a Minister, but discounted it because I was up to my eyes in work.

The prospect of working in Nairobi for a few years obviously had many attractions and if I missed any of them, Ruth was quick to remind me. Both of us had fallen in love with Kenya and it was obvious that it would have been a great adventure. On the other hand, the one thing we now needed in our lives was stability. How on earth we would have dealt with educating the children was a significant problem, especially as I valued being close to them all once again. We were both concerned about leaving Ruth's parents behind, as we were both close to them too. There was also the problem of Ruth's practice, which she was reluctant to give up. The final blow which killed the prospect stone dead was that the Executive Director of UNEP was expected to travel widely throughout the world and Mostaffa Tolba had made an art form of doing just that. With his good looks, greying hair and moustache, he looked what he was – distinguished. The standard joke amongst all Environment Ministers, be they from Developed or less Developed Nations, was 'What is the difference between God and Tolba?' The answer: 'God is everywhere. Tolba is everywhere except Nairobi.' Clearly the travel might have had its attractions, but again I wouldn't see very much of Ruth and the family. I thanked everyone for their support and rejected the offer.

For weeks after I got knocked out of Parliament, there was an amusing cameo which would occur night after night until I filled my life with work. Ruth would return home in the evening and give me the benefit of one of her widest smiles. 'Ah,' she would say. 'I see you are here again. Don't forget, I married you in sickness and in health, but not for dinner.' Ruth had brought up the family single-handedly and in order to handle three boys and prepare for her court cases, had developed a rigid routine. This would mean that the older boys would be set to work on their homework; George would have to be bathed and a meal would be prepared at a set time. But now I was home every evening, I would be expected to help with both the meal and bath time. It was a terrible shock to my system.

Ruth enjoyed giving me my instructions. She would say, 'Now that large white rectangular thing is a fringe. You open the door and – surprise, surprise! – you discover food in it. You take the food over to that black rectangular thing, which is called an oven. You slap the food in and turn those knobs. Hey presto! A meal comes out the other end. Simple, really.' My sons would be choking with laughter and in the early stages choking with the food I served up, but eventually I got into the routine. The alternative was death.

When much later in the evening the house went quiet, because all the boys were tucked up in bed, I safely assumed that we would have a long chat over a glass of wine. However, that was the time when

Ruth sat down at the kitchen table, spread all her briefs out and started to talk to her dictaphone instead of me. Often I would have gone to bed long before she had finished.

Once back in the fold, I realised that Ruth and her parents were not the only people hard at work to keep the home fires burning. What do the armed forces say? For every man in the field, there at least four keeping him there. We had the tremendous support of Cindy Kay, who helped look after the house, Bill Howarth, who acted as our chauffeur as and when needed, and Geoff Crewe, our gardener, who confidently but wrongly assumed that I would have the time to help out when I had lost my parliamentary seat. Ruth called them the 'cement brigade'. It was only when I returned home permanently that I realised what she meant. They held everything together.

Fortunately my portfolio of business activities was slowly but surely filling up and although I saw Ruth and the boys at some stage most evenings, and ten times more than I would have seen them had I still been in Westminster, to the intense relief of my sons, they were soon back in the old routine where their culinary demands were dealt with by their mother rather than me.

Offers of work continued to come in and things seemed to be going remarkably well. Peter Fisher, the founder and Deputy Chairman of P and P PLC in Rossendale, a Computer Service company that I had helped on a number of occasions when I was an MP, telephoned asking me to become a non-executive director of the company. Don Allright from Halliday Meecham, the architects, invited me to become a consultant to the company and Alec Craig and Clive Garston from Halliwell Landau, a leading firm of Manchester Solicitors, also invited me to become a consultant.

When I lost my seat, I was expecting to enjoy the benefit of receiving twelve months' redundancy money free from tax. As I had not received a letter from the Fees Office in the House of Commons to confirm this, I telephoned them instead and was told very politely that I was mistaken. My assumption that a former Member would receive a year's payment of salary if he had served for more than ten years was correct, but with the notable exception that he would have to be fifty years old or over. As I had lost when I was only forty-five years of age, I was only entitled to six months. Typical of me to get my timing screwed up! Now I suffered because I was too young.

At this time I received the letter from Buckingham Palace stating that I was expected to appear at an Investiture in July to receive the honour of knighthood. The accompanying letter from the Imperial Society of Knights Bachelor informed me that Ruth would henceforth become Lady Trippier. The latter was the best news ever. It was clear to me that for all the years she had supported me, to say nothing of building a successful career, bringing up the children and finding her own way from the fridge to the oven, she richly deserved it. The letter inviting us to the Palace made clear that apart from Ruth, we were only going to be allowed two extra tickets for personal guests.

Instinctively I knew that one of them must be for my father, and I said so when I visited him in Rochdale soon after. To my surprise and to his eternal credit he said, 'That's very kind of you, David, and of course I would love to see you dubbed, but I think one of the boys should have my ticket. I have been lucky enough to go to the Palace to receive the Military Cross. I will certainly come to London to support you, as will all the family'.

So it was, and I toddled off for the investiture with Ruth, Alexander and Edward. George was too young to be allowed to attend in any event, but as usual stole the show at the lunch we organised at the Meridian in Victoria by walking around for the whole event wearing my top hat.

It was a happy and very splendid event. The cream on the cake was to come when I was waiting for my name to be called, which was the sign for me to walk in front of the Queen and kneel so that she could lay the sword on either shoulder. The voice of the man who called my name was unmistakably that of Ken Clarke and I was dumbfounded. Apparently Ken, in his new guise as Home Secretary, was entitled to appear at the Investiture for awards given for political services and had taken full advantage of this. He read out my name with a little more volume than for the others in the line up, and I looked straight at him and smiled. He beamed back. What are friends for, I thought?

I was overawed by the State Ballroom, which was where the ceremony took place. The ornate decoration of the room was

Investiture at Buckingham Palace.

The Trippier family after the investiture. Left to right: Roddy, Lady Trippier, George, Edward, Heather, Major Trippier, Iain, Bunty, Alex, Sir David.

magnificent. Whilst waiting to be called from the wings I could just see Ruth, Alexander and Edward sitting in the audience beaming at me. Michael Caine was receiving a CBE at the same investiture and to my amazement he seemed somewhat nervous.

I was delighted to find that the Queen wanted to chat away and the atmosphere was totally relaxed. She asked me how long I had been a Minister and when I answered nine years, she said, 'That is a long time.' I said I thought it was too.

Alex and Edward hugely enjoyed the Investiture but couldn't resist a crack at me. Alex said, 'It was particularly good to see that when the Queen wielded her sword, she cut chips on each of your shoulders. It's the only time Edward and I have seen you balanced.' I thought a cut in their pocket money was called for.

Soon after the Investiture I renewed a friendship with a man I had first met when I was Minister for Small Firms and Enterprise – John Lawrence, a very successful entrepreneur. Very fit looking and with a slight Yorkshire accent, he has a smile for everyone. He had built up a company called J.E.L. Ltd, which specialised in energy-efficient electrical installations and was eventually taken over by Thorn EMI in 1989. At the time that I first met John, he was the man in the north-west of England who was held up by the DTI to be a superb example of entrepreneurship in action. When Peter Walker was the Secretary of State for Energy, he appointed a 'Panel of Experts', some of whom would appear on a breakfast road-show which Peter would take round the country. John was on this panel and for his success in energy conservation, was awarded the MBE when he was only thirty-nine years old. He was always a delight to be with and despite originating from Yorkshire, a fact that I constantly refer to, he was charming, bright, good fun and very accomplished.

The coming together of Lawrence and Trippier – post-my demise as a politician – was one of the greatest benefits, leading to my re-establishing myself on the Manchester scene. Not only have we worked together in business, but we frequently meet socially. Ruth and John's wife Pam get on very well and the four of us escape from the madding crowd and occasionally snatch an odd weekend away. Not everything John and I have touched has turned to gold, but we have achieved more success than failure and the four of us have benefited from a tremendous friendship.

John was responsible for recommending my name to Colin Davenport, the Managing Director of a regional merchant bank called Davenham Ltd, which was on the lookout for a Chairman. Colin is an approachable man, quiet and self-effacing but with an underlying warmth of manner which makes him popular. It transpired that Davenham had a subsidiary, W.H. Ireland, which was a stockbroking firm and one of the oldest in Manchester. John attended a dinner in Scotland arranged by Murray Johnston – an Investment House also heavily engaged in Venture Capital – which was a substantial shareholder in Davenham. John Lawrence happened to be sitting next to Colin Davenport at this dinner when Colin confided in him that the company should appoint a Chairman soon and that their stockbroking subsidiary would need sorting out. John suggested me and I soon met Colin. We got on immediately like a house on fire. Jonathan Diggines – whose responsibility as a director of Murray Johnstone covered their investments in England and who was also a non-executive on the board of Davenham – was already known to me and he supported Colin's suggestion that I should become Chairman.

I was proud to be the Chairman of Davenham and the company was undoubtedly a success. It was clear, however, that sooner or later the company would either float on the Stock Exchange or be taken over. Needless to say, Colin and I would have preferred to float, but when we received two simultaneous offers by way of takeover, the principal shareholders, Murray Johnstone, were perfectly entitled to prefer a takeover than to take any risk associated with a float on the Stock Market.

Prior to the rival bids being dropped on the table, I had been keen to improve the fortunes of W.H. Ireland, whose reputation was sound but whose turnover needed a boost. Knowing most of the stockbrokers in Manchester, I went on the hunt for a Chief Executive and eventually approached a broker called Laurie Beevers to undertake the task. Laurie, an outstandingly able and intelligent individual with a well-developed sense of humour, had a close working relationship with David Youngman, a very accomplished analyst who was also a stockbroker, and they both joined W.H. Ireland. David is clever, tall, with spectacles and an urchin's haircut. The two of them transformed the firm and it soon began to take off. As I was also the Chairman of W.H. Ireland as well as the holding company, Davenham, I had a vested interest in its success and its success was very real.

The company which made the most attractive offer for Davenham was the Butterfield Bank of Bermuda, and although they wished Davenham to continue trading under their original name, they expressed no desire to take over the stockbroking firm as they were principally bankers and had little or no knowledge of stockbroking. Laurie, David and myself decided to complete a management buy-out of W.H. Ireland immediately prior to the final completion of the takeover of Davenham. The offer was accepted and I remain Chairman of Ireland's to this day with John Lawrence as a very valuable non-executive director. I would never have guessed that I would have returned to stockbroking and found it as exciting and rewarding as I had prior to going into politics.

On the 29th August 1993, one day before his 84th birthday, my father lay dying in Bury General Hospital. I stood beside his bed, holding his hand and looking at the face of a man who had been such an incredible influence on my life.

On the one hand, especially in my youth, he had seemed to be so autocratic and demanding. On the other, he had always been a man to look up to, admire and respect. In so many ways he was my hero – not just in a military sense, but in a much wider context. No-one I had ever met replaced him in that position. For the last few years his confinement to a wheelchair seemed at odds with his sporting prowess, his gallantry as a major in the War and his success in business. His brain was active to the end, but his body had failed him and he suffered recurring bouts of pneumonia after his stroke two years earlier. His passing was a blessed release from the pain he had suffered.

He had seen many things in his life and achieved much. After his intense distress at my mother's death, nineteen years before, he had never married again. In some ways he had been a difficult man to live with and work alongside. In other ways, his satisfaction in the success of his children and grand-children was his reward for setting demanding targets for us to attain and secure and we all loved him to the end. He looked directly at me with his clear blue eyes, smiled and gave my hand a gentle squeeze. I kissed him on the forehead and he slipped quietly away without any fuss.

The funeral that followed in Rochdale Parish Church was packed to capacity. The Vicar of Rochdale, the Reverend Canon Alan Shackleton, who knew my father well, paid him a wonderful tribute in the service and my niece Heather read the lesson in her Royal Navy Officer's uniform. It was a marvellous send off. He would have loved it.

After he died, I was amazed that both *The Times* and the *Daily Telegraph* covered his wartime experiences in such detail in two obituaries. Although I knew some of the details, the scale of his exploits and bravery came as a complete surprise to me.

By the end of 1993, I had decided to move to an office in the centre of Manchester, which turned out to be one of the best decisions I have ever made, primarily because I felt I was at the centre of things again. Philipa Kershaw became my Personal Assistant, and has been invaluable to me ever since. As Ruth often points out to me, not many would be prepared to do the job, so I am deeply grateful to Philipa for putting up with my eccentricities.

At about the same time that I was becoming Chairman of Davenham and Ireland's, I was approached by the Council of the Stock Exchange to sit on the Committee which they were establishing to formulate a new market-place to replace the Unlisted Securities Market, which had been outlawed by the European Commission. This was certainly a very flattering offer and I attended many meetings in the Stock Exchange, with other like-minded colleagues, striving to formulate an entirely new market which would be called the Alternative Investment Market (AIM for short). I had also introduced to the AIM Committee Giles Weaver, who was the Managing Director of Murray Johnstone, and whose ability and judgement I had come to respect. Despite the cynicism surrounding the launch of the AIM market, it has become a great success, with many more companies floated on that market than any of us had ever dreamed of.

I was also becoming increasingly impressed by Murray Johnstone as an investment house and acted as an adviser to them or as a non-executive director on one of their Investment Trusts. They were very keen to be the first Venture Capital Trust to float on the Stock Exchange and I was approached to become Chairman of it. The VCT, as they are best known, was an initiative introduced by Ken Clarke when he was Chancellor of the Exchequer as a means of encouraging funds subscribed to by shareholders, which would then invest in smaller companies in the United Kingdom. The ethos was quite brilliant and the tax-breaks for shareholders were very attractive. Nonetheless, the principle ambition of the Government was to stimulate enterprise in smaller companies and try to bridge the gap which had previously remained unfilled by investment and support at the lower end of the financial scale. Needless to say, the principal ambition of Murray Johnstone VCT as a fully quoted PLC, and the first to secure a quote on the Stock Exchange, was to ensure that our shareholders would receive rewards which would match the risks they were prepared to take. John Simpson became the Manager of the fund and he deserves high praise for leading a team which can focus on those businesses which would succeed, whilst turning down those companies which they thought would not. I remain the Chairman of Murray VCT and it is challenging and exciting work that keeps me at the forefront in the entrepreneurial spirit which I have always found fascinating. The success I had achieved in my dealings with the Stock Exchange was becoming more widely known, at least in the north-west of England.

In 1997 I became Chairman of Vector Investments, which is the builder and owner of the indoor arena in Manchester. It was originally known as the Nynex Arena and now, through name sponsorship changes, is called the Manchester Evening News Arena or M.E.N. Arena for short. The *Manchester Evening News* pays a fee to Vector and to Ogden Entertainments, to whom we sublease the management of the arena, and are thus allowed to have the Arena named after them. The success of the Arena is unquestioned and it remains to this day the largest indoor arena in the whole of Europe. It is home to Manchester Storm, the city's ice hockey team, and to the basketball team known as the Manchester Giants. In addition it has staged events ranging from pop concerts to Pavarotti. Most of these extravaganzas are packed with capacity crowds, filling the 18,000 seats available in the arena.

Also in 1997 I became a non-executive director of Nord Anglia PLC, which is the largest provider of private education in the United Kingdom. The founder and driving force behind the company is Kevin McNeany, who started his career as a teacher but quickly saw an opportunity to develop English language teaching schools overseas, private primary schools in many countries abroad, and nursery education in this country. Sharp-witted, with vision, courage and enterprise, and the best of good company at any social event, Kevin was kind enough to invite me to join the board before its successful float on the Stock Exchange. Prior to joining Nord Anglia, I had become a governor of Manchester Grammar School in 1993 – by this time our middle son Edward had become a pupil at the school – and I had developed a considerable interest and enthusiasm for private education. There is nothing better than having-up-to-date experience of being a parent of children who are currently studying. Nord Anglia fascinated me as a company and my association with it is one of my most valuable experiences.

In early 1998 I had lunch with Rob McLoughlin, who was a well-known name at Granada Television and had responsibility there for Regional Affairs. With his youthful good looks, energy and dash, and a special talent for mimicry, Rob was also a presenter for them and had interviewed me on several occasions in the past. Rob – who is a human dynamo – outlined the vision he had for setting up a company from scratch which would become expert in public relations and marketing, media and broadcast, sponsorship and corporate strategy. He wanted to see various skills incorporated in a holding company which would ensure that the service was a 'one-stop shop'. I was very excited by the prospect and acknowledged that there was a huge gap in the market, in which, as my experience had taught me, many companies were dissatisfied with the service given to them in one or all of these fields. Having captured the imagination of myself and Jim Quick, who is one of the UK's most successful design consultants, he contacted other 'names' in the region who would be prepared to join a team to drive the idea forward. Within months we had secured the support and commitment of Mike Davies, who was a popular and respected chartered accountant and a former senior partner of Ernst and Young, and Felicity Goodey, who was well known as a top professional presenter for the BBC.

To remove any political bias, we were backed by the independent peer, Lord Alton of Liverpool, and James Mason, who was a key figure in the Trades Union, Co-operative and Labour Movement. Having received the necessary funding, the company was launched in September 1998 and has never looked back. I serve as the Deputy Chairman to Rob McLoughlin and it is abundantly clear that the company will do well because it offers an unrivalled service and an effective and ethical approach to the business challenges of tomorrow.

In the autumn of 1998 I was invited to open a brand-new factory in Haslingden in Rossendale. The company concerned was called Camfil Ltd, and is the largest air filtration company in the UK. The invitation was sent to me by Brian Taylor, the Managing Director of the Company, and we met for a lunch together with the Finance Director, Bill Wilkinson, so that I would be properly briefed prior to the official opening a week later. I instantly hit it off with Brian and Bill and I began to understand the manufacturing process for which they were responsible. Brian is a tall, powerfully built man, with a pleasant, approachable manner. Bill Wilkinson, by contrast, is small, with a sharp mind. The parent group of CAMFIL is Swedish and I was told that at the opening I would meet Jan Eric Larson, the Swedish President and Chief Executive of the Company and Alan O'Connell, the Director of European Operations, who was resident in Ireland.

The official opening of the plant turned out to be a huge success, not least because Brian Taylor gave a brilliant presentation on the company to a huge invited audience. Unbeknown to me, Brian had been discussing with his fellow directors the possibility of me joining the company as a non-executive director, and he put the proposition to me shortly before I left to return to my office in Manchester. I was delighted as it was important to me that I should become involved in a manufacturing company. For such a long time I had recognised the importance of manufacturing to the country and it was about time for me try to learn from, and hopefully contribute to, this sector of the economy. Although I have only been involved with them since December 1998, it is clear that the company has an exciting future. I never realised at the time I accepted the offer to become a director that what I had learned about air pollution during the passage of the Environmental Protection Act 1990 would be as useful as it has turned out to be.

To be wanted is more important than to be praised. Any fool can lavish praise on another and it may confirm that the man is a fool if he believes the praise half the time. For seven years now I have been very lucky to have been wanted in a variety of businesses. I have accepted from the beginning that some of my directorships will fall by the wayside and some companies I have been involved in have come to naught. What has been vital to my pride and self-esteem is that the vast majority of those companies have been very successful and to have played any part in that success is worth a great deal to me. Whatever experience I had collected in the small firms area, I always tried to bring common sense to the boardroom and hopefully a higher profile to the company I was involved in.

I know that I have been profoundly lucky to have left Parliament when I did. The Conservative Government between 1992 and 1997 had a miserable existence, with rebellion after rebellion making the lives of John Major, Michael Heseltine and Ken Clarke a regular living hell. To be in Parliament as a Conservative MP in Opposition in 1999 can hardly be described as a bed of roses either. In retrospect I think perhaps I was lucky to be knocked out when I was, and the electorate's timing was better than mine.

CHAPTER XXV

Manchester

'We will build a better city now.'

EVERYONE WANTS TO BE associated with success and although it is clear to me that the City of Manchester is a success today, I am even more certain that the many achievements I have witnessed there in the last twelve years will be built upon to achieve even greater success in the next century. It has given me more pleasure than anyone could imagine to have played a small part in a partnership which has given some direction to the strategic development of Manchester as a European regional capital. In this I have played two separate roles.

The first was when I was Minister for Inner Cities and Construction and set up the Central Manchester Development Corporation, as well as taking responsibility for the nearby Trafford Park Development Corporation, which had only been established for a relatively short time prior to my appointment. There were those who were opposed to the setting up of Urban Development Corporations because they saw it as the heavy hand of Central Government descending from on high to impose a strict autocratic framework on the development of the economic and physical environment. They were wrong for a number of reasons. UDCs were only set up because it was thought that without them the strategic development would not take place for some considerable time, if at all. Their principal role was to stimulate the necessary energy to bring the public and private sectors together to achieve what everyone wanted to see – a transformation in the built environment and the bringing of jobs to the area. First and foremost they were a catalyst for change and without doubt that change could only be brought about through an effective partnership of central government, local government and the private sector.

Whatever powers central government may have, they can be

effectively neutered without the support of a local authority. Likewise, the local council needs the support and financial assistance of the Government if any major project is to be delivered. The simple fact that central and local government need each other as an essential ingredient for the recipe of success was clear to me when I was the Leader of Rochdale in Greater Manchester and I had to work with both Labour and Tory Governments. Perhaps the fact that I was an unqualified supporter and devotee of local government was to help me through the many frustrations I experienced in some inner cities, and stopped me sticking my head in the gas oven. It was also glaringly obvious to everyone, with the exception of those on the far left of the political spectrum, that even if there was a perfect partnership between national government and the local authority, absolutely nothing would happen without the private sector having the confidence to invest. Those who thought that the local authorities could handle everything by themselves were flying in the face of reality. Quite apart from anything else, they would never have enough money to achieve the goal.

Although the words 'partnership' and 'confidence' are synonymous with Manchester today, it was not always thus. The ideological tripe which was peddled by those on the far left may, for a time, have convinced a few zealots who were against us being a democratic nation with a mixed economy. For that same length of time, however, nothing – but nothing – positive happened. Infrastructures began to crumble, economic activity ground to a halt and the private sector, fearful of investing in the face of such ideology, withdrew, with the result that unemployment rocketed.

I believe that the watershed for Manchester was in 1987 and the man who led the city out of the shadows was not me, but Graham Stringer. I was simply one of the people who were in a key position at the time and who made him face reality. Graham didn't have to 'read the tea leaves' to tell him what was going to happen, as he had seen the adjoining authority, Salford City Council, make great strides with the private sector in the development of Salford Quays. He had seen me give extra money to Salford, which was also Labour-controlled, when I found I had an under-spend in my budget in the Department. He had seen what had happened to Liverpool as a result of Derek Hatton declaring a fortress policy which was hammering the Merseyside economy and driving the private sector away. He had seen that I would only give Government assistance through the City Grant I had created if the private sector were in the lead and calling the shots. He had also seen that the Urban Development Corporation that I was to set up in Central Manchester was inevitable. Things had to change and to his eternal credit, he also changed. A man of immense intelligence and integrity, he moved his position not by a whisker but by 180 degrees. Despite our political differences, which will never be reconciled, we shared a deep affection for Manchester, which ensured that we were able to work together and bury the political hatchet for the sake of the city and its future.

I did not realise at that time that his acceptance of the need for partnership would develop in such a dramatic way and the growing success of the city today owes much to the fact that he displayed so much vision and commitment whilst he was the Leader of the Council – a position he relinquished when he became a Member of Parliament for a Manchester seat in 1997. It was almost as if he had invented the word 'partnership' himself. Even so, I will always claim that I was the one who attached two 'jump leads' to fire him up and point him in the right direction. He certainly required no further help from me, as he worked tirelessly to achieve great things for the city. I only hope that Tony Blair recognises his ability and that he soon becomes a Minister.

The second occasion on which I was delighted to play a part in developing confidence and partnership in Manchester came many years later in 1996, four years after I was careless enough to lose my seat. It involved the setting up of an organisation called Marketing Manchester, whose principle task would be to promote the city region both nationally and internationally.

The idea of a central marketing initiative for Greater Manchester had been floating around in the minds of many people for some time. The need for it became pretty evident when Manchester set out to bid for the Olympic Games of 1996 and then 2000. Even though those bids were not successful, they demonstrated the value of partnerships between the public and private sectors to promote the entire region and create a greatly enhanced perception of Manchester as a leading world city. All this crystallised when Manchester, Salford and Trafford produced the City Pride programme in September 1994. This was in response to an initiative taken by John Gummer when he was Secretary of State at the Department of the Environment.

One of the many ideas that was mooted to take the area forward to the year 2005 was that of a centralised marketing agency. The idea of a marketing 'umbrella' for the region was such a good one that, following City Pride, it was taken forward by a number of agencies working in partnership. They included Manchester Airport, Greater Manchester Visitor and Convention Bureau, and Manchester Chamber of Commerce. In the process of development, the idea spread beyond its original area to take in the whole of Greater Manchester. That was the background to Marketing Manchester.

The principal task during the setting up of the organisation was to find a chairman and I was amazed and immensely flattered to be approached to carry out this role by none other than Graham Stringer himself. By this time I was already well entrenched in the private sector and had no thought at all of ever getting involved again with local authorities or central government. This role was very different from anything I had undertaken before. It was essentially a marketing operation to promote that which was best in the city region and to bang the drum for an area for which I had enormous passion.

It is true to say that there were a few raised eyebrows at my appointment. Within Greater Manchester there were ten authorities, nine of which were Labour controlled, and Stockport, which was Liberal. Not a 'blue' Council in sight. As it was clear to all that I would be principally remembered as a former Tory Minister, it must have been a source of amazement to those on the other side of the political spectrum that I was approached in the first place. They would naturally have preferred someone who was from the private sector and at the same time had a Socialist allegiance, and I completely understood that.

Recognising that there might be antagonism in some quarters arising from my appointment and the subsequent public announcement, I thought in the bath one morning that I had better whiz round all the Town Halls and meet the various Leaders and Chief Executives as quickly as possible. The exercise was completed within a couple of weeks and in every case the meetings went very well. If there had been resentment amongst Labour Leaders and their Chief Executives, it was quickly superseded by their desire to co-operate in a scheme which they immediately realised could only bring benefit to the areas they represented. They could not have been more charming and helpful, which was a good start.

Within a matter of weeks of my appointment there was a devastating incident in Manchester. On the 15th June 1996 an IRA bomb exploded in the city centre. The bomb was the largest which had exploded on land since the Second World War and it created £300 millions worth of damage. Fortunately no-one was killed, thanks to the superb efforts of the Greater Manchester Police, who moved 70,000 people away from the bomb area in forty-five minutes. I doubt if any other police force in the world could have acted so speedily.

When the bomb went off, it ripped through the Arndale Shopping Centre, the Marks and Spencer store and many other buildings in the vicinity.

The initial reaction to the bomb explosion was one of horror; then the second reaction was one of relief because no-one was killed. The third reaction was 'We will build a better city centre now' – a typical northern response. The last reaction was, 'Well, we never liked that part of the city anyway.' No-one in Manchester had a love for the aesthetic appearance of the Arndale Centre, with its unattractive tiled walls giving it a well-earned reputation as the largest 'public convenience' in Europe.

Within a few days the City Council had organised a clear strategy to assess the damage and a plan to rebuild the city. I was asked to invite some leading figures in the private sector to a meeting at the Bank of England in Manchester where, together with Richard Leese, the new Leader of the Council, and Howard Bernstein, then the Deputy Chief Executive of Manchester City Council, we met with Michael Heseltine in his capacity as Deputy Prime Minister and Alistair Burt, who was the Minister for Manchester and MP for Bury North.

Very few cities, if indeed any, could have responded so quickly and rallied round the principal players, who were already used to working together in partnership for many years. Michael Heseltine suggested that we should run an international competition amongst architects who would submit proposals for the re-design of the city centre.

A new company called Manchester Millennium was formed and charged with the task of rebuilding the city. Howard Bernstein would be the Chief Executive of this company, Sir Alan Cockshaw of AMEC PLC was to chair it, and Councillor Richard Leese became the Deputy Chairman. It was a small board consisting of Marianne Neville-Rolf, the Regional Director of the Government Office in the north-west, Councillor Kath Robinson, Deputy Leader of the Council, Tony Strachan, the Agent for the Bank of England in Manchester, and myself.

Progress has been so impressive that by the end of the year 2000, more than £1.2 billion will have been invested in the damaged area, nearly four times the cost of the damage caused by the bomb.

For me the reaction to the bomb blast was of immense significance. Those of us from the conurbation had not the slightest doubt in our minds that we could turn what appeared to be a tragedy into a glorious opportunity. Once again, the confidence of the people living in the area shone through. I am not entirely certain that had the bomb gone off ten years before, the same degree of confidence would have been in evidence.

In any event, life had to go on and I quickly realised that in the strangest possible way, the IRA bomb actually helped me in my new job as Chairman of Marketing Manchester. As one of my principle roles was to promote Manchester internationally, it was clear that on the day of the bomb blast, the name Manchester was given publicity throughout most of the world. Within a week I had to visit Georgia and Alabama in the USA to promote Manchester, and most people I met had seen television coverage of the bomb blast, and more particularly the success of our police in ensuring that no-one was killed.

Back home, my initial task was to appoint a team in Marketing Manchester which would effectively promote the area. The board of the company was relatively easy to establish, with the various directors appointed because of their experience and enthusiasm for Manchester. The first Chief Executive of the organisation was Elizabeth Jeffreys, who had done tremendous work for the city as the Chief Executive of the Greater Manchester Visitor and Convention Bureau. Together we built around us an executive team whose principal task was to project the strengths of the sub-region and to add value to the many initiatives which so many different organisations were taking. Marketing Manchester was to act as a catalyst, ensuring for the first time that those who wished to be ambassadors for the city should speak with one voice and ensure that we established Manchester as an international city of outstanding commercial, cultural and creative potential. Elizabeth Jeffreys was eventually to move on, in 1998, to become the Director of Tourism for Jersey, a job I'm sure she will carry out with distinction.

The current Chief Executive of Marketing Manchester is Vicki Gregory, a highly perceptive lady who, with her beautiful speaking voice and ready laugh, is able to win the minds of all-comers. Her success in that role is already widely acknowledged. Her previous role in the city had been as Chief Executive of the new Bridgewater Hall, which was a very successful concert hall and home to the Hallé Orchestra. Vicki will achieve great things for Manchester. She is extremely competent, a great enthusiast, attractive, very witty and is a delight to work with. The fact that she is scrupulously honest is perhaps her most outstanding characteristic. Like me, she believes that there has never been a better time to promote Manchester. There are so many 'good news' stories that it is difficult to focus on the ones which will have the most resonance for the various audiences which have to be addressed.

One thing is certain: the Commonwealth Games, which comes to Manchester in the year 2002, must be a huge success and be remembered as the jewel in the crown of the city. The task of organising the city in readiness to host the Games is enormous, but under the excellent leadership of the Games Committee Chairman, Robert Hough, I have no doubt that once again Manchester will rise to the challenge and it will be one of the most successful Games ever staged. Marketing Manchester will do all it can to assist Robert Hough and the fact that Vicki Gregory is ably supported by a key senior member of her staff, Lis Phelan, who is an expert on the organisation of sporting events, will ensure that the support is focused

Vicki Gregory.

and relevant. Small and with unquenchable energy, Lis is a live wire par excellence.

In the three years that I have been privileged to be Chairman of Marketing Manchester, I have taken the message of Manchester's success to many parts of the world; from the European Continent to the United States, from Malaysia to Japan and from Indonesia to Scandinavia. All of the Trade Missions have been organised to encourage inward investment into the Manchester city region and many of them have been very successful, not least because they have resulted in the establishment of new direct airline routes to Manchester Airport. Given that the airport is the largest sponsor of Marketing Manchester, and accessibility to the region is essential to its growth and prosperity, the increase in direct flights is one of Marketing Manchester's principal aims.

Marketing a city may be a little more difficult than marketing a product or a service, but the message that one needs to get across is uncomplicated and easy to understand. The truth is that the vast majority of people who have never visited Manchester in recent years could not be expected to appreciate the dramatic changes which have taken place, which have transformed the landscape beyond recognition.

It is now clear to me that whilst people living abroad may have heard of our excellent airport or Manchester United, they are unaware that the city is the birthplace of the first computer, the brain and body scanner, the splitting of the atom, the first Rolls Royce and the first steam train.

Notwithstanding the perceptions of those who live abroad, there are many people who live in the United Kingdom who do not know that we have the largest medical school in the country, that we have one of the largest university campuses in Western Europe and the largest indoor arena in the whole of Europe.

The fact that these achievements are not well known is no-one else's fault than our own, for as a nation we have never been particularly good at marketing ourselves. We much prefer to be modest and self-critical rather than boastful, and whilst that may be a laudable characteristic, modesty won't gain us business or secure a larger proportion of visiting tourists, and for sure it won't create jobs. So we have to stop being so modest and promote the positive.

Manchester will be sweeping into the new millennium with a city region almost bulging at the seams with new facilities and attractions, thanks to a huge amount of confidence, new ideas and, of course, investment from many sources. A lot of it is already taking shape, or soon will be; from a new Commonwealth Stadium to the Lowry Centre in Salford (which is the national millennium landmark for the arts in whole country) and from the new Imperial War Museum in Trafford to the state-of-the-art Convention Centre in Manchester's city centre.

Having completed the three-year term of office I initially agreed to serve as the Chairman of Marketing Manchester, I was proud to hand over the batten to Professor Bob Boucher, who is Vice Chancellor of UMIST University. He, I know, will be an excellent Chairman and a very worthy ambassador for the city. I moved on to become the President of Manchester Chamber of Commerce and Industry, which is a key partner in Marketing Manchester. Bob Boucher, Vicki Gregory and the wonderful staff at Marketing Manchester will prove to be a first-class team and, like all the people who have a keen interest in the economic and social health of this corner of Europe, will work in partnership to ensure that the quality of life in Manchester continues to improve not only for this generation, but for the next and all who follow.

CHAPTER XXVI

The High Sheriff

'The finest county that God ever gave to man.'

MOST PEOPLE WOULD REALISE that I am enormously proud to be a Lancastrian and lose no opportunity to emphasise my antecedents whenever the opportunity arises. It is often a source of amusement when I visit Yorkshire, which I'm lucky enough to do quite frequently. If my friends on the other side of the barbed wire don't regularly refer to me as 'that Lancastrian', I insist on reminding everyone that I do indeed hail from the finest county that God ever gave to man. It's probably a miracle that thus far I have avoided any trouble from a few who can't take a joke, but I do try to return to my native county before the gates are slammed shut at midnight.

In 1994, I was privileged to be appointed as a Deputy Lieutenant of Lancashire by Sir Simon Towneley who was then the Lord Lieutenant of the county and whose distinguished service as the Sovereign's principal representative spanned some twenty years. He retired as Lord Lieutenant in 1996 and it was widely acknowledged that his success in office owed much to the unfailing support of his wife, Lady Mary Towneley, who was a tower of strength in Lancashire.

One of the duties of the Lord Lieutenant, in Lancashire at least, is to submit a name to the Queen and the Chancellor of the Duchy of Lancaster for consideration as a possible High Sheriff, having taken extensive soundings within the county. In 1994, Sir Simon nominated me to become High Sheriff of Lancashire for the year 1997/98, but it was made crystal clear that it had to remain top secret until there was a public announcement in the early part of 1997. To keep a secret was something I had perfected in my life, but to keep a secret for three years was difficult to say the least. Nonetheless it had to be done, and even the children were unaware of what was to take place. Ruth was the only one allowed to be let into the secret for the three long years.

The business of keeping secret the names of those High Sheriffs 'in nomination' only applies to four counties in the land: the Duchy of Lancaster's counties, namely Lancashire, Greater Manchester and Merseyside, as well as the Duchy of Cornwall. All the other counties in England and Wales know full well who will be their High Sheriffs for each of the three years preceding their appointment, as they are published in the national press.

The secrecy associated with Lancashire and the other two counties within the Duchy of Lancaster is based on specific tradition, whereby the office of High Sheriff of Lancashire is an appointment made by Her Majesty the Queen in her capacity as the Duke of Lancaster, and the persons for appointment are recommended by the Chancellor of the Duchy, who annually, at a private audience, places the Lites before the Queen. The Lites is an engrossed parchment offering the names of three nominated people for the Queen's final selection. It is the usual practice for the Queen to prick the first name on each list with a silver bodkin. The second and third people on those lists can expect to serve in the following years. This practice is steeped in history and goes back to the time when Queen Elizabeth I was sitting in her garden, doing her needlework with her bodkin, and was approached to select her High Sheriffs from a more extensive list. As she confessed she was unaware of many of the names submitted, she pricked them at random with her bodkin. The fact that the practice is still continued to this day says a great deal for British history and tradition.

The office of High Sheriff, which is known as 'the Shrievalty', is the oldest secular office in the kingdom after the Crown, and dates from Saxon times. Throughout its long history, the office has been connected with the maintenance of law and order. Some Sheriffs led contingents at the battle of Hastings. The Normans continued the office and added to its powers and also rewards.

I have always thought that it was nothing short of a tragedy that the powers of High Sheriffs have been steadily eroded since the twelfth century, which is when they were at their height and very extensive. In those days, the High Sheriff judged cases in court – originally jointly with the Bishop. He had police powers and would raise the 'hue and cry' in pursuit of the felons within his shire. On behalf of the Crown he collected taxes and levies and all dues on Crown lands, and he nominated and arranged for representatives of the county to be sent to Parliament. I'm not entirely sure which of those powers – now all disappeared – I would have enjoyed the most.

From the once great powers and official duties of the Sheriff, there remain principally the execution of High Court writs in his name, the duty of attending upon and looking after Her Majesty's judges, of acting as electoral returning officer in certain constituencies, and above all, the upholding of law and order and the uniting of all the Sovereign's subjects in loyalty to the Monarchy.

The preparation for my year in office was considerable, although it is incredibly difficult to organise events when you can't tell anyone why you are doing it. Nonetheless, Ruth has had a lifetime's training in organisation and she had the added advantage of knowing quite a number of the High Court judges, before whom she had appeared from time to time. One thing was certain: however much hard work might be associated with this new role, we were determined to enjoy it whilst at the same time preserving the dignity of the office.

Fortunately there were two significant costs which, through luck, I was able to avoid. I was able to avoid buying a High Sheriff's uniform or the court dress, as I was allowed to wear my own Royal Marines uniform as a Colonel. This had the added advantage of promoting the Marines in the county during my year. The second cost I avoided was having the College of Arms design a family coat of arms, which would be hung in the Shire Hall in Lancaster Castle along with those of my predecessors, who numbered 574. I already had a coat of arms which had been designed for me when I became a knight in 1992, and I certainly didn't want another.

The elaborate swearing in ceremony took place at County Hall in Preston on the 22nd April 1997, and our close family attended. I was supported by my chaplain for the year, who was our local vicar, the Reverend Simon Aiken, and my magistrate, Judith Nuttall, who sits on the bench in Rossendale. Judith and her husband Clive are near neighbours and good friends. I can honestly say that Judith was the most glamorous magistrate any High Sheriff could have wished for.

The ceremony was presided over by the new Lord Lieutenant of Lancashire, Lord Shuttleworth, who was an old friend. His appointment was widely applauded in the county because of his immense popularity. Charlie Shuttleworth is himself physically immense and must be the tallest Lord Lieutenant in the land. He is also probably the youngest, being a few years younger than me. Although he was undoubtedly my boss, as I was one of his Deputy Lieutenants, ironically I had been his boss for a time when I had been a Minister of State in the Department of the Environment and had appointed him as the Chairman of the Rural Development Commission, an office he discharged with considerable skill.

On his appointment as Lord Lieutenant, the county was to get two for the price of one, because Charlie's wife Anne was as well known as he, and had a distinguished career in her own right. Like her husband, she too is unusually tall, with dark brown hair and elegant good looks. She is a brilliant conversationalist and interested in everyone. This charming pair will be an enormous asset to Lancashire. Little did I know at the time that one of the last tasks that Sir Simon Towneley performed in the latter months of his term as Lord Lieutenant was to nominate Lady Shuttleworth as High Sheriff for Lancashire for the year 1999 to 2000. That was certainly a well-kept secret.

Although Ruth and I enjoyed a hectic and exciting time in office, during the twelve months there was a family tragedy which depressed us beyond belief. Bunty's husband, Roddy, died of cancer in January 1998. It was a tragic time and devastated my sister and her children Heather and Iain. At Bunty's request, I gave the eulogy at the funeral and found it to be the most difficult speech I had ever delivered as I was so full of emotion. The only comfort was that he had lived to see his daughter Heather become a regular officer in the Royal Navy, marry a naval colleague, Rob Rimmer (who, like herself, is a Lieutenant-Commander) and start a family. He had also seen his son Iain become a chartered accountant, marry Kath and have a family too. Ruth and I are as proud of Heather and Iain as is their mother. Sadly nothing compensates for the fact that Bunty had lost a wonderful husband and I had lost a true friend.

For my year as High Sheriff, Ruth and I spent a great deal of the time tearing around the county attending official events, opening bazaars and presenting awards. It may have been hectic but it was pleasant and we discovered parts of Lancashire that even we didn't know existed. In contrast to our years in politics, I didn't have to kiss the babies and pass the cigars around. It was in every sense an enjoyable privilege, a very memorable twelve months, and whether we were entertaining or being entertained, it was always essential to maintain the dignity of the office. Although in one circumstance that wasn't easy.

There is a sizeable group of my friends who, like me, occasionally frequent my local hostelry in the village where we live. They didn't quite appreciate the niceties of anyone being High Sheriff, let alone me. Since losing my seat in 1992, I had been blessed by being accepted in my local pub as a fairly frequent visitor, who has been content to enjoy an occasional pint of wallop, enjoy 'the crack', munch the pork scratchings and generally relax amongst my mates. It may have been a contrast to having a pint in the 'Kremlin' in the House of Commons, but in many ways it has been better. This small pub is a 'free house' and its owner and cheery landlord is Colin Ruleman, a small, thickset man with a well-cultivated paunch. He has a wonderful way of sticking his chin out when about to crack some dry witticism. It is essentially an old Lancashire pub. Unlike many which have been modernised, rumferised or 'chef and brewered', it retains the character of everything which is best in the British pub short of sawdust on the flagged floors and spittoons in the corner. Even dogs are welcome – especially if they drop in with their owners after a walk in the rain.

It is, in every sense, my kind of pub and seemingly it is for many others too, since it is always packed, particularly on an early Friday evening. Colin never has to bother enticing customers with beer at half price in a 'happy hour', although he constantly assures me he has a 'happy minute'. It's just that I always seem to have missed the crucial 'minute'.

Apart from the attraction of the material furnishings of the pub, it has an ambience which is naturally created by those who are regulars and whose company I always enjoy. It doesn't matter who you are or what you have done in life – it certainly wouldn't impress. There is a cross section of society there whose company I value, and any attempt by anyone to be in the least bit stuffy is seized on and ridiculed in a jocular, though never malicious, way. In short, it is a great leveller and I love it.

You can imagine that given this background, my fellow locals enjoyed the 'crack' that I was High Sheriff. The fact that the pub is called 'The Robin Hood', and that that name is synonymous with a certain sheriff, was a gift to the comedians. Whenever I walked into the pub, some of the remarks were hilarious, ranging from 'Will you be seeing Maid Marian tonight? Is she cooking dinner or is it Friar Tuck?' to 'Have you collected the taxes yet? I've paid mine, High Sheriff – honest!'

Then of course we had the Wild West jokes (where they would play on the theme of the cowboy sheriff). 'Left your horse outside then? Hope it's tied up, bad lot round here... There's only room for one of us in this town... 'Can I join your posse? Is Doc Holliday riding with you?... Eh up, the sheriff's in town, guns on the bar lads' and 'Goodnight, sheriff. Don't forget a man's gotta do what a man's gotta do.'

I might have preserved the dignity of the office of High Sheriff everywhere else in the county, but I don't think I did a fantastic job in the Robin Hood.

Two of my very close friends who have been known to darken the doors of the Robin Hood are Stephen McGuiness and David Bangham.

Stephen and Colleen McGuiness are near neighbours and have two sons, Philip and Peter, who are close in age to Alexander and George. Stephen, is a builder and one of the most popular men I have ever met. He is good company and always cheerful – the only exception being when his beloved football team, Manchester United, lose a match. Colleen is exceptionally kind and very witty. Like Ruth she enjoys cooking and Stephen bores everyone to death by describing each and every meal in elaborate style. Rommel's Panzer Divisions would never stop Stephen getting to his food and it's probably the only thing in life which is prized as highly as Manchester United.

David Bangham is a partner in Baker, Wilkins and Smith, Quantity Surveyors. He is a gentleman and, like Stephen, first-class company. His wife Pat, with her beautiful long red hair, is good fun and very warm-hearted. Whenever the six of us get together, there is non-stop

Rome 1998. Left to right: Pat Bangham, Ruth, the author, Colleen McGuiness, Stephen McGuiness and David Bangham.

fun, although I suspect anyone listening to us would think we were very loud. We all had a wonderful holiday together in Rome in 1997 and it's clear that there will be other holidays to come.

On a separate occasion Stephen and Colleen took Ruth and me skiing in Chevenia in Italy, together with our respective families. For Ruth and me it was a first, which seemed to surprise everyone. Our children were already accomplished at the sport; Ruth took to it immediately while I disgraced myself by falling down more than I was upright. I shall persevere.

Our new-found friendship with the McGuinesses and Banghams has been one of the most rewarding we have experienced since I came out of Parliament and they, like many of our friends, were particularly kind and supportive during the year I was High Sheriff.

The principal highlight of my term of office was the shield-hanging ceremony in Lancaster Castle, where in June of every year, the High Sheriff attends the Priory Church with those High Court judges who are sitting in Lancashire at the time, a number of circuit judges, and

The Royal Marines Band Scotland at the author's shield-hanging ceremony at Lancaster Castle.

the Chief Constable of Lancashire and the Constable of the Castle. The congregation is made up of some official guests but primarily the event is attended by the High Sheriff's family and his personal guests. The church service precedes the shield-hanging ceremony in the Castle before everyone retires to have lunch in Lancaster Town Hall. The organisation of the day was in the capable hands of the Under-Sheriff, Andrew Wilson, who did a wonderful job. The lunch was in the expert hands of Ruth.

The day was made complete for Ruth and me because of the Royal Marines. The then Commandant-General of the Royal Marines, Major-General David Pennefather, gave his permission for the Royal Marines Band, Scotland to play throughout the church service, to Beat Retreat on the lawns outside the castle, and entertain us over the lunch. It was magnificent and they were as splendid as ever.

In true Lancashire fashion, my Chaplain, the Reverend Simon Aiken, gave an excellent sermon where he occasionally pulled my leg and yet delivered a serious message suitable to the occasion. The shield-hanging ceremony was carried out with enormous dignity and shocked a number of our friends who came from the south, who had previously believed that pageantry on that scale was something confined to London. At the lunch, a splendid speech was delivered by Judge Brian Duckworth, who had previously been a senior member of Ruth's chambers, and I replied.

As a pleasant surprise, Lieutenant Chris Davies, who was Director of Music for the Royal Marines Band, Scotland, had composed a special fanfare for me for the occasion. This was played by the Royal Marines trumpeters when I walked into the Shire Hall in the castle to hang my shield alongside those of my predecessors. It was truly wonderful and he later presented me with a tape of the trumpeters playing it and a copy of the music he had composed.

I had never had my own personal fanfare before and I ruminated as to where I could place the copies of the tape in the future. Perhaps I would wire it up to the doorbell at home. Perhaps I could have one in the bathroom. Perhaps even the bedroom. It would have the advantage of keeping Ruth awake – possibly the disadvantage of giving her a genuine headache. Perhaps it could be played when I walked into the Robin Hood.

On second thoughts – better not.

CHAPTER XXVII

Epilogue

I ACCEPT THAT THE LAST CHAPTER of this book should be carefully crafted. I don't want to be writing a sequel in a few years time and go through all this again.

At the same time, at 53 years of age, I would hate to think this is the final chapter of my life. Hopefully I will move on, but it is something of a leap into the unknown. So the book isn't so much an unfinished symphony – more a progressive barn dance.

For some time I have harboured two secret ambitions. One was to write a book, as I was always moved by the old maxim that there is 'one book in everyone'. The second ambition was to compose a serious piece of music. As I have now achieved the first ambition, I must find the time to achieve the second. I'm daft enough to think I would enjoy it.

Of course I have regrets in life. I wish I had been more academically minded at school. Less swash and more buckle would have made life a little easier for me. I'm sad that my mother isn't here so that I could tell her that she was wrong and that politics wasn't too dirty a game for me and that I had found it rewarding. Although I regret my father didn't see me become High Sheriff and Colonel, he saw most of what happened to me. I can smile now when I recall that in my teens he used to say, 'No-one is useless David. They can always be held up as a bad example to others.'

It would have been nice to have had a daughter, if only so that someone could have worshipped me for part of my life. But who knows – in time I may get a grand-daughter who will do the same thing. As I clearly crave that adoration, I think that in the next life I would like to be an Italian baby.

With our three sons, life has been fascinating – sometimes frustrating but never dull. They bring sunshine and big telephone bills into our home. The shock has been that we ordered babies and we were sent people.

George, Alexander and Edward.

There will be a yawning chasm when Alex leaves home this year, but at least his bedroom will be tidy. Life seems worthwhile because he occasionally asks me to go for a pint in the Robin Hood and he still doesn't realise how flattered I am to be asked.

Edward is the most sentimental, the most organised and the most infuriatingly tenacious of the bunch. It is impossible for me to imagine that he won't do well in life, even if he drives a few people 'crackers' on the way.

Please God, George will go into the Royal Marines. Someone else in this family has to keep up the military tradition and George is the likely candidate. He may be only 11 years old, but he is permanently 'armed and dangerous.'

So that is it – for now. As we approach our Silver Wedding Anniversary in the year 2000, I marvel at the fact that Ruth is as lovely as she was on the day I married her. As I look at myself in the mirror, I realise that I was built for comfort, not speed.

The future is where I want to spend the rest of my life. The only sure certainty is that when I turn my toes up, my will makes clear that my ashes should be scattered over the new Marks and Spencers store in Manchester – then I know that Ruth will visit me twice a week.

Index